Sporting Rifles

Sporting Rifles

BRUCE POTTS

THE CROWOOD PRESS

First published in 2009 by
The Crowood Press Ltd
Ramsbury, Marlborough
Wiltshire SN8 2HR

www.crowood.com

British Library Cataloguing-in-Publication Data
A catalogue record for this book is available from the British Library.

ISBN 978 1 84797 107 4

Dedication
For Jan, Jake and Billy

Disclaimer
The author and the publisher do not accept any responsibility in any
manner whatsoever for any error or omission, or any loss, damage,
injury, adverse outcome or liability of any kind incurred as a result
of the use of any of the information contained in this book, or reliance
upon it. If in doubt about any aspect of selecting, purchasing or using
a sporting rifle, or any subject covered in this book, readers should
seek professional advice.

Designed and typeset by Focus Publishing, Sevenoaks, Kent

Printed and bound in Singapore by Craft Print International Ltd

Contents

Introduction

The sporting rifle as a type encompasses a wide spectrum of designs, reflecting the range of quarry species that the sportsperson can legally pursue. In Great Britain there has always been a healthy respect for sporting rights and outdoor pursuits and the unique sense of primeval instinct that comes from an early morning's foray into the woods. For me, shooting is more about the quality of the stalk than the final conclusion, although every sportsperson should be aiming for a humane, one-shot kill. In reality, more game has been taken with a bow or spear than a firearm, but as human nature and laws have evolved we are constrained by legalization yet have a plethora of firearms to choose from. The wise person will consider the fieldcraft first, and then settle on the equipment he will need.

As you will see throughout the book, the choice regarding equipment is truly huge, but I would have more respect for someone who buys a cheap rifle but shoots every day and loves the natural world, than for a sportsperson who has the best equipment money can buy yet has no interest in Mother Nature and her fickle ways. However, true to human nature, we all tend to be seduced by the latest craze or fashion, whether we know about it or not, and firearms for all the quarry species in Britain reflect a general trend towards adaptability, greater choice and synthetic materials. Thankfully there is still a place for the true specialist gunsmith capable of producing exquisite works of art, just as the 'old world' artisans once did.

In Britain today the red deer is the largest game species one can shoot, followed by wild

OPPOSITE: Sporting rifles come in many guises, from the traditional wood stock and blued steel to modern-day synthetic materials and a stainless-steel finish.

RIGHT: A quality gunsmith such as F.A. Andersons of East Grinstead is a good place to start with regard to advice and choice of sporting rifles and accessories.

boar, small populations of which have become established as a result of escapees from captivity. These two species obviously need a different rifle than that used for rabbit or vermin, but many similarities remain, and indeed it is often only the calibre, cartridge and application that differ. This book is here to guide both amateur and experienced shooters in their choice of firearm, to advise them in the uses, limitations, calibre and maintenance of the guns available, together with a brief description of quarry species, and the accessories that might be needed to become a safe and responsible sportsperson.

Most modern rifles have their origins in the firearms of yesteryear, and none more so than the fabled Mauser from Germany. This bolt action design has systematically inspired a whole progeny of derivatives, clones and variants from all corners of the globe, and it is testament to the fact that once a good design has been established it is often difficult to progress beyond it. Indeed today, the Mauser-type bolt action design is still the most popular form of rifle design in use and demand throughout the world. Variations on the bolt action theme have progressed, with the fine tuning of actions and bolt smoothness and lock up – but the principle is largely the same.

It is not just the mechanical design that determines whether a rifle will be suitable for the specific task in hand: its style or aesthetic appeal is often what decides a purchase, and there are several specific designs to choose from, such as Sporter, Classic, Varmint, Mountain, Stutzen or Bull pup. The Sporter is usually a slim build, handy rifle for everyday sporting use, with wood or synthetic stock, or blued steel and stainless finish. Classic rifles reflect a more traditional design of yesteryear, with straight-lined stocks of elegant proportions. Varmint rifles may have the same actions as their Sporter brothers, but they have a heavier stock and wider fore-end, with longer and heavier barrels to help accuracy when they get hot. Quite the opposite are the Mountain rifles that are stripped to the minimum to save weight. They have light, whippy barrels and are designed to put the first shot on target under arduous conditions. Stutzen rifles do not suit everyone, because they have an extended fore-end section of the stock that comes flush with the muzzle, and often have a barrel clamp that can cause problems with barrel vibration and accuracy.

Bull pups are rare, but have the action bedded in the rear portion of the stock with an extended trigger reach, thus allowing a very short rifle but with a standard barrel length. Similarly, grip-cocking rifles such as the Sommer and Ockenfuss are short and manoeuvrable, but rarely seen in the field.

Each design should be considered before you make your final choice.

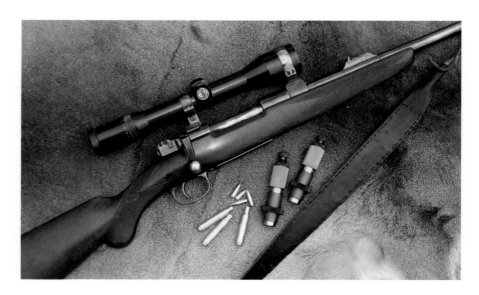

The classic Mauser has spawned more modern sporting rifle designs than any other; one such is the Rigby, the timeless sporting 0.275 calibre rifle.

Bull pup rifles have their action bedded further back in the stock than conventional designs, making them very short and handy as a sporting rifle, as is this B and M .22 BSA rifle.

RIFLE ANATOMY

Bolt actions, slide actions, straight pulls, doubles and single shots all serve one purpose, and that is to manipulate the cartridge in and out of the rifle, and to produce a positive and safe lock up on firing. I will deal with all action types in the following chapters, but the most common is the bolt action, which I will discuss here in more detail.

The heart of any rifle is a good action from which the trigger, barrel and stock are secured. It is important that an action is as concentric and true in manufacture as possible, because any deviation will result in poor bedding to a stock, or unsquare barrel unions or a binding or sloppy bolt.

Take a Remington M700, which is an industry standard rifle with a well respected action: like so many other similar bolt actions, the

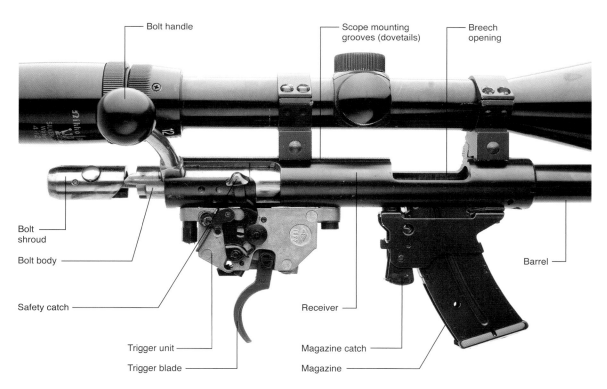

All the important parts of a modern rimfire bolt action rifle.

Take-down rifles are very popular among stalking enthusiasts, because a swift barrel or stock change can transform a deer rifle into a fox gun in an instant.

receiver is a solid piece of ordnance. In this case it is rounded, and has race ways cut internally so that a cylindrical bolt with twin opposing locking lugs can slide back and forth. At their forward position the bolt lugs travel through a 90-degree arc that locks them against the action's face to support a cartridge within the barrel's chamber that is secured immediately in front of it.

In its rear-moving position an extractor claw grips the case's rim in the head and withdraws the fired case from the chamber; it is then ejected from the rifle's action via (in this case) a plunger recessed within the bolt face. All this movement is governed by an external bolt handle. This design has changed very little over the years, with manufacturers having differing variations on a theme but all basically performing the same duty.

Actions come unstuck if out of true, and many people may want to have their rifle's action blue-printed or trued with the idea that if everything is made to be concentric, there is the best possible chance of reaching the best accuracy potential. This means that all the threads and unions are squared and recut to a precise fit, and bolt lugs are lapped, race ways ground and polished, load-bearing surfaces lapped or trued, recoil lugs squared and even collars fitted to bolts to provide a more precise fit.

Alternatively you could elect to go the custom route and order a custom action that has all these processes built in.

Triggers

Triggers on most rifles supplied from the factory are more than adequate for most sporting purposes, and certainly err on the side of caution with regard to safety rather than pure usability. Trigger pulls are often heavy to avoid

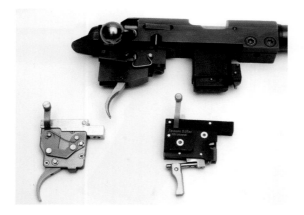

Factory-fitted triggers are better these days, but aftermarket triggers such as the Jewell and C G Universal transform the feel and performance.

unwanted discharges, and trigger blade creep and lack of feel are common. However, most triggers are adjustable or can be worked on by a competent gunsmith – though you should be extremely cautious if you decide to do this yourself.

Most triggers perform the same task: to allow a controlled and predictable release of the sear to allow the firing pin to be released and thus initiate the firing sequence. There is a huge variation, but what you are looking for is a clean, precise, perfectly safe trigger release that will help accuracy. There are three main types: single-stage triggers, two-stage triggers and set triggers.

Single-stage triggers are just that: the release of the trigger sear is achieved with a single pressure to the trigger blade. There should be no creep or movement, just a clean, predictable let-off point enabling a speedy firing cycle. Two-stage triggers differ in that the first pressure point is there to take up the slack and settle your aim to a point where the sear is finally let off by a small crisp second pull that concludes the firing sequence. Proper follow-through on the shot for consistent aiming and accuracy is paramount, especially on some actions where the lock time is slow, for example external hammers such as the T/C G2 carbines.

Set triggers are popular on the Continent, and many centre-fire factory rifles are thus equipped as standard. Operation is via twin trigger blades or the bi-directional use of one traditional blade. A set trigger allows the shooter to 'set' the trigger pull to a small release by pushing the existing blade forwards, as on Mannlicher Pro Hunters, or pulling the second blade on a two-blade system. Whichever one you choose the trigger release can be very light, and in all but perfect weather conditions you should be wary of premature trigger release, especially if you suffer from 'buck fever'.

Stocks

In times gone by most sportspeople only ever had a choice of one stock material, and that was wood: cheap beech on rimfires, or sturdy or well figured walnut on more expensive rifles. But from the nineteen-eighties onwards I can remember seeing new 'plastic' stocks appearing on the market, showing the virtues of their

Today, sportspersons can benefit from the weather-resistant and unshifting zero potential of synthetic and laminated stocks.

weather resistance and strength. Nowadays synthetic stocks are commonplace, not just as an aftermarket purchase but also as a standard trim or option on most factory rifles. One reason is the cost and lack of availability of really good quality walnut, and the price increases have meant that synthetic stocks are actually a more viable option, quite apart from the practical benefits.

Synthetic stocks can take many forms, from the standard factory profile to a true custom item with unique design. But whatever they look like, there are definite benefits to the shooter who really uses their rifle, not least the fact that synthetic stocks are usually much lighter than their wooden alternatives and so a lightweight sporting rifle with more weight in the barrel, or a Mountain-type gun, can be achieved. This is usually accomplished by using two hollow halves of moulded plastic or synthetic polymer, which can be less rigid than a standard wood stock. This has the problems of twisting and bending on firing, especially in the fore-end region, which is detrimental to accuracy.

The best advice is to go for a make such as McMillan, H-S Precision, Robertson's or Bell and Carlson, which use solid or laminated layers of polymer with built-in colour patterns or external finishes; and some, like the H-S Precision, can come with integral bedding blocks for stiffness and precise bedding. The non-warping impervious nature of synthetic stocks makes them a favourite with custom makers, and they can have synthetic bedding or pillars added after purchase to make a totally reliable rifle.

This is not to say that traditional walnut stock is out of vogue – it is not, and many wood stocks are now being furnished with factory bedding blocks and/or synthetic bedding pillars to go some way to avoid moisture-induced accuracy problems.

Laminates are a half-way house because they use numerous thin layers of wood veneer bonded with a resin to form a super strong, weather-impervious 'sandwich'. These stocks give good stability, which is great for accuracy. Depending on the wood veneers used, they can look very striking; but most suffer from the same problem of being heavy, so are best used for static shooting rifles.

Barrels

Dependent on application, be that small game or varmint or deer stalking, each shooter will have their own preference to barrel length,

The precise bedding of action to stock to provide a solid platform to achieve maximum accuracy from a rifle is now becoming standard on some factory rifles such as this T/C Icon.

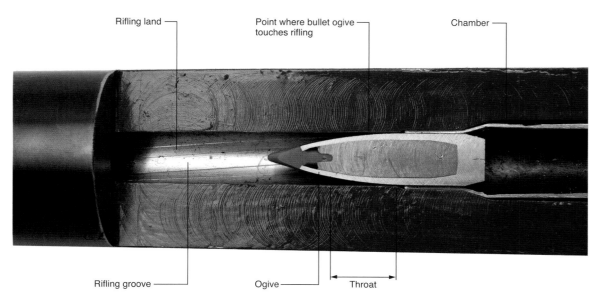

Rifling land

Point where bullet ogive
touches rifling

Chamber

Rifling groove

Ogive

Throat

Cut-away of the barrel showing the relationship between the rifling and bullet's seating depth, and why it is crucial to think about the whole firing cycle, and not just pulling the trigger.

contour weight, material and finishes. With a factory rifle you have a choice of chrome moly steel that is blued externally or stainless steel that has a bead-blasted, non-reflective finish with a contour that suits the calibre or application. For instance a .17 Fireball can have a slim sporter profile in a lightweight sporter stock for use as a walking vermin or fox rifle, or if you prefer a heavier rifle in full blown varmint trim, then the same calibre can be had in a heavyweight varmint contour and longer barrel.

Light barrels heat up more quickly than heavy ones, so this may be your consideration especially if you intend shooting a lot of rounds at one sitting, such as long range varminting.

More important to me is the internal make-up of a barrel, as the barrel is the most crucial item on a rifle with regard to accuracy potential. Choice of calibre from a factory gun means that the manufacturer has already settled on a chamber dimension with correct throating and barrel twist to give the average cartridge shooting a variety of bullet weights.

You choose a .223 for fox work with a 1 in 12 twist rifled barrel which is fine for fast moving lighter bullets from 30–55 grains but when you start to reach the 60 grain plus bullets there is

not enough rotational spin to stabilise the bullet weight and to achieve a load with the heavier 60, 70, 75, 80 or even 90 grain bullets the rifling twist rate must increase or become faster and so a 1 in 9 or even 1 in 6.5 twist is appropriate. Some manufacturers offer two twist rates but they are rare, and this is why a custom barrel tailored to your needs is a good option.

The inside of the barrel is a volatile place, and great pressures and stresses are put on the barrel as a cartridge is fired and a bullet starts up

Manufacturers usually make a sporter and varmint version of a popular rifle in their range, such as these Tikka rifles.

There is a style of rifle to suit any need or just personal preference, from full stocked Stutzen to classic walnut sporter.

the barrel. Any imperfection will culminate in minute vibrations and a bullet not starting in a straight line and thus at the muzzle the harmonics of the barrel resonance will make the bullet depart the barrel at slightly differing points, causing inaccuracies.

That is fine, but shooters can certainly benefit from understanding that to achieve optimum performance from a calibre, a custom barrel is a far better option. If you rebarrel a rifle you can choose your own barrel contour that governs weight, barrel vibrations and heat dispersion. You can also choose that contour at differing lengths to suit both the cartridge's ballistic characteristics or your needs i.e. a short fat 18 inch .308 calibre barrel would make a great deer gun in woodland giving a short yet barrel vibration deadening heft to it. Or you could elect to go for the same calibre with the same length but with a sporter profile to achieve a lighter rifle for hill work. Alternatively if weight is a concern but you like the longer heavy barrel for velocity reasons then why not elect to have the barrel fluted that removes weight from the barrel but keeps the overall profile the same with better heat dispersion.

The main area to consider is the inside of the barrel where the real work is done. Choosing a rifle with a standard chamber but match grade barrel material is fine but why not go the whole hog and have a tighter than average chamber to minimum specs with a tight neck to achieve better concentricity. This will require special case and reloading prep and then have a custom throat cut to suit the specific bullets you want to shoot and have them seated so the maximum powder capacity or load density is achieved further enhancing the rifles true performance so long as it cycles through the magazine still. Options are endless with barrel twist rate as discussed and even throat angles to support the bullet before entering the rifling all can be considered and even rifling profile or number of lands to control stability and reduce barrel fouling all have great merit. This subject is an entire book in its self.

FINISHES

Shooters are becoming more demanding with regard the coatings or finishes used to the exterior of their rifles. Traditionally the blued steel and oiled walnut would suffice but as trends change there has been a swing towards more durable and hunter-friendly finishes with regard to weather resistance and subdued surfaces so as not to spook one's game. High polished blueing looks great on a traditional or classic firearm and if well cared for will serve you well enough but unwanted reflections from high grade lacquered stocks can and do betray your presence if not careful plus you are always mindful of not scratching that well figured stock that your mind is often not 100% focused on the field craft. You can still have a traditional blued finish, but I prefer the underlying pre-treated surfaces to be shot blasted with grit to give an even yet satin or dull overall look.

Alternatively you can elect to have one of the many after market treatments applied to your rifles exterior. For metal parts be they chrome moly or stainless finish you can choose many paint, bonding or surface treatments such as Mil Spec paint that is impervious to acids and fouling as well as water or have a tough Teflon coating applied for the same reasoning. Treatments such as KG or Duracoat are oven baked heat treatments that bond a tough exterior jacket to metal parts that is available in many colours to suit terrain, foliage or personal bent!

Indeed the firm of Hydrographic specialise in very personalised rifle coatings for part or all of the rifle including scope mounts and acces-sories. Coatings can be plain bold colours to graduated patterns or abstract designs although camouflage patterns are very popular for concealment purposes but may raise a few eye brows in the traditionalist camp. These are highly practical, durable and in some finishes are non-slip that will enhance an old gun, or finish off a custom project.

CUSTOM ROUTE

There is a trend towards custom rifles that utilise the very best of each component discussed above. Often a custom rifle designed and made to your requirements far outweighs any additional costs, which will be considerable, but what you get is a highly accurate and functional rifle that will deliver humane shots year after year. If you can afford one then the expense of buying two or three cheaper models is soon outweighed.

Custom centre-fire rifles such as this Steve Bowers sporter are at the pinnacle of rifle design and performance.

The Sommer and Ockenfuss rifle utilizes an unusual grip-cocking action and has the format of a bull pup rifle; in a tight spot this rifle performs admirably.

Custom rifle builders in Great Britain are on the increase, but Callum Ferguson, Steve Bowers and Norman Clark are still at the top of their game. Rebarrelling an old but favourite rifle to breathe new life into it, or finer tune the calibre choice to perfectly match your quarry species, is a great option.

One need not necessarily go to the expense of a complete custom rifle build. Often if your existing rifle's design fits you, then a Match grade barrel refit will revitalize a treasured arm. It is a good time to consider calibre choice too, and if the bolt from the donor gun is the appropriate size then any calibre can be chosen, as long as the action length will cycle it as will the magazine if desired. I have done this on many an occasion when experimenting with Wildcat calibres. If they do not work out it is just the cost of a rebarrel job; if it works then the same applies but with more smiles. I favour the old Tikka M55 and M65 actions along with the old Sako pre-75 actions, when build quality and non plastic parts were still key ingredients and not governed by cheap overseas competitors.

Regardless of choice, hopefully there will be something in these pages that will interest you and guide you through the maze of technical jargons.

Perfection in custom rimfires is the Norman Clark silenced .22lr BSA Martini rifle; this is a serious longer range rabbit rifle.

Chapter 1
Quarry Species

No sportsperson should venture into the great outdoors without first fully familiarizing himself with the quarry species he hopes to shoot. This is not only essential with regard to a successful conclusion to the shoot, but ethically any sportsperson should respect the game he seeks. Take time to learn about the quarry's lifestyle and habitat, and you will gain far more from a day's shooting than purely filling your bag.

The best way to have a truly hands-on experience of wildlife is to venture into the woods not with a rifle but with binoculars and a camera. Mastering the art of stealth, fieldcraft and stalking using this equipment is far more difficult than with a rifle, and when you have mastered the skill of successfully stalking to within camera shot, changing to a rifle will seem second nature. I spend just as much time out in the woods with my camera as I do with my rifle, and have learnt so much more about my quarry animals and their habits by studying them than by just shooting them the instant I see them. Animals have far keener senses than you and I, and are very adept at avoiding humans however good our equipment, and without a little 'insider' knowledge our stalk will be nothing more than a pleasant walk in the woods.

We are fortunate in that in the British Isles we have a great diversity and a plentiful supply of quality quarry species to shoot, from the humble rabbit, the hated rat to the crafty fox, right up to the majestic stag and now the wild boar that is making a comeback – we have never had it so good. This great diversity is in itself the challenge for the sportsperson, because to master the differing skills necessary to hunt such a wide spread in quarry species would take a lifetime – and this in a nutshell sums up the sport that so many of us enjoy: if it was too easy we would not feel that tingling exhilaration that we do now from, say, a successful deer stalk, and this is why a good sportsperson keeps coming back for more.

Fair game can be split into three categories: small game, foxes and deer.

SMALL GAME

The smallest species provide a challenging and plentiful sporting prospect, but as in all categories, safe and sensible shooting practices must always be observed. Feathered game and squirrels are usually tree bound, but whether in the trees or on the ground, if a safe shot is not possible then you should never attempt it.

The Brown Rat (Rattus norvegicus)

Probably the most universally hated mammal on the planet, this long-tailed verminous rodent is actually a great quarry species for fledgling shooters, or just for pure sport at close range; an evening spent sitting patiently can often result in fast and furious personal sport as day turns to dusk. But knowing a few basic facts about the rat's lifecycle can reveal a lot about their habits and therefore how best to achieve a good bag.

The brown rat is the only rat species that is legal quarry. It forms part of the mouse family, and usually weighs anything from 10oz (280g) to over 1lb (450g), though some that have fed on well stocked grain stores grow to monster size and become a sporting challenge in themselves. Their body can be 10in (25cm) long with a further 7–8in (18–20cm) added for the tail, but they have a dumpy appearance as compared with

Scourge of the inner city, the rat has always been on the vermin shooter's list, especially in grain stores and around farm buildings.

the more slender black rat. The fur is browny grey, graduating to a paler underbelly, but the feet and ears are characteristically bald, as is the long scaly tail.

As regards habitat and distribution, I do not think there is anywhere that does not have a population of this vermin species – they have indeed become endemic in our society, and their proliferation is often encouraged by our own slovenly social habits. From a sporting point of view, farm buildings, outhouses or grain stores are the most obvious habitat: wait patiently and they will inevitably emerge.

They are usually active at dawn or dusk and more often throughout the night, and with their fast and furious feeding habits, typical of any rodent, they are extremely adaptable and will swim, climb and jump remarkable distances if they have to. They form a typically hierarchical family system, predominantly living in their own, often large, dug burrow systems, beneath buildings for security.

Their prolific nature is partly due to the fact that they enjoy a year-round mating season, unless the climate is very cold. The gestation period is between twenty-two to twenty-four days, and they can have up to six litters of between five and twelve young every year. With only a fifteen-day weaning period and independence within six weeks, you can see why they are considered undesirable world wide.

Their eating habits relate to the donor source, and being omnivores they enjoy a very varied diet of plants, seeds, fruit, carrion, fish, eggs and human food as well as mice. They live communally in related groups of up to sixty rats, and there is a strong family bond; one female will mate with many males, and surrogate mothers are commonplace. This means that if a mother is shot, another is there to replace it.

From a human point of view it is essential never to touch a shot rat with the bare hands as rats carry diseases such as salmonella or, more importantly, Weil's disease. Wear gloves and burn the corpses.

The Rabbit (*Oryctolagus cuniculus*)

If ever there was a classic sporting game animal, it has to be the humble rabbit. Not only does this prolific yet wary quarry species offer a real challenge to the shooter, but after a successful stalk it yields fantastic meat to eat. It is undoubtedly my personal favourite.

Commonly 12–16in (30–40cm) long and weighing anything from 2lb (1kg), the rabbit is instantly recognizable from its relative the hare by its smaller size and ears. It is normally salt and pepper brown grey in colour, although I have seen varied colours from buff to black, depending on habitat and interbreeding. The universal white underside of the tail is usually only seen after it has winded you and is scurrying towards the hedgerow!

Now widespread throughout the British Isles and Ireland, I have shot many a rabbit on the outer reaches of the Scottish Hebrides – so it is genuinely a universally adaptable animal.

Its habitat is extremely varied, from sandy dune systems, low-lying plant cover to heaths and woodland areas. All rabbits like to be warm and dry, and they rarely venture past an altitude of 1,250–1,500ft (375–450m). On a fine morning you are most likely to find them sunning themselves in a spot sheltered from the prevailing wind; then you can take a careful stalk downwind to within range.

Ultimately their diet is the reason why they

OPPOSITE: Close encounters with wild animals are always exhilarating!

The mainstay of any small game shooter, the humble rabbit offers very good sport and its meat is delicious.

live in large communities: purely vegetarian in their preferences, rabbits forage for grasses, bulbs, bark, roots and herbs, and this dictates that they must live on the fringes of cultivated areas or woodland margins. They do so in several large family groups in burrows called warrens, where there is safety in numbers. The mating season is usually between February and July, but with global warming a year-round breeding season is now commonplace.

Gestation is between twenty-eight to thirty-one days, and a doe will have four to six litters a year of between four to six young; this allows a rapid and successful regeneration of rabbit numbers despite heavy hunting pressure. Suckled for less than four weeks, the young are then independent.

Clearly hierarchical, rabbits will frequent territorial marking areas and will scent mark from a chin gland, rubbing areas that are obviously specific rabbit landmarks such as logs or stones. Learn to look for these, and a clear rabbit living pattern will emerge.

In some areas it is in pursuit of the rabbit that the novice shooter is introduced to sporting shooting. And after thirty-five years this particular shooter still ranks the rabbit as one of the best quarry species.

The Hare (Lepus europaeous)

The brown hare is more common than the mountain hare, and is the variety that shooters will probably encounter most often. Substantially larger than the rabbit, the hare can weigh upwards of 10lb (4.5kg); it is between 15–25in (40–60cm) long, with yellowish brown fur and distinctive long black-tipped ears. The posture is decidedly more bulky, with the hindquarters being longer and more powerful than the rabbit's.

The hare lies up during the day in a shallow depression known as a 'form', in the open fields or in long grassy outcrops; when undisrupted it can be seen cantering across the fields with its characteristic lolloping gait.

Hares become most active in about March, when the males fight for dominance of the females, who will chase away unwanted suitors. Gestation is forty-two days, and a female will have three to four litters a year of two to five young; they are suckled for no more than three weeks, and are fully independent at four to five weeks.

Much like the rabbit, the best times to shoot the hare is at dawn and dusk, although a stealthy stalk during the day can provide some keen sport.

The Grey Squirrel (Sciurus carolinensis)

Often described as a 'tree rat', the grey squirrel is fast, tough and scatty, and can be hard to drop instantly. A real challenge to shoot, the woodland floor-feeding squirrels offer a safer shot than the varieties that colonize the trees.

From 8–10in (20–25cm) long, with a tail of three-quarters that length on average, the squirrel weighs 1–1.5lb (450–675g) and is instantly recognizable as a squat, tough little mammal. It is grey-white in appearance with a hint of orange to the head and rear end; the underbelly is almost white. The short, sharp pointed ears are always on the alert.

A North American species, the grey squirrel is endemic throughout most of Britain and has ousted the smaller and more attractive native red squirrel. As with so many invading species, it has been a fast colonizer and is at home in both mixed and broad-leaved woodland as well as in gardens and open urban spaces where food is abundant.

Grey squirrels spend more time on the ground than reds, so potentially offer a safer shot (note that the red squirrel is legally protected); however, they nest high in the fork of a suitable tree, the nest being called a dray. They have a reasonably long gestation period of forty-two to forty-five weeks, with only one litter of between two to four young born in the warmer spring months; very occasionally a second is weaned at ten weeks.

The normal food source consists of acorns, and they like any kind of nuts; they can also be attracted by fruit as long as it is sliced and sweet-smelling. This can be a good ploy to entice them within range, as too is mimicking their chatting call.

Squirrels can cause tremendous damage to forestry plantations and so numbers have to be controlled.

Carrion Crow (Corvus corone) and Hooded Crow (Corvus cornix)

The crow generally offers a very good opportunistic shot, and this can range from a close-up farmyard distance to extremely long range with specialist equipment. The wariness of the wild crow is legendary, and in my view, any crow bagged with a rifle is a sporting achievement.

The most common is the carrion crow, which is widespread throughout England and Wales and southern parts of Scotland; further north the hooded crow is predominant. Both male and female are 12–14in (30–35cm) in length and all-over black in colour including the beak; the call is a characteristic 'Kaa, kaa' uttered in quick succession, or a lower, more guttural ronking tone.

The crow is a solitary nesting bird, and usually builds its home high in the branches of a tree

RIGHT: Crows are very good at keeping just out of range of your rifle; they have superb eyesight, which makes them worthy adversaries.

or cliff edge. Here the female lays a single clutch of between three to six eggs, light blue-grey in colour and dappled with mud-brown spots, towards the end of March or in early April, although later clutches are now commonplace. The chicks are strong enough to leave the nest after thirty-five days, but may rely on the parents for food until spring arrives.

The crow is considered to be vermin, especially by farmers, who blame them for pecking out the eyes of newborn lambs and stealing grouse eggs. Certainly they will do this, but successful crow control keeps numbers to a tolerable level and minimizes this risk. The crow's regular diet includes small reptiles such as frogs, small birds, insects, grain, worms, fruit, nuts, occasional fish and root crops. I have also spent many a morning watching hooded crows, a northern variety of the carrion crow, feasting on small crab and mussels on the shorelines of Argyll.

Crows by nature are far more solitary than rooks, which live in large family groups. Their eyesight is very keen, and they can spot the slightest bolt movement from a rifle at a good distance; they are also extremely wary, and will only return after a long while, when the hunter has probably given up all hope of a shot. Stalking the crow with a rifle is therefore a real challenge, because a missed shot from a long stalk or wait may be all you will achieve in a morning's work. Long-range varminting involving specialist equipment to tackle crows at extreme range is exciting, and as far as sport goes, one of my personal favourites: stealth and extreme accuracy with correct wind judgement are necessary to connect with a small-bodied crow at over 400 yards.

Magpie (Pica pica)

The pied villain of the hedgerow, magpies are extremely abundant and offer good sport and at the same time valuable pest control to the landowner over whose land you shoot.

The magpie has certainly exploited the urban sprawl in England. In some areas they exist in intolerable numbers to the point that fifteen to twenty can be shot in succession, only to be replaced by the same number a week later. Magpies mob other species, and will also give away a fox or deer's presence with their characteristic chatter. One shot magpie attracts another, which if it is shot attracts another, and so on.

Identification cannot be confused with any other species as no other bird is like the magpie: with its very striking black and white plumage and pronounced chattering 'kak-kak-kak-kak' call, it stands out in our woodland environment. Both sexes are alike, about 14in (35cm) in length and the tail half as long again. Most happy in woodland edges, its nest is often perched precariously on branches and bush cover. Breeding and nest building starts in February, with a normal clutch of between six to eight eggs laid in April to May. With an incubation period of only twenty-two to twenty-four days, the fledglings then leave the nest after only twenty-four days.

Magpies are prolific in some areas, and their characteristic chattering is an essential part of the rich tapestry of the British countryside.

Magpies feed on flies, beetles, worms, small mammals, carrion, cereal, fruit, frogs, nuts, human food waste and roadside casualties.

Rooks (Corvus frugilegus), Jackdaws (Corvus monedula) and Jay (Garrulus glandarius)

You are more likely to encounter crows than these three species, but where they proliferate they offer sport in their own right.

The jay is a predator amongst small bird species and is hence legal to shoot, but I have never shot a jay and feel no compunction to do so; I always like to hear their screeching call and see their brightly coloured plumage in the woods.

Jackdaws too are egg thieves, and are therefore no favourite amongst gamekeepers, but they do not devour crops as pigeons do, and are more of a pest around farm buildings as they tend to form large groups and their roosts make a mess.

The rook, on the other hand, offers a better sporting prospect. It can be distinguished from the carrion crow by its bare-skinned face and whiter-coloured and thinner bill, and on the ground it walks with a definite waddle, and the leg area is more plumped up with feathers than a crow's.

Rooks favour grassland and coppiced woodland, where they form large and very noisy roosts from April onwards. Young birds are called branchers and are commonly shot with rimfire where safe to do so; the breast meat is traditionally made into pies.

Like most of the crow family, rooks have good eyesight, and when armed with a rifle, the sportsperson's total concealment and minimal movement is essential for success.

Wood Pigeon (Columba palumbus) or Collared Dove (Streptopelia decaocto)

Usually the domain of the shotgunner, there is no reason why the pigeon or collared dove cannot be taken with a rifle of the correct calibre where it is safe to do so. Both are a more opportunistic quarry for a rifle than, say, a rabbit. I usually only shoot pigeons if I am on a woodland

Pigeons should only be shot on the ground for safety reasons, and then only head shots taken.

edge or within a concealed ride within the wood, ostensibly out shooting rabbits with a silenced rimfire, and one lands within range and offers a chance shot.

Widespread now throughout Britain except in the remotest or wettest hill areas, the pigeon thrives on the intensive farming regimes in certain areas of the country. However, they need woodland to roost and breed, and the ideal situation is to shoot them as they fly to and from their feeding grounds.

Particular care must be taken to identify the woodpigeon correctly from other protected pigeon species; from a distance it can be identified by its characteristic flight. The predominantly grey plumage is striped with distinctive white wing bars that are visible from a distance, as is the black tip to the tail. At closer range the neck can be seen to have a white patch on each side.

Collared doves are much smaller and have a more overall buff/pink tinge to the plumage.

Foxes need to be controlled, but I still admire their tenacity and guile.

Both sexes are similar, and measure 10–12in (25–30cm) in length, as compared to the wood-pigeon's 16in (40cm).

Diet varies between predominantly greens and grain, according to seasonal availability. The successful shooter will familiarize himself with the rotational nature of the crops in the farm landscape, and plan a suitable course of action to intercept the hungry birds. Pigeons can eat their own bodyweight of over 1lb every three days or so, and will feed at least three times a day if possible, and more often on colder days.

During the winter, clover, ivy and holly berries and seeds from weeds are the main foods, although rape, kale and sprout leaves will also be taken, so site your hide near these. In spring and summer the birds will move to sown grain crops such as maize, beans, peas, clover, kale and rape, whilst in autumn they will seek out the stubble fields of grain and ripe maize, enjoying the occasional slug or worm.

The pigeon's eyesight is supreme, and it can readily spot the white areas of your face and hands and the slightest movement. A wary shooter will always wear gloves and at least a hat, but better still is to set up a hide with a light-weight camouflage mesh and sit patiently.

Collared doves can provide great sport around grain stores, using reduced velocity rimfire ammunition. Culling is necessary to keep these hungry marauders down to tolerable levels.

THE FOX (*VULPES VULPES*)

The red fox can offer a great variety of sporting opportunities to the rifleman. Shooting from a fixed position at dawn or dusk can be very profitable, as is calling them up, using both hand-held and electrical devices; and if human disturbance is high, lamping for foxes at night really does pay dividends. Alternatively, where foxes are 'lamp shy', night vision equipment is becoming increasingly popular.

The fox has successfully colonized all environmental regions, and far from being more docile as compared with the urban fox, the true farmland creature is every bit as clever and elusive as it always was. Its diet includes small mammals, birds, insects, carrion, berries and worms. Depending on the availability of food, the average weight of an adult fox can vary greatly from 10lb (4.5kg) to over 20lb (9kg); normally from the nose to the tip of the tail it is some 40in (1m) long.

Mating usually takes place between January and February; when courting the fox will make a characteristic screaming call. Gestation is fifty-two days, and there are commonly four to six cubs in a litter, sometimes more; the vixen stays in the earth with the young cubs and the dog fox brings them food every day. The dog fox can be stalked above ground during the day as he sleeps curled up in crops or thick vegetation. The cubs become independent after five months.

Foxes are highly territorial, territory size depending on population density and how easily food is available. Left undisturbed they will routinely patrol a set path, and this can be their downfall because you can intercept them en route. They will scent mark their territory at well defined sites with urine or anal gland secretions, and with secretions from glands in the feet, particularly at night.

Their sense of smell is good, but not as acute as their hearing, which can instantly pinpoint an incautious metallic clank as your binoculars touch your rifle barrel. Often when you are calling up a fox it will come downwind unseen and then melt back into the undergrowth, with you none the wiser that it was there at all!

Although foxes do take lambs and young roe deer – almost certainly sick ones – they also eat a large number of small rodents and rabbits, which is actually of benefit to the land where population densities are high. So with foxes, a balance in control is always the best policy.

DEER

There are six species of deer available for sporting shooters in this country: red, sika, fallow, roe, muntjac and Chinese water deer (CWD). Only the red and roe are indigenous, the others being introduced or park escapees.

The differing size and natural habits of each

The red deer stag represents most people's perception of deer stalking in Britain, and no finer a day's sport can be had than stalking red deer in the Scottish Highlands.

species can really test the ability of any shooter, and keen stalking techniques and appropriate rifles and calibres are needed. These must comply to the differing legal requirements in certain parts of the country, and will be discussed in more detail in Chapter 6 on cartridge ballistics.

Red (Cervus elaphus)

The largest of our deer species, the red deer has an uncanny knack of being just out of range or over the next hillock when you stalk it. There is no doubt that the heart stirs when you are in close proximity to these beasts. They are often 75in (2m) in length with a shoulder height of 50in (1.25m); in weight, adult stags often exceed 300–400lb in nutrient-rich feeding areas. They have a reddish coat in summer, which coincides with the stag's antler growth prior to the rut, or mating season, between September and October; thereafter the pelage changes to a dark greyish brown, though it retains the prominent yellowish rump patch.

Like most wild animals and deer species, the red deer's habitat is varied and depends on the availability of cover and natural food sources; this means that deciduous woodlands, forestry, mixed woods, moorlands and beyond the tree line can all be suitable for the red deer to survive.

The females, known as hinds, live with the calves apart from the stags for most of the year, but join up with either a solitary male or a 'bachelor' groups for the rut. This period is truly magical, especially in the Highlands of Scotland where the stag's roaring call echoes down the glens announcing his presence to his harem of hinds and as a signal of his prowess and intentions to other would-be suitors. Stand-offs between stags involve much body posturing, and if intimidation is not sufficient, they will engage in a head-to-head battle of strength with interlocked antlers.

It is at this time that a stalker can watch and assess the health of the herd to some degree, marking out stags suitable for culling. It is also a good time to mimic the stag's roars to bring a selected cull animal within range either for closer observation or a safe shot; many stalkers 'rattle' cast antlers to mimic two stags in battle

Mature fallow deer are almost nocturnal where I live; often there is only a glimpse of them at dawn and dusk, which makes managing their numbers very difficult.

– although if done incorrectly this can have the reverse effect and scare the stag off.

Gestation is eight months, and usually a single calf is born. It is suckled until it is nine months old, but even after weaning it will stay close to its mother until the following year.

As with all deerstalking, the aim of the stalker is to improve the health of the herd and thereby maintain a healthy, viable stock of deer for the available food cover per acre. This means that more hinds should be culled each year than stags; however, the lure of the red's magnificent antlers often results in an imbalance in the sexes shot by paying guests if this issue is not closely regulated. Couple this to the fact that hinds are shot largely over the winter months when the young have had time to become more independent, it takes a dedicated stalker to fulfil their hind cull on time and with the correct percentage.

Fallow (*Dama dama*)

Fallow are most commonly associated with country houses and estates as the deer of choice to fill big parklands. Their varying coloration – from white to menil spotted and black – obviously has its appeal. However, the truly wild fallow is an altogether different deer. Being a true dawn and dusk beast for its feeding activities it has a cunning knack of disappearing from the fields and melting back into the woods just as the first legal amount of light breaks in the sky or fades away.

Smaller than the red at about 65in (1.5m) long and 35in (90cm) at the shoulder, it has a characteristically long tail of about 10in (25cm). The largest buck can weigh in at 150–200lb (70–90kg).

Fallow prefer a mixed or deciduous woodland environment in lowland regions, and feed on grasses, herbs and fruit, with acorns and beech mast being favourites, too. They rut in the autumn, as do the red deer, but usually later, often going into November. The buck will mark out a 'stand', and utters a guttural belching call to attract does and warn off rival bucks.

A buck will mate with many does. The doe usually produces a single fawn, though sometimes she will bear twins, after a gestation of thirty-two weeks. When the calf is born she will conceal it in undergrowth for several weeks until weaning at six to nine weeks.

The bucks grow interesting antlers, which progressively become bigger and more elaborate after each annual casting in April or May, as long as the feeding is good. The characteristic palmated antler instantly identifies the fallow deer, as does the long tail with black borders. A useful adjunct when stalking this species is a thoughtfully sited high seat that offers a clear view into vegetation and puts you out of the fallow deer's range of vision.

Sika (*Cervus nippon*)

The sika is a species of deer introduced from Japan. It has colonies in many parts of Scotland, England and Ireland, and has now successfully interbred with our native red deer. Smaller in stature than the red and fallow, it is up to 60in

Prettiest of the non-indigenous species is the Sika deer, the stags with their upright antlers and rich brown pelage.

(1.5m) in length and has a long tail of up to 5in (13cm). It has a reddish-brown coat with distinctive off-white spots in summer; these fade in winter, and the pelage changes to a dark, nutty-coloured grey-brown.

Like the fallow deer, the sika is a grazer and browser, preferring grasses, fruits, berries and tree shoots. It lives in separate-sex herds in woodland areas or close cover hill land.

The sika can be very secretive, and has a reputation for being very tough to stalk. From my own experience, for an early morning stalk it is essential to get into position before sunrise to maximize your chances of success.

As with most deer, the rut is a good time to see more activity involving often large stags that do not otherwise make themselves known outside the hours of darkness. You will know when the rut has started with sika because in October to November you will hear the stags' high-pitched, ear-piercing whistling call – a very primeval and unnerving sound on a misty autumn morning.

Again, a single calf is born (rarely twins) after a thirty-two week gestation period, and although independent from weaning after nine months or so, it will stay with the hind until the following year.

The sika is recognizable from the red by the 'V'-shaped brow to the face and the very obvious white hock glands. The antler growth is similar to the red but appears more upright, with a mature stag having eight tines to the beams, typically four on each side.

Roe (*Capreolus capreolus*)

My favourite and, in my view, the most beautiful of our deer species, the roe is a challenging and highly addictive deer to stalk. The bucks regrow their antlers each year, typically with six points, but roe have a very wide variation of antler growth and form, making them difficult both to age and to recognize – yet they are highly desirable amongst hunters.

Their frame is altogether smaller, perhaps 48in (1.2m) in length and 30in (75cm) at the shoulder, and weighing some 55lb (25kg) for the buck, and they move daintily. They have a vivid red summer pelage with no spots or visible tail,

Nothing is more handsome than a roe buck in summer coat. Shy and elusive, stalking the roe with rifle or camera is my favourite pastime.

but a white rump that they fluff out when alarmed. In winter the coat changes to a coarser dark brown/grey, with white throat patches.

In winter the bucks also shed their antlers and grow new ones; these are covered in velvety skin until they are fully formed from March onwards, depending on the maturity of the bucks, when they rub them against trees and bushes until the velvet is removed. The older bucks are the first to cast, grow and then clean their antlers so they can fray and mark territories in the spring. Their intention is to pair up with a doe for the rut, which starts earlier than other deer species, in July to August. This involves the buck chasing the does, often in rings formed in the fields, with the does egging the buck on with a repetitive feeping call.

For the stalker there is a plethora of man-made imitations of the doe's call, which can bring an eager buck to within range for observation. In fact, collecting roe calls is a hobby in its own right.

Roe have a delayed implantation gestation period, so the foetuses develop from December until the fawns/kids, usually twins and sometimes even triplets, are born in May.

Roe are more commonly browsers, favouring buds, leaves, twigs and especially brambles with cereals, fungi and grass/herbs also being taken. If you find a good source of these foods at the appropriate time of year, then this will be a good place to stalk roe. Roe also bark, and with practice a stalker can imitate this, either to stop an alerted and fleeing deer (both sexes bark) or to lute in a buck during the spring when he is actively marking his territory and will respond to barking, thinking it is another rival buck.

It is important to form a balanced deer management plan for the land you shoot on, and this means shooting more female deer than males, in this case a roe doe, to keep the population equilibrium.

The Muntjac (Muntiacus reevesii)

The muntjac is a foreign import, and the wild population in this country originates from parkland escapees; it has spread to many counties in England, with populations throughout the Midlands, parts of East Anglia, to the borders with Wales and as far south as Sussex.

Muntjac are small, highly active deer measuring only 18in (45cm) at the shoulder; a good buck weighs 35lb (16kg). They prefer dense undergrowth but are active, mobile feeders, taking a nibble here and there on grasses, fruit, brambles and ivy as they patrol their territory.

Their pelage in summer is a very sleek chestnut brown with a pale underbelly. They have primitive short antlers measuring at most 4–6in (10–15cm) with a short brow tine emanating from very long pedicles that form characteristic brow ridges. They also have a pair of short protruding tusks in the upper jaw.

Muntjac are prolific breeders, hence their quick colonization. The doe produces a single

Short, squat and a prolific breeder, the muntjac deer has quickly colonized most counties in England and can provide challenging stalking as they always seem to be on the move.

fawn every seven months, as breeding is non seasonal. This poses a real problem for the stalker not wishing to orphan young, as the doe is either pregnant or has a fawn at foot, and so there is no close season.

The muntjac is a very vocal deer, barking profusely at intruders during the mating process, or at noisy stalkers!

The Chinese Water Deer (CWD) (Hydropotes inermis)

Like the muntjac, the Chinese water deer is a foreign import, the wild population in this country originating from parkland escapees. CWD are more contained around the counties of Bedfordshire, Buckinghamshire, Northamptonshire and adjoining counties.

The CWD is 20in (50cm) high at the shoulder; typically a buck weighs 40lb (18kg). It is more like the roe than the muntjac, but is distinctive in that neither of the sexes has antlers, but instead they grow tusks in the upper jaws. The buck's tusks can be nearly 3in (7.5cm) long. By comparison the hindquarters are higher than

the roe's, and from the front the face has fluffy ears and a prominent button nose. The rut takes place in December, and fawns are born between June and July; they are mature at six months old.

CWD are happy on lower-lying farmland, scrub or woodlands alike, and offer the stalker an unusual and unique deer species to hunt.

CONCLUSION

Each species requires specific characteristics in bullet design in order to achieve a clean kill. What is right for a rabbit rarely works on a fox, and is certainly wholly inappropriate for deer. There is also the legal requirement necessary to achieve correct velocities, energies and minimum calibres. There have been many changes to the law with regard to close seasons and legal calibres for individual species. Chapter 6 deals with cartridges and ballistics, and discusses in depth the correct calibre needed for each species, with effective ranges, bullet choices, terminal velocities and energies, and also some of the new legal issues.

Chapter 2
Clothing and Ancillary Kit

CLOTHING

'There is no such thing as bad weather, just inappropriate clothing' – how true that statement is. There is a bewildering array of clothing on the market today, with some spectacular claims to stealth and weatherproofness, and prices to match – the buyer beware! The needs of a sporting shooter with a rifle are different from those of a game shooter with a shotgun. The latter traditionally wears some form of waxed cotton jacket that is smart, weatherproof and ideally suited to the country lifestyle. However, by the nature of the material it is usually noisy if stalking through foliage after rabbits or deer. Therefore you will need something that is quiet as well as waterproof and well insulated, and in a subdued colour so you blend with your surroundings.

Due to the widely varying temperatures in different parts of the country and at differing times of the year, you will probably want a couple of clothing options to satisfy your needs. Alternatively you could use layers of clothes, and many jackets offer a waterproof outer shell with a removable fleece lining. This way you are kitted out to be comfortable in the coldest Scottish winter or on the warmest summer day whilst out stalking for roe.

The trend these days is for your clothing to have some form of camouflage pattern; this usually comes from the huge popularity of such garments from the USA. There is no doubt that some of these patterns are incredibly lifelike, representing broken tree limbs, leaves or stubble fields. If you like this type of coverage then they can certainly add good concealment outdoors in the correct seasons – but camouflage has a funny way of making you stand out to non-shooters! I use camouflage jackets on occasions but find them somewhat non politically correct these days, and can do without the attention or stigma they may bring you from the general public.

I never leave on a sporting trip without my trusty roe sack; apart from carrying roe deer, I can stow all my other shooting kit in it and it still allows a hands-free operation.

Camouflage clothing can be very effective at making a hunter blend with his environment, seen here using an Attleborough call and Wetlands camouflage pattern.

Swanndri wool clothing from New Zealand and I have been shooting partners for years: it is warm, tough, weather resistant and silent, and the checkered pattern offers good camouflage.

Jackets

I prefer either a plain dark colour, or a nature check or Harris Tweed-type fabric. It is movement and noise that will alert your quarry more than just your body form, and if you sit quietly downwind dressed in plain green clothing you can still see a lot of game. More importantly the fabric should not make too much noise, so when purchasing a jacket be sure to ruffle the arms and collar to see how much the material squeaks or rustles. Usually waterproof jackets are noisier because they have a waterproof layer such as Gore-Tex beneath the outer layer, and this is often very rustly. Some outer fabrics snag and squeak too when touched, which is to be avoided, whilst other types of outer layer, such as saddlecloth, are quieter but still have a noisier inner waterproof layer. You will have to decide how much noise is tolerable to you.

Fleece jackets are certainly the quietest, but most are not fully waterproof unless they have a waterproof membrane; however, when weather conditions are not wet they make a good shooting choice. The only real down side is that burrs can attach themselves easily to the soft woolly surface of a fleece, and in no time at all you can end up covered in them — which, if you think about it, is really good camouflage! They come as smocks or zipper fronted, and I prefer the zipper because if you get too hot it is easier to undo the zip and let the heat out — although having said that, a smock is more weatherproof — ah, choices!

The best choice as far as I am concerned is either traditional Harris tweed or Swanndri. Harris tweed is supremely hard wearing, has good waterproofing, and the pattern is a good nature camouflage. This is also true of my favourite jackets, which are Swanndri. Made in

New Zealand they are made from 100 per cent wool which has been treated to be waterproof. They are silent in use, very hardwearing, and available in many check patterns in good, natural, earthy tones that make you blend into the surroundings whilst still not offending anyone. I have had my Swanndris for more than twenty years and they refuse to die, and that includes the shirts, which on their own make a good replacement for a fleece.

Loden is a traditional European fabric of tightly woven wool usually in a dark green colour; it is nicely weather resistant and quiet. Some of the Loden capes disguise a human's form by being knee length in nature. Again the woolly exterior is prone to picking up burrs so the shooter ends up looking like a Christmas tree with baubles on, but nothing is ever perfect and I like them.

Trousers

Trousers are easier. I usually wear a plain green pair of triple-layered trousers, the outer layer being made from moleskin, which is a hardwearing cotton fabric, the middle layer a Goretex waterproof membrane, and the smooth inner layer avoids chafing, which is a blessing especially on an arduous stalk after deer or rabbits. If you shoot as I do, then you are usually on your knees and elbows a lot, and some form of weatherproofing in the trousers is beneficial. If the weather becomes too hot and these garments, although breathable, still become hot, then I choose a single layer moleskin trouser.

A good feature is to have pockets on the sides of the legs to avoid crushing contents when crawling and making you uncomfortable, and zippered pockets means you avoid losing your car keys. It is easy to retro-fit a zip to any trouser pocket, and I would recommend you do so.

If the weather is really horrendous or extremely cold, especially if you have to remain still for any length of time, such as up a high seat, then it may be wise to invest in a pair of waterproof insulated overtrousers. I use a pair of Sportchief from Canada; although camouflage patterned, these have a fantastically waterproof breathable membrane with a thick fleece lining and so are toasty warm.

Traditional stalkers like the hard-wearing Loden cape because not only does it give good weather protection, but it also disguises a human's outline very well.

Footwear plus Socks

Never skimp on a good pair of boots: there is nothing worse than a pair of cold feet to make you fidget and scare your quarry away. I tend to get through a decent pair of boots every other year, but I do wear them every day. Depending on the style of your shooting you may want a couple of pairs, one for wet days and one for warm ones, as well as a pair of Wellington boots.

For everyday shooting I favour a three-quarter height hiking-type boot with a leather outer skin for flexibility but with a thin insulated and padded section with a good waterproofing membrane. The sole must be pliable enough to give good grip on all surfaces, from mud, snow, rocks and wet grass, and be aware that not all treads work as expected. The key is to be able to feel the ground beneath you, enabling a feedback so you can adjust your gait and weight accordingly and avoid cracking a twig and scaring any animals.

Where it is particularly cold a boot with an inner thermal bootie is ideal and will keep your feet very warm; however, it may make them sweat more if you are a more active stalker. For long periods aloft in high seats these thermally insulated boots are a good choice. I use a pair of Sorels from Canada, which after a day's use in the worse snow or mud are still comfortable and warm. They are expensive, but worth every penny because you are not distracted by cold or wet feet and can concentrate purely on shooting.

Matching the sock to the boot is also important. Always choose boots and socks together, otherwise they may be a tight and uncomfort-

able fit. A blend of wool and synthetics offers good thermal qualities coupled with sufficient lifespan. Being knee high makes them comfortable when gaiters are worn, and helps repel the dreaded midges and ticks.

Hats and Gloves

Often forgotten items are gloves or a hat, but they are really good way of shielding you from the elements and also covering up the most obvious parts of your body to game – nothing spooks animals more than the movement from a pale pair of hands or face, or reflected light off them.

Gloves are cheap, and I use thin cotton pairs with the trigger finger cut off; these are delicate enough to be able to feel through if I need to change scope settings or the like. I always keep several pairs dotted about jackets, trousers and in the car so I always have a pair to hand.

The same is true with a hat. This will cover your face to a certain degree depending on design, and a wide-brimmed hat can keep rain from dripping down your neck and on to the eyepiece of a scope or binoculars. Quite often a face mesh or shield is useful when game is encountered at very close quarters, and you may want to cover all your exposed parts to avoid any detection. Midge nets are great, but unless they have a clear Perspex front, peering through mesh can cause eye strain after a while.

ANCILLARY KIT

It is inevitable that as one's interest in a sport grows, so does the desire to spend more money on kit to make that experience more enjoyable; but it is also true that there are many gadgets and gismos that are really unnecessary. Over-burdening yourself with fancy equipment will not necessarily make the shoot more successful, and these days I travel light and rely on fieldcraft as my main accessory. There is, however, a minimum level of equipment, and the amount you spend on each item is up to you. Each sport of vermin, fox and deer stalking will require certain specific differing kit, but a common base kit is always the same.

Quiet, hard-wearing and waterproof trousers and boots are essential items for any shooter.

Roe Sack

Regardless of the species being tackled, I am never without my roe sack as a carrying aid. Although specifically designed to carry an adult roe deer from the woods after field dressing, a roe sack is an item of kit that serves many other uses. All your paraphernalia can be stored within the sack, safe from the elements and more importantly allowing stress-free progress through fields and woods, allowing the hands free operation to steady yourself with sticks on those tricky Scottish ridges or instant access to your binoculars.

Although there are many differing models, most share a common format as a rather over-sized form of rucksack with a multi-pocketed exterior. Fabric material varies from canvas to Loden models. I use a cheap canvas model and have done so for more than ten years, and although battered, torn and blood-stained, it refuses to die and allows me real comfort out in the wilds. The canvas exterior is easily washed, but you have to take care when slinging it over the shoulder when fully laden so as not to tear the retaining flap. Loden is a special, tightly woven wool material; it is aesthetically pleasing and tougher, but is a little more difficult to keep clean. All models have some form of removable inner sack, which in the case of carcass extraction prevents any fluids seeping out to the outer layer. Usually made from tough synthetic material, it is easily cleaned and disinfected.

The real advantage of any roe sack is to store all the other essential items, itemized below, besides those bulky bits of equipment that would otherwise be stuffed inconveniently into one's pockets. Most have at least two external pockets with weather or storm flaps, which are great for stowing less valuable items such as toilet paper, rope and disposable clothes. I often use the buckles and straps to fasten camera bipods if I am testing equipment at the same time as shooting.

The roe sack soon becomes an indispensable item of equipment.

Carcass Loops

I always carry a set of carcass loops just in case a strap breaks on the Roe sack or two deer are needed to be carried. These take the form of two straps made of leather or a synthetic fabric such as Cordura. They either have loops cut at their

All the kit you are likely to need can be conveniently stored in a roe sack.

ends to allow the quarry's feet to be secured, or have bindings at the end that serve the same purpose. These are simple designs that are quite often the best. Inexpensive and taking up little room they soon become very useful for a variety of other tasks such as dragging out deer from rough terrain.

If you do drag deer, especially the larger species of red and fallow, then a purpose-made deer drag will help. Again, simple is best: a one-piece handle made of soft foam is easy to manage and more comfortable on the hands, and it is attached to single corded loop, which makes carcass extraction much easier and safer.

Ammunition Pouches

Although spare ammunition can be left in the factory cartons, the need for easy and quick access usually requires some purpose-built container. This can be rifle-mounted to the butt stock or fore-end in some cases, or more commonly is some form of pouch that you keep on your belt or in a convenient pocket. Whichever the case, it must be silent in operation because nothing spooks game more readily than metal clinking on metal. It can be made of high class crafted leather or a factory-made leather equivalent, while synthetic neoprene and cordura are both light and waterproof and far cheaper. Generally these hold about ten rounds.

For a long-range vermin foray you will probably carry more than ten rounds, and will need the MTM plastic cartridge box, divided into specific calibre compartments. This is waterproof and easily stowed in the roe sack.

Bolt Carriers

There are times when you will want to take the bolt from your rifle, for safety reasons and for security, and using a bolt pouch or carrier is a very convenient way of keeping it safe. This eliminates the risk of it becoming uncocked, and therefore nigh on impossible to recock before fitting into the rifle without proper tools. The ones I have seen are one-piece leather with a fold-over flap to keep the bolt secure, with a slotted side to allow fitment of any bolt length. Either fit it to your belt or in your pocket.

Muzzle Covers

A purpose-made muzzle cover is undoubtedly useful, but is easily replicated by a piece of insulating tape. The idea is to keep debris from getting into the bore, which is a good idea as a blocked bore can be disastrous. Traditionally made of leather, it is slipped over the muzzle. However, as stated, the same can be achieved by a piece of tape, which has the advantage in that when you need to take a quick shot it does not have to be removed because the bullet can be shot through it without detriment to accuracy.

Torch

On early morning forays or late night lamping trips it is always prudent to carry some form of illumination, not just for finding your footing but for retrieving that lost item. Any torch will suffice, but there are purpose-made units available that are designed to be tough, compact, waterproof and powerful.

I use a Streamlight Sidewinder model that has LED illumination with the option of clear, red or green lights with non-strobing or strobing illumination as a carcass indicator if you have to retrace your footsteps.

First Aid Kit

An often overlooked accessory is some form of personal first aid kit. Hopefully this is one item that you will never need, but life being life it is inevitable that sooner or later an accident will happen. A common problem is cutting yourself when gralloching, when an immediate plaster is advisable. There will also be occasions when a scope can bite you in the eyelid, if shooting from an awkward angle and the recoil is stiff.

Drop Tube and Bore Snake

These two items directly relate to problems with the bore of a rifle. There are times when rain, debris, mud, ice and dirt get into your barrel, causing an obstruction. Usually that is game over, but if you take some form of collapsible cleaning rod you can remove the culprit; for

Fieldcraft and knowledge of your game are both far more important than the latest fancy gadget, so spend more time in the woods and not at the gunsmith's.

example, the Rapid Rod from Sinclairs is ideal, and takes up very little space.

I always carry a bore snake, which is a cleaning mop and brush all in one with a weighted end so you can give your rifle an in-the-field clean as necessary. They are calibre specific, so keep several handy – they have saved the day for me on many occasion.

A newer item is a drop tube, which is more useful than it might first seem. If you are a reloader and you have made your ammunition too long or very close to the maximum overall length of your rifle's chamber, there is a risk when chambered that the rifling can grip the bullet tightly. This is no problem if the rifle is then fired, but problems arise if you open the bolt to remove the unfired round and the case comes out but the bullet stays where it is, dumping all the powder in the magazine! Again you

are in trouble unless you have a drop tube, which is a calibre-specific length of brass rod that you literally drop down the barrel when the bolt is removed to knock out the stuck bullet.

Map of the Shoot

From a purely legal and safety point of view, a detailed map of the shoot is essential. All the bridleways, footpaths and dwellings should be noted, as well as clearly defined boundaries. I always note down the owner's name and contact number and any relevant landowner's details, both for my own benefit but also to advise them should I notice a trespasser or sick livestock.

I also jot down where I see the game on my journey, together with the weather conditions so I can transfer the details into a more detailed journal at home. This is to build up an understanding of the movements of both animals and humans in all weather conditions and at all times of the year.

FAC and Permission

Always carry your firearms certificate (FAC) whilst out shooting, detailing permission to shoot the rifles you own on the land that you are actually shooting on. If you are stopped, and quite often this will happen as stalkers tend to be active in the small hours, it is much easier to be able to show the constabulary all your relevant documentation straightaway.

To back up the FAC I always carry an additional letter or purpose-drawn document detailing the landowner's permission for me to shoot on the named land, and what I am allowed to shoot. Again this avoids any awkwardness with the police: the last thing you want is for them to phone the landowner at 2am to verify your permission – he will not thank you for that.

There are several purpose-made certificate holders, and this is a good idea to stop the paperwork from becoming dog-eared and wet.

The Mobile Phone

Love them or hate them, a mobile phone is a safe and sensible option for any rifle-carrying sportsperson these days. Disputes can be quickly and easily settled, and more importantly in case of an accident the relevant emergency services can be contacted.

Walkie-talkies are also very useful if used conservatively when out shooting with a colleague, but there is always a tendency to use them unnecessarily and risk spooking game.

Toilet Tissue

Essential not just for the obvious (which should be avoided if possible), tissue has many other uses. At a push it can be used to wipe lens and glasses on scopes and binos, although I prefer a lens cloth wherever possible. Carry about twenty sheets, but put them in a sealed plastic bag and make sure they are separated to stop any dampness sticking them together.

Lens Cleaning Cloth

As stated above, a proper lens cloth or lens cleaning equipment is far better than a tissue. I use several alternatives, the most convenient of which attaches to the rifle's sling fitments and so is accessible at all times. Swarovski, famous for scopes from Austria, makes a great all-in-one lens cleaning kit; it comes in the form of a green cordura-type pouch with pockets to hold the lens cleaning fluid bottle, lens brush pen, moistened lens wipes and packet of lens tissues.

In a similar vein Leupold produces a lens pen system, which is a double-end application in the shape of a pen with a brush at one end and a non-fluid lens cleaner at the other. Reasonably priced, it represents good value for money and is easy to use and keep in a coat pocket until needed.

Another really handy piece of kit is the Bushwear Spudz. This is a cleaning cloth that is stitched into a protective elasticated waterproof pouch measuring no more than 2×1.5in (5×3.5cm). You pull out the cloth, which is a triangular lint-free fabric, clean your lens and pop it back in. Because there is an ABS clip attached, it makes for easy location on any rifle sling or clothing, so it is always handy.

Disposable Gloves

Contamination when gralloching a deer is to be avoided at all costs, and a packet of disposable gloves takes up no room in the roe sack. Wearing disposable gloves avoids transferring blood to your rifle or equipment, and they are also invaluable for handling vermin such as rats.

Wash Box and Carcass Box (in the Car)

This is another indispensable item if you use the family car for your shooting exploits. The facility to hold a bloody carcass or scores of rabbits will leave the boot of the car stain free. Purpose-built boxes designed to carry the weight of the game you intend to transport is far better, and collapsible versions take no room at all. They are easily washed out, and some contain tray liners that lift up the deer so the meat is not sitting in any body fluids on the way home. Once bought, it will last you forever. A wash box holding water

Never leave home without a pair of good binoculars; they are literally your eyes in the field, and allow you to spot your game animals before they spot you!

and disinfectant simplifies the task of cleaning up after the shoot.

Repelling Midges and Ticks

Any way of repelling midges is an extremely good idea, and relief from either of these pests is welcomed by any sportsperson out in the field. Midge repellents can be highly variable, and their effectiveness depends on coverage, repeated use and exposure. The Expedition Midge repellent in aerosol form, whose active ingredient is myrtle and a blend of other plant extracts, really helps in deterring the dreaded midge.

If you have an embedded tick, its swift removal is highly desirable. A pair of tick pliers is the easiest, most cost-effective way to remove ticks. The thumb-operated extending tick pen has a head that lifts the tick out of the skin without squeezing it and thereby transferring tick saliva into the skin. The saliva is known to contain bacteria that could carry Lymes disease or other disease.

There is also a medical patch that safely removes embedded ticks from the skin. The Rid-a-Tick patch is 1in (2.5cm) in diameter and made from 3M medical tape that is hypoallergenic latex free. Simply cover the tick and press the patch into place; no air can then reach the tick's body, and after several minutes, it literally backs out of the skin. Once it is free from the epidermis, the patch is folded around its body and it can be safely disposed of.

Secateurs

An absolutely essential item for any shooter. It is highly annoying to sit down in a hedge or up a high seat only to find your vision obscured by some foliage or tree twigs, and a brief prune with a pair of secateurs soon remedies the problem. Any garden centre set will be fine, but a model made by Leatherman's is a combination tool, with the secateur's grips containing an array of additional useful devices such as screwdriver, blade and saw.

Binoculars

After your ancillary equipment the most indispensable item other than your rifle or ammunition is a set of binoculars. Regardless of the quarry species you shoot, a pair of binoculars will help fill your bag more than any other gadget. Whether you are shooting rabbits or stalking deer, your rifle should always be slung over your shoulder so your hands are free to hold your sticks and binoculars. Binos enable you to pre-empt your quarry from spotting you first, and to judge terrain and spot other wildlife that may give your presence away; without them I would miss that roe buck bedded down in the brambles or squat rabbit in the hedgerow or fox peering out from the undergrowth tracing my every step. You do not have to spend a fortune on glassware, but if you can, then all the better because you will be rewarded with much improved low light performance and reliability.

Because you will be using your binoculars constantly, this may influence the size and weight you choose. Indeed, many people buy too large and heavy a set, and end up regretting the weight around their neck. Unless you shoot from a static high seat or go long range varminting, then choose a medium-sized pair. More important is the relationship between the objective lens and the magnification that will influence the light-gathering properties. Lens coatings will either enhance your image or not.

It is said that the human eye can only accommodate an exit pupil dilation of 7mm, and many manufacturers base their range of options around this. The exit pupil is determined by taking the objective lens diameter and dividing it with the magnification value: thus an 8 power into a 56mm objective diameter would yield the magical 7mm value. These would be rather big and heavy, especially with a glass lens, so the 'norm' has always been 7 × 42mm, giving a 7mm exit pupil and enough light-gathering abilities.

The more you pay, the better the lens quality and coatings, which not only improves brightness and low light capabilities, but will reduce flare and reflections. This will increase contrast and improve distinction between game animals and the foliage they are undoubtedly hiding in, so they can literally pop into focus.

I usually have a pair of cheap binoculars, costing no more than £80, in the car at all times as a back-up, then a good pair that I use all the time. Expect to pay upwards of £750 minimum for a pair of high quality European binoculars: Swarovski, Zeiss, Kahles and Leica dominate the market, but you can get some very good sets for a more modest £200 to £300, such as Steiner or Leupold. Regardless of price, they must all be fogproof, shockproof and waterproof, otherwise they are just a dead weight round your neck.

Knives / Carcass Preparation Tools

I like to travel light and need kit that is dependable, but cheap enough so that if it is lost, as often happens, it is not too much to replace. I would choose a budget price stalking knife, carcass saw and chest spreader; these three items will cope with 90 per cent of all your shooting needs, and certainly greatly help in carcass prep and safe handling as well as gutting rabbits.

The Bush knife represents unparalleled

Carcass preparation tools might include a stainless-steel rib spreader to gain better access to the chest cavity, a ribcage saw, and knives with synthetic handles that are easily disinfected after use.

quality at a bargain price. The blade is 4in (10cm) in length and is made of 4290 stainless steel. The grip or scales are a hygienic rubberized textured handle that fits snugly into a synthetic and equally hygienic plastic sheath with integral belt attachment. The blade holds a good edge, is hard wearing and very stain resistant. This is a great do-anything knife, and personally I have several at hand in various coats in case I lose one. Having said that, a custom-made knife offers pride of ownership and utilizes some of the best edge holding steels and scales (or handle) available. In my view Alan Wood makes one of the best knives in the UK, avidly collected but equally appreciated by professionals for its worthiness out in the field.

In similar vein is the Bush saw, a stainless-steel hunting saw that can be of real benefit in cutting through the rib cage on larger deer. There is a well designed curved tip that protects against accidental puncture of the intestine or even bladder. A cheap tool that comes complete with a cordura sheath.

The final carcass prep tool is of real benefit in allowing a fuss-free gralloching of deer in the field: a spreader made from quality stainless steel that has been designed specifically for the British deer species. It comes in two sizes, 7.5in (19cm) or 4.5in (11cm) in length. Their design with twisted section gives a strong integrity that holds open the ribcage allowing the stalker ample room to work within. Whether in the field or back at the larder, as an aid to carcass cooling the 4.5in spreader I use on roe is easily slipped into the stalking jacket and is a welcome addition out in the field.

Sticks / Rests / Bipods

Supporting your shot is essential to gain maximum accuracy, and this can take the form of two options: rifle-mounted bipods or hand-held sticks of some sort. Most stalkers take a shot whilst standing so any aid to steady the shot is beneficial.

I would not be without some form of sticks. They are invaluable, not only as a steady shot but also when traversing rough ground, aiding in climbing or descending a steep hillside, or checking out suspect boggy areas before you

Alan Wood custom knives are the best available to British shooters; they are not just things of beauty, but offer a superb cutting edge and handling traits.

take the first step. Also a good stiff stick can be used to hoist a small deer to perform the gralloch.

Simplicity is often the best policy here, and the use of straight wooden hazel sticks can be all one needs, providing a stiff, non-bending rest — and eco-friendly to boot. However, as with everything, modifications on a theme can bring forth a better product.

Two sticks offer a much steadier rest and can be as easily deployed as a single stick. The use of two garden canes were my first hand-held bipod secured with a leather strap just to the top to form a crux from which a supporting hand can cradle the rifle.

One problem with all sticks is that the one height can be tiresome if you want to sit in a hedgerow and wait for a shot and the sticks are just too long. An option here is the introduction of telescopic legs, made from aluminium to keep the weight down, with a padded strap and

Austrian shooting sticks are unique in that they have four supports to cradle both the front and the rear of the rifle, and are therefore very steady to use.

stick ends. These can be very useful and hard-wearing and add little weight to your shooting kit. I was doubtful at first as they can be expensive, coming from Europe, but now I would not be without them because they are so useful, and have made many impossible shots very possible and satisfactory.

There are also three-leg versions, which take longer to deploy but are superbly steady; these are best used as a static rest or where you have a client out stalking.

One of the best steady stick systems I have used is the Austrian version; this uses four wooden sticks joined in an inverted dual 'V' formation, and forms an unbelievably steady shot in the standing position. Again, though only one length and best deployed from a more static position so the set-up does not alert quarry you are hunting.

Rifle-mounted bipods that fold up under the fore-end of the stock have always been popular. They are offered in many lengths, with models that have fixed or extendable legs as well as swivel and tilting options for use on uneven ground. They can be great for static prone shots at rabbits, foxes, deer or long-range crows, but there will be an impact shift if the fore-end is flexible as the rifle recoils.

Slings

These are an absolute 'must'. Rifles should be slung on the shoulder at all times, allowing the hands to be free for steadying yourself, holding your sticks or more importantly holding your binoculars as you slowly scan for game.

Materials and designs vary widely, with traditional leather still being popular, but synthetic or cordura are good choices as they need less attention, and some have rubberized panels to the underside, which increases grip at the shoulder area.

Calls and Attractants

Calls, be they synthetic in nature, organic or electrical, can be spectacularly effective or thoroughly disappointing if they are not used in the correct way. People think that a few mimicking noises will have game beating a path to your rifle! Sometimes this can certainly be the case, but animals that rely on sound to survive are far better at determining real sounds from bogus ones.

You can buy wood, plastic, combinations of the two, use leaves on site or turn on electrical gadgets for most species. But take note that it is illegal to attract birds with electronic calls only to be shot. Nevertheless, calls offer good practice to entice birds to observe or photograph them.

Foxes can come readily to the call of a distressed rodent or rabbit, thinking they are in for a free meal. However, the frequency and volume of the call is crucial, because foxes learn very quickly and, as with lamping, can become 'call

ABOVE: Electronic fox calls such as this Fox Pro and Jack-in-the-box can be very effective in attracting foxes to within range, but use them sparingly because if you miss, then old Charlie will remember his mistake.

ABOVE: Another essential item is a good sling to carry your rifle so your hands are free to use your binoculars or shooting sticks.

RIGHT: Shooters like to tip the odds in their favour and so a variety of calls are used for vermin, foxes or deer. Practise first, however, otherwise all you will see will be rear ends disappearing into the woods!

shy'. In these cases a product called the Jack-in-the-box adds an audible stimulus with a visible attractant, too, in the form of a mechanical moving prey on top of the caller.

Deer can also be successfully called in, by mimicking either does in oestrus or barks, roars and whistles from males. Roe calls are very numerous, and become an art form in themselves. Available as single units or boxed sets, they are worth trying during the roe's rut in July/August, for which they are designed. Having said that, I have had deer coming to investigate calls at most times of year if they are inquisitive, and muntjac deer will often come to roe calls to investigate.

Game attractants are not a new idea. Salt licks have been used to attract deer for years, but now there are also aerosols and pastes. Broadly based, they can contain an aniseed flavour that is known to attract deer, with the addition of vital vitamins and minerals to encourage proper growth. The salt paste constituent is primarily sodium chloride and magnesium, with a binding

The ploy of using attractants to lure game to a particular spot is not new, and there are now many types on the market; I have used them with mixed results.

agent that gives a highly saturated salt paste consistency. This acts as the basis to which the aniseed attractant is added at 0.1 per cent. Being a paste, it is easily applied to tree stumps or trunks and allowed to dry to act as a long-term deer attractant that can be topped up regularly and sited on known deer tracks or feeding locations.

The second item is an aerosol version of the aniseed attractant, which is a very concentrated aniseed solution that can be sprayed on vegetation, tree stumps, and in fact anything to attract deer. It is also useful for masking the human scent on clothes, and I have had some success in photographing deer in this way. As with all these products, some deer will be attracted more than others, depending on the availability of natural salt and minerals in their environment.

Wind Meters

This may seem to be a spurious item of kit, but shooters will tell you that although you can learn the trajectory of a bullet and determine the range accurately these days, judging wind conditions can make or break a shot. Wind meters are now cheap. A good model that gives instant wind direction and strength readings will allow you to make an educated judgement as to how far to aim off in order to make an accurate shot.

If you do not take the wind meter out on every trip I find it useful to go out on differing strengths of wind, get readings from it, and then see how that translates to the movement of the trees, leaves or grasses on a shoot. In this way if you can memorize these movements or make a cheat card you can gain a very good indication of wind strength on any areas you shoot.

Rangefinders

These are fast becoming a 'must have' item with regard to giving a shooter an accurate and instant reading as to your distance from the target. This allows for a correction in your aiming to allow for trajectory drop, so long as you have the trajectory tables for the ammunition you are shooting at the time, with the corrected velocity for your barrel length. This can be viewed in

Rangefinders and wind meters are good accessories because they will give you an accurate reading and so enable you to place a more humane shot.

two ways with regard to ethical behaviour. Firstly, with an accurate range you are far more likely to place your bullet where you aim – if you are a good shot, that is. But some say that with the confidence a rangefinder affords you, you can be tempted to shoot at far greater ranges, possibly beyond your abilities.

Mechanically rangefinders can work in several ways. The older types use a split image optical unit rather like older generation camera view finders, with a range being read from a sliding scale. More common are the laser-type hand-held units that are more practical in terms of carrying and for field use with their instant accurate results. A laser beam is sent to the target and then reflected off that target, and the receiver within the laser unit converts the time taken into range.

This is very practical and fast, but the drawbacks are that the usable distance measurable can vary widely, depending on the quality of the range-finding device and, more importantly, the reflective quality of the target subject – and rabbits, crows, foxes and deer are not known for being reflective! Far from it, and so under field conditions the terrain, weather, fog, mist, rain and ground cover can all influence the true result gained from these devices. Rangefinders can be very good at teaching yourself to estimate ranges to a target if you leave it at home or the battery goes dead!

Lamps

The realm of the fox shooter or rabbit controller will usually involve some nocturnal forays. If you can afford it, you might prefer night vision equipment, however, more commonly used are the hand-held or rifle-mounted lamping systems. These might be a single self-contained rechargeable unit; however, more commonly a lamp is purchased as a separate item with a desired illumination strength for the distance

Fox shooting is often conducted at night so a lamping kit with spare differing coloured lenses and a rechargeable battery gives a good degree of flexibility to 'lamp' shy foxes.

High seats can be used for all forms of shooting, not just deer. They allow an elevated, unrestricted view of your shoot with the advantage of keeping your scent away from game and enabling a downward-angled shot for safety.

and species you intend shooting, and then a separate rechargeable battery pack, usually contained in a belt-mounted pouch.

Many have replaceable lens colours, from red (the most common) to blue, grey, orange or green; through experience on your own foxes or rabbits you will find out which works best to hold them in the light beam, and not have the adverse effect of spooking them.

High Seats

A high seat is not essential, but is extremely useful if you shoot in an area where the deer, or other game for that matter, are hard to see due to foliage growth in the spring/summer months. High seats are also recommended from more practical or safety reasons, if first, the ground is frequented by dog walkers, or is so flat that a ricochet may carry for a long distance. The angled shot afforded by a high seat is far safer from this elevated position, and many farmers or landowners may insist on you using one, especially if cattle or farm stock roam freely.

The importance of one's scent and its impact on wildlife cannot be underestimated, as an unfamiliar scent trail will alert game more quickly than any other invasion into their natural world. Here the high seat has a further benefit, in that the elevated position carries your undesirable scent at a higher plane, and it can be dispersed further downwind without too much risk of giving your position away.

CONCLUSIONS

A sportsperson can own the best, most expensive and up-to-date equipment on the planet yet still shoot no game if their fieldcraft and mental attitude towards the quarry is incorrect. Less is certainly more with regard to equipment, especially if you have to hike with all this paraphernalia for any length of time. It is best to choose a few essential items and carry them conveniently in a backpack or roe sack. I despair if I leave my binos or gloves at home so I now keep a cheap set of both in the car, plus a spare knife and plastic gloves and water for the gralloch.

'Beware the man with one rifle or kit, he probably knows how to use it' is as true a saying today as it ever was.

Chapter 3
Vermin Class Rifles

Much maligned as the poor man's full bore, the humble rimfire reflects the attitude that less is often more. Among the sporting fraternity the rimfire calibre, be it the .22 or now the .17, represents an ever-evolving rifle design and manufacturing technique. It is no surprise that a cartridge spawned in the nineteenth century still continues to outsell any other firearm in existence, and the combined advantages of low recoil, noise and cost make the .22 the rifleman's rifle.

It originated way back in the mid-1840s with the introduction of the salon cartridge Flobert BB caps, although a more common case dimension appeared in 1857 with Smith Wessons .22 calibre short round. This makes it probably the oldest cartridge having a self-contained design with primer component with the rim for ignition. The rimfire's ease of manufacture and low cost is the reason for its longevity and the fact

that it still survives today, whereas the larger calibre rimfire rounds have all but disappeared in favour of the centrefire primed cases that allow the potential to reload the spent case, giving the shooter a good degree of flexibility when it comes to fine tuning their rifle. The rimfire round cannot be reloaded and thus you must rely on proper manufacturing techniques to ensure accurate ammunition and consistency.

Today, .22 rimfire ammunition ranges from BB caps, through the short and long varieties to the standard and most widespread long rifle (lr) version. This has led to the greatest diversity of loads, ranging from squib air rifle velocity loads to the subsonic – below the speed of sound (1050fps) – and into the target and high velocity rounds that exceed the speed of sound, and right up into the hyper velocity categories, some over 1500fps.

Lightweight hyper velocity rounds certainly

The .22lr rimfire has to be the most popular calibre of all time as a vermin tool; this Browning T-Bolt is a superbly accurate rabbit rifle and very well made.

exert extraordinary appeal among shooters, but their ballistic performance has little to offer the serious sportsperson in Britain, where a rimfire and sound moderator using subsonic ammunition is the preferred and more practical choice. All these will be explored in the chapter on cartridges.

There is also a new wave of rimfire rifles that uphold the rimfire ethos of 'less is more'. The .17 Mach 2 and .17 HMR represent a departure from the pedestrian and often maligned performance of the .22 rimfire variety, and bring the rimfire class of rifle right up into the twenty-first century with lightweight, highly frangible, high velocity projectiles.

TYPES AND MANUFACTURERS

.22 rimfire rifles can be sourced in the widest range of configurations, from single shot, bolt action, straight pull, lever, pump and semi-automatic designs. This means there is a rifle out there to suit every style of shooting scenario for the sporting shooter. Each has its advantages and disadvantages, usually relating to speed of operation, but more importantly with regard to accuracy potential and reliability.

The slowest to operate are the single shot

designs, often with a simple flip-open mechanism or bolt action, with a manual manipulation of bolt necessary to cycle the action close behind. These are followed by the short up-and-down movement of the lever action, with pump and straight pulls being far rarer, but offering another design that might enthuse certain shooters allowing a more rapid reloading operation.

Fastest by far are the semi-automatics, where a new cartridge is fired on every press of the trigger. However, this usually comes with a loss in accuracy, as bolt actions are generally the most accurate actions available – although increasingly, the demand for ever more accurate semi-automatics is closing the gap, with a host of aftermarket custom parts and barrels.

Among the best selling rimfire rifles in Britain today are a mixture of European, American and Scandinavian designs from manufacturers such as CZ, Sako, Anschutz, Weihrauch, Walther, Remington, Ruger, Savage, Marlin, Thompson Center, Henry, Browning, Taurus, Weatherby and Rossi. And this is by no means a complete list, as there are many custom rimfire makers; certainly Kimber and Cooper Arms are noteworthy manufacturers.

In my years of testing firearms for many shooting magazines I have come across most of

.22 lr rifles can also benefit from a little customizing; here a Sako Finnfire wears a Wenig extra fancy walnut stock, C G Universal trigger, Leupold EFR scope and V-Mach silencer.

RIGHT: Rimfires come in all sizes depending on your own personal preferences; visit a gunsmith's or a game fair to view and handle each model before you buy.

BELOW: T/C Contender in .17 HMR is a flat-shooting crow rifle despite being a single shot design.

what is on offer to the British shooter, some good, some not so good. What is important is to buy the best you can afford, and really analyse the type of shooting that you have on offer to you. If you want to stalk rabbits with a variety of shots at differing ranges, then a bolt action will suffice; but if you intend to shoot a lot from the back of a 4 × 4 as part of a pest control service, then a semi-automatic would be far more useful to you.

BOLT ACTION RIFLES

Most common are the bolt action rimfires that incorporate a difference in full bore bolt action designs, in that the bolt locks via rear-acting lugs, rather than the more conventional forward-locking system. The bolt handle operation and rearward cocking action is still employed and offers the shooter potentially the best design for accurate shooting.

Rimfire rifles for sporting use will certainly come with a magazine of some sort. This can take the form of a magazine mounted forward of the trigger guard or tubular feed system. In this way as the bolt moves back, a cartridge from the magazine is raised which is engaged by the bolt in its forward motion to cycle the round into the chamber. This action also cocks the rifle's trigger, but is the most 'hands on' in terms of movement and operator input.

A repeat of this sequence lasts as long as the magazine is full – slow, yes, but the finer tolerances in manufacture in a bolt rifle allow a greater degree of potential accuracy.

Scopes are essential items these days, and receivers are cut or drilled for some form of scope mounting, although some manufacturers still supply their rimfires with rudimentary iron sights.

Increasingly the trend amongst shooters has been towards stainless steel metalwork and synthetic stock materials in favour of the more traditional blued steel and walnut furniture. In a sporting arm it is undeniable that the latter is better at repelling inclement weather or adverse field conditions to which owners will subject their rifle; nevertheless the sale of wood stock and polished blued rimfires, however less prac-

tical, still remains strong among more traditional sportspersons. You will know what suits you, and most manufacturers recognize this and offer the same design in both configurations.

A description of the best known and most widely available bolt action rifles in Britain will give a more detailed idea of the good and bad points of each individual rifle. In this way readers can make an unbiased decision as to the various designs, operations and price ranges that will fit their individual requirements.

CZ (Ceska Zbrojovka)

Beyond doubt the most popular and hard-working .22lr is the CZ rimfire in any of its many guises. Its longevity of production is testament to its build quality and its popularity with shooters, yet it retains that 'old world' quality of build with real value for money.

Manufactured in the Czech Republic, the CZ harks back to an era of traditional rifle design and quality, but fulfils the ethos of giving the shooter exactly what he wants and at a fair price.

The American model best typifies the classic design aesthetics, incorporating classic profiled walnut stock and cut checkered panels for grip with beautifully polished blued steel parts. The shortened, fully synthetic models, such as the Style, are designed for extreme use in all weather and fulfil this role very well. The range provides both sporter or varmint barrel profiles – that is, lightweight or heavyweight – .22lr, .22 WMR, .17 Mach 2 or .17 HMR calibres allowing CZ to equip the shooter for any outing to the woods or fields.

I have never shot a CZ that would not shoot accurately and reliably, and I know many examples that still bring home rabbits after twenty years of service.

CZ continue to use the well worn, tried and tested petite Mauser design action and bolt assembly that has served them so well for so long, and is common to all their rimfires. Its tubular all-steel receiver has integral dovetails for scope mounting with plenty of length to accommodate most scopes on the market today. The bolt is beautifully proportioned with a short, angled, rearward profile, adequate ball bolt knob and short bolt throw. The bolt has a twin extractor claw arrangement with affixed blade ejector that is simple yet works very well and is suitably robust.

The magazine, now polymer in construction, feeds directly from a floor plate capture hinge, and again, whether you fit a standard five shot or ten shot magazine, feeding is flawless. The safety catch is a horizontal-type lever straddled on top of the rear bolt shroud, with operation dictated from the right side. Set at right angles to the bolt, the rifle is set in the fire mode and a red dot can be seen on the side of the action. Pushing it forwards engages the safety, and the lever covers the red indication dot, which tells the shooter the rifle is safe – a useful feature when out in the woods or bumping along in the back of a Land Rover.

The trigger blade is a little skinny but there is just enough room for a gloved hand in the trigger guard, although a little limited on adjustment; the shooter must rely on proper follow-through to achieve maximum accuracy. Having said this, there are many after-market trigger sear and spring replacements that bring the trigger up to modern-day standards. The Rifle Basix CZ52 model is notable as it allows adjustment for sear engagement and weight of pull, and still uses the factory safety for convenience. Pull weights from 10oz to 2.5lb transform the CZ into a great vermin tool by eking every last inch of accuracy out of the rifle's performance.

The CZ Synthetic Style design does away with the traditional walnut and blued action, and comes in a practical nickelled finish to the metalwork and synthetic plastics for the stock. Whilst some may baulk at this, it actually offers a very practical exterior for real life shooters. Outwardly the barrel and action seem to be made of stainless steel, but are in fact nickel-plated to offer a good weather-resistant finish. This is very hard-wearing and not too shiny, to avoid spooking any wary game from unwanted reflections. Any dirt or blood from messy hands is easily wiped off without any detriment to the finish, which allows the shooter to concentrate on the shot and not worry that their rifle is getting knocked about.

At last here is a synthetic stock that does not feel synthetic. Most plastic stocks have a very hollow moulded profile and feel to them, but not so the CZ Style. The black synthetic stock has a drab finish (perfect for hunting) and stippled finish, excluding the need for checkering, and gives a real sense of stability and workman-like endurance. The form represents a high combed Monte Carlo cheekpiece and Schnabel fore-end, complemented by a solid black fixed recoil pad.

If ever there was a hunter-ready, off-the-shelf, call it what you will .22 rimfire for pest control, then the CZ Style has to be it.

Probably the best selling rimfire in Britain today is the CZ 452 rimfire in its many forms; here the Style synthetic rifle is accurate and utterly reliable.

Remington

A name synonymous with American ingenuity and longevity is Remington. Their early model 541 rimfires certainly shot and looked great, but now Remington have drawn in their range and offer just a few select models. The first is the premium grade 504 model bolt action offering a choice of walnut or laminated stock designs and a detachable magazine, whilst the Model 5 is a more modestly priced rifle and a practical hunting tool.

The 504 is a new introduction from Remington and is available in .22lr and .17 Mach 2 in classic sporting trim or .22lr and .17 HMR in a laminated stock, heavy barrelled version. In either guise they are little gems.

This .22 is no normal run-of-the-mill rimfire. Taking the form of a full blown stalking rifle, the overall weight is 6lb (2.7kg), evenly distributed throughout the 504's large-build profile. It feels like a centrefire rifle, and the only clue that it is a rimfire is the small ejection port cut into the receiver side. With the quality walnut stock in a classic sporter form and satin blued steel parts with substantial receiver block, it all adds up to an impressive rimfire rifle.

The receiver walls are 0.25in (6mm) thick in places and ensure a well bedded and straight bolt operation and vibration damping effect, conducive to good accuracy. The bolt is no small item, measuring 5.75in (14.6cm) long with a weight of 8.2oz (233g), using twin dual-acting opposed extractor claws in the bolt's face that make short work of engaging and extracting cases. The bolt handle is short but nicely bent rearward to the shooter, with a good smooth bolt handle that aids in effortless cocking operation. With the .22lr version, and indeed the same with the .17 Mach 2, the bolt travel is short and fast – a travel of only 1.26in (3.2cm) is necessary to load, feed and eject a cartridge. The top of the receiver is drilled and tapped for scope bases such as B-Square Weaver style, which allows a secure and quick detachable option to the scoping system.

The safety is a fairly standard push-and-pull lever-operated unit, forward for 'fire' and rearward for 'safe'. In the rear 'safe' position the trigger sear is blocked yet the bolt can still be operated to remove a chambered cartridge if desired. The trigger blade has a slim, smooth, silvered finish that operates a single stage trigger movement, which is set at the factory for optimum pull weight, sear engagement and let-off, and is a clean 4lb (1.8kg) pull.

Rimfires do not have to be cheap: the Remington 504 is a beautifully crafted and appointed rimfire that inspires a confident shot when taken into the field.

The Remington 504 is unusual in that it is bedded in two places using aluminium pillars that stop stock wood compression and inaccuracy due to stock warpage. The magazine, with plastic black base and light alloy casing, resembles that used on the semi-auto model Rem 597, being single stack fed, and but it holds six rounds in .22lr and only five rounds in .17 Mach 2 and HMR. It has a barrel length of 20in (50cm) and is highly practical on a rabbit gun. There are no unsightly redundant open sights either, which gives the 504 a clean line, and the bore is a 5-R button rifled in .22lr configuration for good stability of most rimfire ammunition.

The stock dimensions compliment the metalwork and give the humble rimfire that 'big gun' feel. Well balanced, the 504 comes to the shoulder very naturally and instinctively and has that cliché, pointability. Crafted from American walnut, the standard grade tested showed really good colour and vibrant figuring, all finished in a satin lacquer. There is a 13.75in (34.92cm) length of pull, which is nominal, with a 1.18in (2.8cm) drop at the comb and 1.25 (3.1cm) drop at the heel, and with no cheekpiece the comb is sufficiently high enough to support the cheek for good scope-to-eye positioning. To top it off, there are well executed checkered panels to the fore-end and pistol grip but no palm swell, with the addition of a lightly engraved and embossed pistol-grip cap with the Remington 'R' centrally placed.

For anyone wishing to own an up-market, quality rimfire for vermin control, then the Remington 504 sporter model has to be a very good contender.

Ruger

Ruger is also based in America, and like Remington, they offer great value and reliable rimfire rifles. Their M77/22 model is legendary as a superb sporting arm, and is offered in both classic trim or up-to-date synthetic or laminated materials. The price is competitive, and the quality and features are more akin to more expensive centrefire Ruger M77 rifles, which it mimics.

The primary differences are that the rimfire version utilizes the same rotary ten-shot magazine from the 10/22 semi-automatic rimfire, and the bolt-locking mechanism uses a mid-bolt rotating twin-locking bolt arrangement. The M77/22 is available in .22lr and .17 Mach 2 or .22 WMR or .17 HMR, the only difference being the size and capacity of the magazine size.

The M77/22R model is the basic grade with no sights, but it sports a good walnut stock and still offers an accurate and reliable rimfire hunting tool. For the British market the barrel comes threaded for a moderator and is available in three lengths of 20in (50cm), 22in (55cm) or 24in (60cm) dependent on calibre. Scope mounting on all models is via the Ruger proprietary one-piece ring system that mounts directly into the receiver bridge via thumb screws and a recessed slot for and aft of the action.

Ruger triggers are safe and competent for the task required, but benefit from a bit of adjustment; for a complete overhaul, replacement triggers are available from Rifle Basix. These are 100 per cent drop in and utilize the factory safety. Adjustment range is from 1.5 to 3lb (0.67 to 1.36kg) weight, which will then maximize any potential accuracy from the rifle.

For more arduous use, the synthetic stock or laminated models may be more suitable, being more readily able to repel the elements and take the knocks of everyday sporting use. The laminated stock 77/22VMBBZ version is a smart rifle, and in .17 HMR is a great small rifle with a barrel length of 24in (60cm). Its overall target-grey external finish to the stainless-steel metal parts combines hunter-ready attributes with a smart overall look. Accuracy from all Rugers is legendary, and the high capacity, ten-shot magazine in .22lr makes for a very practical sporting rabbit or vermin rifle, whichever guise you prefer.

Sako

Anyone involved with shooting will certainly recognize the name Sako, a firm based in the frozen regions of Finland. As a boy my first gun magazine in 1974 had a review on a Sako stalking rifle, and I was hooked. Sako stand for innovation and excellent build quality. Not the cheapest, but if you want a rimfire that will last a lifetime, look no further.

Sako always make good rifles, and the Quad rimfire system allows a shooter to swiftly change between .17 Mach 2, .22lr, .22WMR and .17 HMR barrels with one screw: great versatility.

Hugely popular, the old Finnfire rimfire range was the benchmark for rimfire users in terms of accuracy and quality. The five-shot or nine-shot magazine-fed bolt action rifle was available in both varmint and sporter guise, equipped with a superb barrel and good trigger. Sako then took the bold move to discontinue the marque and replace it with a design that was a total departure from any rimfire that had come before. The Sako Quad seemed to offer four rifles in one, with its quick change barrel facility. All four popular rimfire calibres of .22lr, .22 WMR, .17 Mach 2 and .17 HMR were offered in a sporter weight 22in (55cm) barrel that could be replaced by a simple single barrel-release retaining nut. Offered in synthetic or hunter grade walnut, the Sako Quad is a versatile, top quality sporting rimfire.

Many pest controllers own both a .22lr and a .17 rimfire of either guise. This of course means two rifles with the expense that this entails – but if you buy a Sako Quad you have a swift barrel change facility, where you simply exchange the barrel and magazine assembly and leave all the other components the same. This will not only save you money, but you will have a common chassis, where familiarity encourages proper shooting techniques.

I can see most owners of the Quad settling on having two barrels: firstly the .22lr, the work-horse of the vermin controller, which enables the use of subsonic ammunition and sound moderation for maximum discrete shooting; then when the occasion dictates it takes just a swift couple of turns on the barrel-release clamp and a .17 HMR barrel can be inserted for some fox/crow control work.

The .22 WMR, although a capable round, has been eclipsed by the .17 HMR cartridge, and the new .17 Mach 2 still has to make its mark on the British market as a shorter-range rabbit round. Whichever way your cartridge choice lies, the Quad offers versatility for most shooters.

The action is essentially the old Finnfire design, with adaptations for the barrel-release mechanism. This is a compact little action that has had the ejection port enlarged to accommodate the longer .17 HMR and .22 WMR rounds. The integral scope mount dovetails are atop, whilst the trigger guard is still the polymer-moulded unit, which some like and some do not. The bolt is beautifully swift in operation due to the low bolt lift angle and very short bolt throw; this makes for fast and accurate manipulation that keeps the right hand and bolt handle out of the way of any mounted scope. The bolt handle has been given a moulded plastic shroud that not only gives a positive grip but is faceted for optimum comfort.

Extraction is accomplished with a single extractor claw on the bolt's face, and because all the four calibre choices share the same rim dimensions, extraction is good. So too is ejection, despite this being accomplished by a small sprung piece of steel located on the left rear of the inner action, which has always looked a little flimsy.

The trigger remains the same single-stage unit, with a nicely thin, curved trigger blade and positive feel. Set at the factory, the Sako trigger breaks when cocked at a precise 4lb (1.8kg) weight, but feels lighter as there is zero creep and let-off is very precise. You can adjust the mechanism, but as a sporting trigger weight for all weather conditions I personally would leave well alone. The safety is the simple rocker type found on most of the Sako range, with a two-position operation: forward is 'fire' and rearward is 'safe' – simple, uncomplicated and relatively quiet in operation. The magazine still remains the plastic affair as on the Finnfire but remodelled, which feels a little cheap and is restricted to only five rounds regardless of calibre, and fits the longer HMR and WMR as well as the smaller .22lr and .17 Mach 2 rounds by use of a back-positioned polymer filler plug.

The barrel-change mechanism is the really interesting bit, and is in essence the strength of the Sako Quad system. All the barrels have the same profile, weight and length of 22in (55cm) so as not to hinder a swift barrel change, and they now come threaded with a ½in (13mm) UNF thread for fitment of a sound moderator (varmint profiles are now available). For easy recognition of calibres each barrel is colour coded by means of an o-ring sited just forward of the barrel/receiver join: blue indicates .17 Mach 2, yellow is .22 WMR, orange is .17 HMR and green is .22 lr.

In order to change the barrels for a differing calibre, Sako have profiled the chamber end of the barrel to allow a slide fit into the receiver. There is a machined flat on the bottom of each barrel, which allows a raising locking section to marry up with this area and thus secure the barrel and receiver as one unit. This is achieved by a long Allen key provided with a large plastic handle that needs only a few turns to release the barrel or tighten it.

This system takes the rimfire rifle into a new era with regard to versatility and user friendliness. The sportsperson on a tight budget who needs a dual-role rifle with good build quality and accuracy need look no further than the Sako Quad.

Anschutz and Weihrauch

As regards higher quality rimfire rifles, it will come as no surprise that many designs for sporter rifles originate from the world of target rifles, and as such, models from a manufacturer's range are often adapted to suit a dual purpose for sporting use, be it cut down or lightened in some way. Anschutz are one such firm from Europe, although Weihrauch have their HW60J and HW66 models.

The Anschutz 1717 is about as good as it gets, with a seventeen calibre rimfire rifle offering unparallel accuracy and superb trigger.

Anschutz's pedigree cannot be denied, and their sporting models stem from their hugely successful Model 54 and 64 target actions, offering unparalleled quality, reliability, and above all accuracy potential, coupled to their own precisely made barrels. The 64 range spans the cheaper end of the market, with models of 1417 or 1517 in both .22 and .17 calibres respectively. The 14 series in .22lr is a slim-weight sporter model available with shortened barrels of 14in (35cm) if desired, iron sights and also left-hand models. The 15 series still uses the 64 action but is designed with a more classic substantial stock design, and is available for the 17 Mach 2, 17 HMR and 22 WMR cartridges, although the option of a short 18in (45cm) thumbhole model is a marvellously handy and accurate little vermin sporting tool.

Finally the 17 series sports the top of the range 54 action and great trigger, and is available in most calibres. The cream of the crop is the 1717 HB model, with a blend of varmint and classic walnut stock and heavy profile barrel of 24in (60cm). This model in 17 HMR is Anschutz's flagship.

But one Anschutz rifle stands out above the rest as a sporting arm, and that is with the XIV carbine models in both .22 and .17 calibres, or 1417G to give it its proper title. Having satisfied myself that .22lr rimfire barrels can be reduced in length with no detriment to either velocity or accuracy, a factory rifle that actually comes thus equipped with a short barrel for sporting purposes, and so fits that niche nicely, is the Anschutz XIV carbine.

The number of times a short, easily handled .22 rifle is used in the confines of a 4 × 4, or whilst rabbiting in heavy undergrowth, makes a carbine rifle length preferable in any sporting scenario. Reducing the barrel to a scant 14in (35cm), and coming complete with screw-cut muzzle from the factory to accept a moderator, makes this a package that is highly manoeuvrable in cover, superbly accurate, and perfect for use with subsonic ammo.

Anschutz utilize the same match-grade barrels on their sporter models as they do on their target rifles, giving a high degree of accuracy. The chrome moly-steel barrel material has really crisp, well cut rifling, and the chamber is

smooth and tool mark free. The medium/heavy profile is a straight diameter ¾in (19mm) from receiver ring to muzzle and finished in a low lustre blueing, just right for a sporting arm. Although shorter in length, you lose nothing in terms of accuracy or velocity – in fact the shorter, stiffer barrel is less likely to flex as a lighter, longer barrel would.

The barrel is nothing without a good delivery system, and the action on the XIV is again the tried and tested match-grade Model 64, which is beautifully machined and engineered to ensure smooth operation and, more importantly, reliable feeding and positive ignition of the cartridge. The bolt is light but beautifully machined with twin extractors that provide very positive case extraction, whilst the ejector is sited in the bottom of the receiver and protrudes upright through the bolt as it is retracted, and hence 'pings' the empty case clear of the action. The bolt lever terminates in a large moulded plastic knob that offers a positive operation and fast follow-up shots as necessary, a feature you will like more than its looks whilst out lamping from the back of a pick-up or when out on a wet day.

The fully adjustable trigger is pure class, which certainly contributes to the rifle's impressive groups on the test targets. The model is 5092, which means it is a true two-stage trigger unit that is set at 1lb 12oz (800g) weight, but can be adjusted by those competent to do so. This makes the XIV a cut above the rest of most competitors' trigger units, its first stage pull allowing you to take up the slack just prior to let off with extreme control, then just a moment's thought of the second pull to release the trigger sear, totally safe and very quick.

Cleverly Anschutz have determined the end user of such a XIV rifle to be a hunter, and thus a ten-shot magazine comes as standard with the carbine series, although optional five-shot models are available. So no more fumbling for small capacity mags, as a couple of ten rounders will keep you shooting whilst others are reloading, a practical facility if a little ugly. The magazine release catch is small and awkward to operate, as you have to push forwards and then pull down on the magazine to release it.

The classic walnut model – a thumbhole is

The Savage 93 R17 BTVS in .17 HMR rimfire with stainless finish and stable laminated stock is very comfortable, and built to take the knocks.

also available – is fashioned in a truly classic, no frills design; it has no cheekpiece but still fits the shoulder well, and allows a reasonable degree of good scope alignment. The walnut is dark and dense, and finished with a tough lacquer; it is chequered on the fore-end panels and pistol grip with some infilling, but still provides additional grip.

The XIV is built to a very high standard and will give a long and accurate life to its owner, nor will it tire him out by being excessively heavy, or impede him when out in the woods because of its shorter overall length.

Savage

Savage is another American brand that has earned a reputation for producing well-priced sporting rifles that are dependable rather than elegant. Basic models have either a hard wood or black synthetic stock, whilst laminated and camouflaged options are available. The MK2 rifle is a budget, bolt action design available in either a blued or stainless-steel finish, with a characteristically curved, detachable magazine. Although conservatively priced, they offer the budget conscious a perfectly adequate sporting arm.

One model stands out above the rest as a quality sporting rifle, and that is the more up-to-date M93R17 BTVS model. This bolt action

model is stainless steel with a laminated stock, and is a real asset in terms of weather resistance and non ingress of debris from any arduous stalk. It is finished in an alternating dark and pale brown wood layer that is pleasing on the eye, and finished in a satin lacquer. The fore-end is hand filling, which I like, and has that all-important ventilated profile of three progressively larger slots that seem all the rage on rifles these days.

Whereas the stock is cutting edge, Savage have stayed with the tried and tested BVSSTB action that has served them well. It is a basic construction with simple tubular form and near mid-mounted bolt handle. The action is long at 7.25in (18.4cm). It is stainless steel in construction, with a finish that is polished but not so garish as to spook your game.

The bolt has twin extractors sited at the edges of the bolt face, which provide a strong extraction of fired cases; these functioned flawlessly in the test. The bolt handle is sited forward of the trigger, which is common to this design, and the bolt travel is a scant 1.5in (3.8cm), only needing to cycle and feed the diminutive HMR round.

The action is finished off with separate Weaver-style scope bases finished in silver to match the action; these are included with the rifle.

The trigger unit is the highly regarded Accutrigger model that has a clean, crisp and predictable trigger let-off coupled with a foolproof safety feature, making it utterly reliable. The Savage trigger can be adjusted from 1.5 to 6lb (0.45 to 2.7kg) weight by the shooter, because a unique safety bar or interrupt system ensures that however much the trigger is adjusted, only a safe let-off is ensured. This is achieved by having an integral skeletonized false trigger preset within the trigger blade, called the AccuRelease, which has to be depressed at the same time as the actual trigger. Then a crisp, clean sear release is accomplished and the shot is on its way. It is actually a relatively simple design executed very well, and it does give the shooter some peace of mind.

The magazine is a five-shot detachable unit; although having a meagre payload, it is stainless in construction. The in-line feed functions very well, but as with all Savage rimfires, the magazine release and retention is awkward, especially when your fingers are cold and wet. The barrel again is stainless steel with a nicely polished finish with a varmint/heavy profile. There is the characteristic Savage step to the barrel profile; from the receiver is a straight taper of 4in (10cm), followed by a 90-degree step down for the remaining barrel length, of which the total is 20.75in (52.7cm).

Marlin

Marlin is another American manufacturer that offers an array of rimfire rifles very similar in design to the Savage line. A model such as the M983 is unusual for a bolt action rifle in that it uses a magazine system more common on a lever action, that of an under-the-barrel tubular feed system. This offers the shooter a twelve-round capacity, which is nice but a fiddle to operate, and may negate the use of a conventional fit sound moderator, depending on size. Available in a choice of laminated, synthetic or wood stocks with blued or stainless steel, the Marlin range is a good choice for the budget-minded shooter.

For those that prefer a box magazine detachable option rather than the tubular system, the model 982 or cheaper 925 series of bolt actions

may be more appropriate. These are in .22 and .22 WMR calibres, whilst the 917 models are chambered in the .17HMR round. Again, blued and wood stock is the basic choice, with synthetic options, although the 917VSF has a stainless barrel with a very nice fluted finish.

.17 Mach 2 fanciers can opt for the 917M2 and 917M2S Marlins, both sporting a 22in (55cm) barrel, but the M2S version has a stainless finish and laminated stock, although the M2 is the basic model with blued steel and wood stock.

STRAIGHT PULL RIFLES

Straight pulls are a small percentage of rimfire sales, but rifles such as the Browning T-Bolt epitomize the quality and functional benefits of the design. Typically this mechanism differs from a traditional bolt design in that the operation is achieved in one plane – there is no upward turn of the bolt handle to unlock the bolt before rearward bolt operation and cocking the action. Instead the rifle is cocked with one smooth rearward movement of the bolt handle that opens the action, cocks the trigger and hammer, and then cycles a cartridge from the magazine.

Browning

The T-Bolt design is a superb rimfire sporter blending traditional build qualities with some very modern design twists. Originating back in 1965, the Browning design lasted until the mid 1970s and offered the hunter a beautifully proportioned, unique little rimfire rifle.

Unlike the forward/back and up/down movement of a conventional bolt operation, the T-Bolt cycles with a single straight pull back and then forth. The bolt handle actually pivots just a little before the bolt opens, which then pulls the twin circular locking lugs/rings from the receiver walls. The design is very smooth, strong and foolproof, the fit and finish have very tight tolerances that glide in their raceways, and there is no binding or lateral play whatsoever. The bolt handle is L-shaped and this pivots on a vertical cross pin sited at the apex of the handle in the receiver. This large pivot allows the twin circular lugs to be unlocked from the receiver with little effort as the bolt moves backwards.

The bolt body is a single unit that has twin extractors to ensure positive extraction and controlled support for the case as it is loaded. Innovation does not stop at the action design: the magazine is a real gem in its own right. It is of a double helix arrangement that enables ten rounds to be loaded into a small overall magazine size. Totally unique, it works very well.

The trigger and safety are contained in a single firing mechanism unit that forms the tang safety location and polycarbonate trigger guard that attaches to the base of the receiver. The two-position safety actually doesn't lock the bolt, only the trigger, so single rounds can be removed or loaded from the action as required.

As with the action, the barrel has a deep blued finish complimenting the walnut stock beautifully. Sporter-profiled for its .22 length, the barrel starts at 0.825 (2cm) diameter at the receiver ring, quickly tapering down to 0.535 (1.3cm) at the muzzle, which has a recessed, properly crowned finish. The barrel is already screw-cut for a sound moderator with a 0.5 UNF thread, and if you think 22in (55cm) is too long, then Browning are now offering the T-Bolt with a 16in (40cm) threaded barrel as an option. It is fully free floated along its entire length, and thus none of the fore-end wood touches the barrel upsetting barrel vibrations, and ensures consistent accuracy regardless of the weather.

A great and viable alternative to any bolt action design, the T-Bolt offers the hunter an unusual but superbly made and accurate rimfire sporter.

PUMP ACTION RIFLES

The pump action rifle, as the name suggests, cycles and cocks the action with a reciprocating pumping action of the fore-end grip. In truth it is a fast and efficient means of cartridge manipulation, but as with semi-automatic designs, they are not designed with the same tight tolerances associated with bolt action rimfire. This is mainly to allow a fast, slick and reliable function of the rifle. The real problem with pumps is that the magazines are tubular under-barrel mechanisms. This is very old hat and makes them slow to reload, and a removable magazine would be much better and practical for use in a sporting scenario.

In reality there are only two pump actions available at present: one is the Remington 572 Fieldmaster, and the other is a copy of an old Browning design called the Taurus M62.

The Browning T-Bolt uses a super-fast straight pull bolt operation and ten shot helical magazine system, which makes it ideal as a rabbit gun.

Taurus

This Brazilian-made rifle has a tube-type magazine with a wood stock, open sights and old-fashioned external hammer. The action is top opening, precluding the use of a scope mount, although the rifle can be easily split into two main sections for storage. The model M62R has a 23in (57cm) barrel and thirteen shot capacity, whilst the M62C or carbine has a 16.5in (41cm) barrel and twelve-shot payload. This is a fun rifle for afternoon plinking, but not a real sporting contender.

Remington 572 Fieldmaster

As uncommon as straight pulls, there is one pump action that stands out as possibly an alternative sporting rifle for rabbits in this country, and that is the Remington 572 Fieldmaster.

The Remington Fieldmaster is a whole different ball game: good build quality, accurate, reliable and capable of mounting a scope, this rimfire is a viable sporting arm should you wish.

Sporting highly blued steelwork with 21in (52cm) carbon steel barrels, the walnut stock has the typically high gloss American finish. With the tubular magazine you are not restricted to one size rimfire from the .22 stable, there is a capacity to shoot twenty .22 short, seventeen .22 long and fifteen .22lr rounds, all reliably.

Weighing only 5.75lb (2.6kg) with an overall length of 40in (100cm), you have a trim, very handy little rimfire sporter – though fitting a moderator could be problematic with that full length under-barrel tubular magazine. Still, its saving grace is being able to mount a scope via the integral grooved receiver, and since nearly all shooters will want to do this, the Fieldmaster makes another option for rimfire hunters.

LEVER ACTION RIFLES

Lever actions have a small but loyal following, and operate with a reciprocating movement from a lever ring attached beneath the rifle's action. The cartridges are cycled from magazine to chamber by a downward motion of the operating lever sited to the rear of the trigger unit. Pushing the lever down not only cocks the action but ejects any spent case from the chamber, and pulling the lever back into position retrieves another cartridge from the magazine, which is then fed into the chamber. Cartridges can be kept in a tube magazine under the barrel, or via a more traditional clip magazine design. Despite its old design, there are several manufacturers who offer this load system.

Pump-action rimfires are rare, with bolt or semi-auto designs being more mainstream. However, the Remington Field Master is fun to use and offers a creditable alternative vermin gun.

Thompson Center offer the old Contender and new G2 single shot rifles that also allow a swift barrel change, and are handy sized vermin rifles.

Browning's BL22, Henry's Varmint Express and Marlin's 39A offer models with a choice of tubular magazine feed, whilst the Ruger 96/22 sticks to its tried and tested rotary magazine, bringing this ancient marque up into the twenty-first century. For this reason we will look at the Ruger 96/22 in more detail.

Ruger

The Ruger 96/22 is offered as a .22 WMR model as well as a .17HMR calibre, and is unique in that although being a lever action it has many of the attributes of a modern rimfire rifle, making it more akin to vermin control as does any other lever action on offer today. Most rimfire hunters will want to fit a sound moderator and use subsonic ammunition, but most lever actions use the old tube-fed under-the-barrel feed system that almost negates the use of a silencer due to the proximity of the access to the magazine with the barrel-mounted moderator.

In my opinion this is where the Ruger 96 wins, because the rotary magazine from the 10/22 series of rifles is utilized, although nine shot in this case, not ten, and it is sited as a unit beneath the action just in front of the trigger guard. More than just a good design, in real

terms it means that the 96 can be fitted with a moderator that transforms this old design concept into a very usable rifle for rabbit or vermin control.

Operation as such is not very slick as compared to a bolt or straight pull, and despite the fast lever design there is a distinct excess of noise with every pull. As a sporting arm it offers an unusual design, but it would not be my own personal choice despite the accuracy from both .22 WMR and .17 HMR models.

SINGLE SHOT RIFLES

Single shot rimfires represent the simplest design criteria, but this does not mean that quality has to suffer, and it is a great rimfire design for the novice to master. A single shot rimfire can take the form of either a cut-down target model or a dedicated single shot design such as the Thompson Contender (TC) or G2 models and Rossi R17.

Whereas the TC and Rossi rifles are break open designs, there is often a propensity to convert a target arm into a sporter by reducing the barrel length and changing the stock dimensions. This means that any target rifle can be converted. The Walther Running Boar single shot is a superbly accurate arm and ideally suited to barrel reduction, but their single shot capacity is their only drawback – that is, if you miss on the first shot.

Thompson Center

The Thompson Center Contender carbine epitomises a rifle that offers superb versatility, and is unique in that the barrel can be quickly detached and replaced in another calibre, thereby allowing a rifle that can be transformed from rimfire to centrefire use with just a flick of the swivelling firing pin switch. Maximum versatility and accuracy can be achieved from the TC design, and it is a good choice to learn on or as a lightweight hunting tool. I have owned many TC rifles, and can still rely on their performance to bring home wild food for the table.

Choice of varmint or sporter profile barrels allows a preference in weight to be achieved, and the stock options also vary, from walnut to synthetic with a simple no cheekpiece profile to thumbhole camouflaged options. The newer model G2 carbines have a stronger and reprofiled action with a clever recock of the trigger sear without opening the action, as on the older models. The trigger, too, has a better pull and feel, which certainly aids in accuracy, making the G2 a very practical and portable little vermin gun. Calibre choice is endless due to the enormous options offered by the well established pool of custom suppliers. All the common rimfire calibres are catered for in a barrel profile or finish, with some very interesting sub-calibres such as 17 Squirrel, 14 Walker or even 10 or 12 calibre Eichelberger rounds.

As a one gun option but with the easy ability to upgrade calibres even to fox and deer sizes, the T/C carbine is well ahead of the opposition.

Rossi

For sheer simplicity and cheapness, the Rossi single shot break-open rifle is hard to beat. Rossi are better known for their lever-action centrefire calibre rifles, but in single shot mode they have a surprisingly good degree of potential as a do-anything rimfire hunter. Either as a low cost training tool or a youngster's first rifle, or indeed as a rifle to sling in the back of the 4×4, the strong, no-nonsense, single shot action is a great safe learning tool for proper firearms training.

For the rimfire hunter models include the R17 that has a set of rudimentary iron sights that will be passed over for fitment of a scope via the drilled and tapped receiver and scope base system. The barrel is 23in (57.6cm) in length, but the overall length of the rifle is short due to the lack of receiver of these single shot rifles, where the cartridge is placed directly into the barrel's chamber manually. The R17 is chambered for the .17HMR round, and is available in a conventional blued steel and wood stock, although a stainless steel and black option is also available. There is also a youth model that sports an 18.5in (46cm) barrel that, once threaded at the muzzle, would make a prize candidate for sound moderator fitment. The external hammer is manually cocked and is foolproof, although a bit sluggish, and the action is broken by a simple catch that, once depressed, releases the barrel to drop open.

This rifle is not pretty, but it is still cheap, and will appeal to the more thrifty among us.

SEMI-AUTOMATIC RIFLES

Semi-automatic rimfire rifles allow the shooter to follow up the first shot extremely quickly if necessary, by a recoiling bolt operation for every press of the trigger. As the rifle is fired the recoil force is transferred from the cartridge to the recoil spring, which allows the bolt to free recoil within the receiver backwards, thus cocking the action. The bolt then returns to the closed state, on its way back stripping another cartridge from the magazine and feeding it into the now empty chamber. Thus every pull of the trigger initiates a fresh round fired without any additional bolt manipulation. Popular as a hunting tool, most semi-automatic rimfires do not have the accuracy potential of their bolt action cousins, although there is a new breed of custom semi-auto rimfires that may finally change all that.

Most manufacturers offer a rimfire semi-automatic: these include Browning's Buckmark,

Remington's Speedmaster, T/C's R55, Henry Survival, Walther G22, CZ511, Marlin M7000, Savage M64 and Anschutz's 525.

Ruger

The standard 10/22 Rugers have the accolade as being the most prolific rimfire semi-automatic ever produced, over six million to date, and at the same time the most popular to customize due to the huge number of after-market options available. In standard trim the 10/22 offers the real world rimfire shooter with a reliable, no-nonsense repeating rimfire.

Offered in styles ranging from standard wood-stocked, blued, sporter barrel profiles to full blown, target, heavy-barrelled, laminated stock models, Ruger have every eventuality covered. The 10/22CRR is the compact version, sporting a barrel little over 16in (40cm) and finished with open sights. The hardwood stock is plain and has a short 12.75in (32.4cm) length of pull with a hard plastic butt pad, but offers a handy little repeating sporting arm for the beginner. Then there is a synthetic model dubbed the K10/22RPF, or 'All Weather', with a stainless-steel action and barrel with a synthetic black moulded stock, suitable as a go-anywhere rifle in any weather conditions for rough

or heavy use. Those requiring a little more refinement would be best served with the deluxe model. Dressed in walnut and checkered stock, gone is the barrel band, and fitment of a rubber recoil pad is far more practical. A heavy barrel version dubbed the K10/22T in brown laminate stock with stainless or blued finish is designed to eke every last drop of accuracy from the design, and gives a nice heft to the rifle to make it more stable in the hold.

Custom 10/22 rifles are prolific and represent a whole industry, but some stand out as exceptional. The North West Custom Parts Hunting Sporter is a blend of the best after-market parts for the 10/22 rifle. Sporting a Bell and Carlson synthetic stock to repel the harsh British weather, this 10/22 is designed as a premium sporter for rabbits and vermin. Every part has been customized, from the Tactical Solutions barrel, which contributes to the incredible overall light weight of 3.75lb (1.7kg), down to the reprofiled bolt and firing mechanism, to produce a reliable and, more importantly, accurate rifle for vermin control.

The trigger mechanism is a drop-out unit and is replaced with a Power Custom hammer and spring; this offers superior trigger pull and reliability and finishes off what can only be called perfection as a rimfire repeating arm.

To get the best from a semi-auto rimfire, people often turn to specialist custom add-on items and services. This North West Custom Ruger 10/22 is about as good as it gets.

Some people like the idea of a quick second or third shot, and this can be an advantage whilst out lamping rabbits; here the Remington 597 is a good, reliable choice.

Remington

For those of us with limited funds, the Remington 597 offers the serious rimfire sporting user a factory fresh, 'out of the box', ready-to-go repeating rifle.

The Remington 597 has to be a worthwhile consideration as a semi-auto rabbit gun. True, there are fewer after-market items for the Remy, but it offers the hunter a good deal as a competent and reliable rimfire hunter. I particularly like the synthetic grey stock; although glued from two halves, the design is comfortable and well proportioned. Better still is the action, which has integral dovetail scope rails and utilizes a good trigger unit with a hold-open bolt system after the last round is fired, and the magazine is easily dropped by a more convenient magazine release than the Ruger design. Furnished with a screw-cut barrel for sound moderator use, the Remington 597 is designed to be used in the field under extreme conditions, and as such offers good reliability and accuracy from a repeater design, and in many respects eclipses the venerable Ruger 10/22.

CONCLUSIONS

Regardless of your personal preference, there are more than enough choices for the British shooter to satisfy his own tastes, in fact more than any other realm of sporting arms in this country. The vast majority will be more than content with the bolt action design, and this should be your first choice. But with the ever-increasing demand for more exotic and higher performance, the semi-automatic rimfires are catching up fast. The crux of the matter is this: choose a rifle that best suits you, your style of shooting, and the range at which you most commonly shoot. Then familiarize yourself with the workings and foibles of your rifle, and learn to shoot it accurately at all ranges and in all weather conditions – and then you will glean the maximum from your sporting forays.

Chapter 4
Fox Rifles

Strange as it might seem, the rifle you choose for foxes, and to a large extent deer stalking, is actually less crucial than getting the bullet choice right. Most modern-day rifles are capable of adequate accuracy for fox work, and often a suitable fox calibre version of a deer rifle is sufficient. However, unlike the wide choice of operating styles in the vermin classes, semi- or pump actions for centrefires are not permitted by law. Therefore the majority of the rifles suitable for fox control are either bolt action, single shot, straight pull or lever actions, and it is the bolt actions that are most widely used.

As in many shooting situations, a quick second shot can be desirable, and no more so than in some types of fox control especially where a fox is called into range or whilst lamping, where shots can be unpredictable. Weight can also be an issue, so fox rifles usually have a varmint profile for steadier shots at longer range, or a light-weight, compact sporter profile to operate quickly and at close quarters.

For closer work there is a crossover from rimfires to centrefires, and some .22lr ammunition is suitable for fox rounds at close range, although the newer .17 HMR rimfire is better.

Foxes live in a varied environment and require a wide range of rifle styles to combat them; this .20 Tactical Custom Rifle Services varminter with PES moderator is excellent for flat shooting against the fox.

TYPES OF RIFLE

The Walking Gun

The epitome of a great all-round fox rifle is termed a 'walking gun', light enough for use in the fields or out lamping on foot, giving good first round accuracy and good handling. It matters not whether the rifle wears a synthetic or wood stock as long as it has fast target acquisition and possibly a quick second round if necessary.

Fitted with scope and moderator, a good fox walking gun should not weigh more than 8–10lb (3.6–4.5kg), and should be robust enough to withstand a few knocks. I would always have a sling fitted, not only to allow hands free binocular use but also to gain a little extra support when shooting off hand. A bipod is also a good idea, such as a Harris, to allow quick deployment if a longer range shot presents itself. So too is a Hunter's cheekpiece that attaches to the stock's butt, allowing you to store extra rounds and game calls.

Static / Longer Range Rifles

Where foxes are shot or lamped from 4 × 4s or from a static position at long range, there is less emphasis on weight and more on a steady rifle. Here we are talking of varmint profile rifles with a suitably larger fore-end to accommodate larger diameter barrels either with sporter or thumbhole stocks but usually all tooled up with an overall weight of 10–14lb (4.5–6.3kg).

Equipped with large, variable scopes for precise bullet placement and low light ability, these fox rifles deliver accuracy at extreme range and are capable of handling more potent cartridges. Most manufacturers make alternative varmint models to their existing sporter range.

Single Shot Rifles

A single shot fox rifle need not be a handicap in the hands of a competent shooter. One well placed shot is all that is needed, and many single shot rifles are so simplistic in design that a rapid second shot is actually very fast to administer. Furthermore single shots are usually smaller and therefore weigh less than their repeating brothers, making them easy to handle when in the woods or bouncing around on a quad bike or in a 4 × 4.

I like the straightforwardness of a single shot, as many also have a swift barrel-change facility that will turn your nimble foxing tool into a deer stalking rifle.

Rifles in this category include the Thompson Contender G2 and Encore models, available in an array of standard or wildcat calibres and facilitating a swift barrel-change facility. Ruger produce a superbly crafted rifle in the No. 1 model of its line of single shot rifles for foxes or varmint with heavy barrel, although the lightweight trim No. 1B would make a great walking fox gun.

This is also true of the Browning High Wall in a calibre such as the .22-250. It is a superb go-anywhere, accurate lightweight fox rifle – as indeed are any of the custom makers' single shots, especially the more readily available Cooper Arms Phoenix Model 21.

Because of their simple design, some single shots can be cheap, as the Rossi rifle: this solid, break open design is a dependable work tool, and not something just to admire in the gunroom. Single shots can also be highly expensive, such as the Blaser K95 from Germany that allows barrel change and differing degrees of adornment.

My favourite is the T/C G2 carbine in .223 calibre: this is a rugged, accurate, simple rifle in a good calibre for foxes, an incarnation of the famous Contender pistol. Its facility to change barrels between rimfire as well as centrefire is legendary, as is its accuracy. There is an automatic hammer block safety, and on the G2 model you can cock and decock without opening the barrel as on older models. This is a truly excellent foxing tool: short, trim and lightweight, with either wood or synthetic stock of sporter or thumbhole design, with calibres as diverse as .17 Mach 2 to 6.8mm SPC Rem for fox use in either blued or stainless barrels.

OPPOSITE: *.17 PPC shooting a 30-grain Woodchuck Den bullet from this Venom custom Sako rifle makes an ideal light but long range fox rifle.*

Lever Action Rifles

This is probably the smallest category of usable rifles for fox control, although a couple do stand out: the Browning BLR and the Ruger 96.

The Browning BLR Rifle

This rifle is more commonly associated with deer work, but it can make a fast, accurate and highly pointable foxing tool if chambered in the right calibre, such as the flat-shooting .22-250. Made in Japan, the quality is good with a 20in (50cm) barrel and four-shot detachable magazine, and a lever action that cleverly retains the trigger blade within the trigger guard whilst operating. Despite its solid feel, the BLR weighs only 6lb 8oz (3kg), and with an overall length of just under 40in (1m), this Browning would make a superb walking fox rifle.

An alternative lever action is the Ruger 96 model in either .17 HMR or .22 magnum calibres. It is a light, fast-handling carbine with utilitarian looks and robust construction for bouncing around in the back of a Land Rover. Introduced in 1997, the model 96/22 was initially available in .22lr and had Ruger's typically styled carbine 10/22 semi-automatic profile with barrel band and detachable rotary magazine system. A .22 magnum version was introduced shortly after, as well as a hard-hitting .44 magnum carbine; the .17 HMR version is the latest incarnation.

At a glance, if it were not for the lever under the action, the 96/22m could be mistaken for Ruger's hugely successful 10/22 repeater .22lr. The action is very similar, having an enclosed design with only a small aperture to the right flank that ejects spent cases. This is to prevent debris from field use getting into the action's moving parts – which is fine, although it makes retrieving a stuck case tricky. The whole action is made from alloy, so it is light, and it has a smooth, black-painted finish with a pronounced curved rear section tang as it meets the woodwork.

The actual lever design is reminiscent of the old Savage 99 system, with an enclosed ring section of 2.8in (7cm) and operating arc of about 3.5in (8.9cm). Although the lever is curved, you still rap your knuckles when operating it.

As befitting a carbine design, the overall length of 37.25in (94.6cm) is largely due to the short 18.5in (47cm) barrel, which is a slender sporter profile without a threaded muzzle for a sound moderator. Better is the one-piece dedicated scope base supplied with the rifle, which enables the use of standard .22 tip-off or dovetail mounts to fit a cut along the mount's length.

The trigger unit has a single-stage pull that is adequate at best, with a lack of feel and 5lb (2.3kg) pull, although the trigger blade, despite being smooth, is wide enough to give a little more control to the firing cycle.

The magazine is a longer version of the 10/22 rotary design to accommodate the .22 magnum round. Capacity is reduced by one to nine shots, but this is more than enough, and gives the shooter enough firepower from one magazine load for sporting use.

The utilitarian stock is made from birch stained a walnut brown colour and finished with a matt but smooth lacquer. The length of pull is short at a measured 13.25in (33.65cm), but in truth the stock is all you need on this sort of rifle. At least you can concentrate on the stalk without fear of damaging any lovely figure wood!

BOLT ACTION RIFLES

Although this is the biggest category, which rifle to choose is actually the most difficult because most of the leading manufacturers offer a good range of fox rifles. For me, what makes the difference is whether you are walking or staying in one place.

Remember that most of us generally only shoot one fox on an outing if we are lucky – maybe more if out lamping, for sure, but to most, a lighter weight one shot is desirable as it is important to get that first shot accurate. Great choices are therefore many sporter weight, barrel-profiled rifles such as the excellent CZ 527, Tikka Lite, Remington LVSF, Winchester Coyote Light and Ruger laminated 77/22H.

Browning, too, offers a fast-handling bolt action in the guise of the A-Bolt. Its lightweight, lightning-fast bolt and great accuracy, coupled to a good choice of calibres including the fast-stepping .243 or .223 WSSM, makes it a very good fox rifle.

Again, personal choice will dictate length of pull on the stock, aesthetics and synthetic components. I like the Tikka Lite, weatherproof for the most part, good value and always accurate. The Remington LVSF is also an excellent, fast-handling little fox gun, even with a scope and moderator fitted – but choose your calibre carefully because the barrel is not free floated. Similarly the CZ 527 series offers a dependable, magazine-fed rifle on a tried and tested action design that may not be the pinnacle of sporting prowess, but it always shoots really well, especially in varmint form; it has a wood or synthetic stock.

As for the others, the Ruger laminated .22 Hornet is a favourite of the fox world – a light, rotary magazine with light recoil and good accuracy, it is a calibre with just enough to get the job done with minimal fuss and bother. It is not too expensive in terms of rifle cost or ammunition expenditure if you shop around a bit. A new design is the Winchester Coyote Light, a synthetic-stocked, fluted, stainless-barrelled fox gun delivering good accuracy at a keen price, which is built to take the knocks in the field and in and out of a vehicle or scrambling out of a barn.

Similarly the third category of a fox/deer rifle encompasses many of the aforementioned rifles, but a Tikka T3 Lite in .243 with a 75-grain bullet has to be a good all-round combination. Sako also offers the Hunter range, with a dual personality of deer/fox combinations; and the Finn light with its fluted barrel and synthetic stock is a hard-wearing, accurate, all-weather fox gun. Mannlicher Prohunter Mountain rifle in .260 Remington is a 6.5mm variant of the .308 case, and really is an all-round cartridge. A 120-grain Ballistic Tips travelling at 2900fps is a serious fox bullet, and is not too explosive on deer as to cause excessive meat damage.

The Prohunter range is excellent value for money, and accuracy is always good for any fox sortie. And don't forget the Weatherby Vanguard rifle, available in a variety of fox calibres that give guaranteed accuracy at 100 yards. A .257 Weatherby version fitted with a moderator is a combination that allows you to shoot magnum-class cartridges with the felt recoil of a standard calibre fox or deer gun – and in my book that makes the Weatherby a real contender.

Magnum calibres such as the potent .257 Weatherby, here in the Vanguard model, can send a 75-grain V-Max bullet speeding along at 3,900fps.

A CLOSER LOOK

The CZ 527

Few designs can be described as classics, but surely the Mauser bolt action is one. Having spurned hundreds of derivatives and similar or modified action types, it is proof that if a design works, then why change it. The CZ 527 is one such variant from that old genre; in fact the term 'Mini Mauser' would best describe the action used on this rifle. Specifically designed by CZ in the Czech Republic to cater for the smaller family of cartridges such as .222 and .223, its diminutive size perfectly balances the cartridge choice and offers no excessive weight. The 527 model offers a micro-sized Mauser action with twin forward-locking lugs coupled to a large external extractor. Combine this with a neat, five-shot detachable magazine, side safety and fine set trigger as standard, and you can see why the 527 model is still so popular. The new variant, called the varmint sports, has a long, heavier weight barrel and is chambered in the new .204 Ruger high-stepping fox cartridge; it can be had in wood, laminate or synthetic stocks.

The whole action has been miniaturized. The bolt has been scaled down, with smaller length and slender girth, but the twin opposed locking lugs are suitably large to provide precise and safe bolt closure. Common to most Mauser designs is the external extractor that is non-rotating and acts in conjunction with the bolt stop positioned ejector spur to positively eject used cases from the action. The bolt cocks on opening, and the rear bolt shroud is used as the cocking piece. The bolt handle is straight and rather short, but the comfortable small ball operating end ensures a smooth and trouble-free cycling action. The initial tightness from a new rifle is soon overcome, and after the range and field tests the bolt runs in nicely. Scope mounting is easy as there are integral dovetails on the receiver top, a system I always prefer.

Common to all model 527 CZ rifles, regardless of calibre or variant, the detachable magazine is a good and preferred option, especially on a fox or varmint rifle where fast successive shots may be encountered, or where trouble-free operation whilst lamping in darkness is beneficial. This is a two-handed operation because the catch has strong jaws, but is one that is easily learnt.

The trigger is adjustable and has the advantage common to many CZ models of having a set trigger fitted as standard. The initial factory setting on the standard trigger pull is heavy at around 5.5lb (2.5kg); it is set thus for safety reasons, but this can be lightened, which would certainly improve its feel. If you want a very light trigger weight of less than 1lb (227g), the trigger blade

The CZ 527 is a classic foxing arm with detachable magazine, bombproof mini Mauser action, and now chambered in the fox's worst nightmare, .204 Ruger calibre.

For hard use in all weathers, a stainless-steel and synthetic stock rifle makes sense. The Winchester Coyote is accurate and built to take hard use.

can be 'set' by pushing it forwards until an audible click is heard, and then used as normal.

The Varmint model has a more slender profile barrel than one would think of from a more traditional varmint rifle, although the length is deceptively long. Measuring 25.75in (65.4cm) from receiver to muzzle, the 527 barrel is actually nearly 2in (5cm) longer than many similar competitors' rifles. Also of importance is the fact that the barrel is fully free floating along its entire length, and so shifting zeroes due to warpage should not be a problem.

The stock is classical in wood trim, but better profiled in laminate and synthetic for scope usage. Some longer-range varminters would prefer a wider fore-end profile, but the stock as it is worked fine shooting with either a Harris bipod or off shooting sticks.

In .204 Ruger calibre the CZ527 barrel twist is that of 1 in 12in (2.5 in 30cm), allowing bullet stability for bullet weights of 32-grain and 40-grain bullets. Remington 32 grainers will shoot 0.5in (13mm) groups at 100yd with a velocity of 3987fps and 1129ft/lb energy. The 40 grains from Hornady give velocities and energy figures of 3735fps and 991ft/lb respectively. Regardless of velocity, even at these figures a 32-grain bullet when zeroed at 100yd will still penetrate the chest cavity of a fox at 275yd (250m) – and that in real life is all that matters.

In fact the more a CZ is used, the more it settles down to be a smooth, highly reliable firearm that knows how to shoot, and takes the knocks that any shooting trip might throw at it.

The Winchester Coyote

The Coyote model is the perfect genesis from the well respected, tried and tested Winchester model 70 bolt action. Whereas the original model 70 was a pure classic rifle with blued metal and figured walnut stock, the new model offers a 24in (60cm) stainless steel with matt blued receiver and synthetic stock in a profile that transcends a hunting model with a blend of varminter.

The barrel profile strikes a good balance, literally speaking, between a medium to heavier weight but with the clever inclusion of flutes to reduce the weight. They not only look good, but they allow a heavier profile barrel and therefore good rigidity and accuracy, whilst also allowing a lighter overall package.

Pure Winchester 70, the action is both simple yet strong. It incorporates a push feed and coned breech design aiding in smooth cartridge transfer from magazine to barrel, and a hinged magazine floor plate with three-position safety located at the rear of the bolt. Cartridges are accurately fed from the magazine into the chamber, and just as reassuring extracted and ejected by the fixed blade ejector at the rear of the bolt raceway on the left side. This controlled round push feed (CRPF) system ensures that the cartridge enters straight into the chamber, thus avoiding damage to the bullet's tip. The large, centralizing Win '64-style claw extractor is the reason here. The bolt body is nicely jewelled for looks and has twin opposing large locking

Laminate stocks offer the benefits of synthetics but with a more natural look. The Howa rifle in .22-250 and thumbhole laminated stock is a great all-round fox rifle, and well priced.

lugs that give a solid lock-up when the bolt is closed.

Winchester have always favoured an uncomplicated and simple trigger design. There is nothing wrong with that, and on the Coyote the trigger pressure was set at a conservative and safe 5.5lb (2.5kg) weight. If this is too heavy the mechanism is easy to adjust, as the threaded shaft contains three lock nuts that in turn affect the trigger pressure and let-off.

The new Lite version of the Coyote stems from the reduced weight of the barrel fluting, and also the use of a Bell and Carlson synthetic stock to replace the heavier laminated version, all with four striking cut-out ventilation holes in the fore-end. Looking like sharks' gills, this gives the Winchester that contemporary look which goes all the way through the fore-end, and is there to assist heat dispersion and cooling after an arduous day's varminting. Extra care has been taken with the bedding of this rifle, and an aluminium bedding block contacts the action, ensuring a positive grip and uniform platform for stock to metal unison. The recoil lug is factory bedded with a synthetic bed material, which although minimal, is ample for positive location, although the rear securing screw has little stock material to actually bind with.

In .22-250 calibre I would stick with the 50-grain loads for flat shooting accurate loads from this rifle against foxes, or shoot a more controlled expanding bullet such as the Sierra 55-grain Game King for roe in Scotland or muntjac in England.

The Howa

The Japanese make very price-conscious rifles, many suitable for fox work. Their laminated lightweight sporter in .204 Ruger is a very capable walking fox rifle, and their heavy-barrelled varmint versions with thumbhole or sporter profile laminated stocks deliver great accuracy and consistency for longer range or steadier shots.

The heart of any rifle lies in its ability to maintain a strong, stiff and reliable action from which all the appendages can synergize together; get the action right, and you are half way to a good rifle. The Howa utilizes a single forged steel action that is machined to the correct dimensions either in steel or stainless steel. This straightaway gives a good strong action, and the top receiver bridge is drilled and tapped for scope bases identical to Remington rifles, and there is an integral recoil lug beneath. The blued finish was a good, rich, deep satin blue-black that complemented the barrel and stock well, and with proper care could cope with some real-life shooting abuse. At the base is a hinged floorplate magazine holding four cartridges in .22-250 calibre with a simple lever operation sited in the forward section of the trigger guard.

One real asset of the Howa action is the large and very well engineered bolt and handle. Stemming from a single piece of steel bar stock, its dimensions give a comforting, robust heft to the whole action. There are two large locking lugs up front, which when cammed into the action, on closure bind or mate true to the action body, thus not imparting any unwelcome torque to the action. The ejector is a plunger type, sprung within the bolt body, and very forcefully ejects spent cases from the action. Primary extraction is accomplished by an M16 rifle-type extractor claw. This is a really good, solid extractor that grips the rim of the case very securely and never fails to extract a case from the rifle's chamber.

As far as varmint/foxing stocks go, it would be hard to find a better designed and finished stock for this class of rifle. Finished in a black laminated wood structure with a tough lacquered external surface, this stock hits the mark in both looks and function.

To further enhance the design there are three slotted ventilation holes to each side that transcend the entire girth of the fore-end. This has a dual role in allowing the barrel to cool quickly after a rapid session of shots, and it looks good, too. The firing hand is supported vertically, and gives a good length of pull to the trigger and thus correct trigger tension. The 'hole' of the thumbhole is large enough to use quickly if the rifle has to be mounted in a hurry, and the swept-back roll-over cheekpiece does a good job of positioning the eye centrally to the axis of the scope.

.22-250 is a great all-round fox/varmint calibre, and readily lends itself to good accuracy potential. The barrel is a heavy, varmint profile tapering from 1.2in (3cm) to 0.82 (2cm) at the muzzle, and is fully free floating, thereby allowing a reasonable number of rounds to be shot before heat build-up impairs accuracy. It is hammer forged in construction and button rifled with a one-in-twelve twist rate and six-groove rifling, and has a properly recessed crowned muzzle. At 100yd, factory Remingtons, Federal and Norma ammunition with bullet weights from 40 grains to 55 grains will all shoot below the inch mark or just over, for a production rifle with factory ammo that is good.

The RWS Titan

The Titan 3 is a synthetic-stocked, stainless-steel rifle design for fox or deer dependent on calibre, and offers the shooter a good build quality with a barrel-change facility. The finish is designed to repel the elements, and is in the ever-popular stainless-steel metalwork complimented with a synthetic stock. The overall size of the action or receiver is suitably large, as the RWS Titan uses a common long action specification so as to accommodate any cartridge overall length, rather like the Tikka T3. The ejection port is 3.25in (8.25cm) long, and this makes for a long bolt operation on the smaller calibres such as .223 – however, this seems to be the way manufacturers are going these days. The bolt locks securely directly into the back of the barrel, thereby alleviating any stress. The receiver at the bottom front also has a split clamping system that retains the barrel shank and facilitates a quick change of the barrel. It is securely retained by a lug and twin securing screws, thus allowing

The RWS Titan, here in .223 calibre and fitted with a PES 38mm moderator, is capable of fox shooting close up when calling, or way out there at long range.

a degree of flexibility to your Titan rifle with regard to calibre choice.

The bolt is very large and solid, with a one-piece construction that is well machined to fit the receiver, which results in a smooth operation. There are three locking lugs up front that fit directly into the barrel recess, and as such allow a short bolt lift to disengage.

There are no scope rails or dovetails, it is just drilled and tapped for scope bases, and the magazine is a detachable variety with a capacity of three rounds in .223, although a five-shot version is also available.

The trigger is nice: it has no set trigger mode, as so many other continental rifles have, and in truth does not need it. The trigger breaks cleanly at 2.75lb (1.25kg), which is very good; you can adjust to your own settings, but there really is no need. The crisp let-off and fast lock time ensures a better placed shot.

The barrel is made from stainless steel with a suitable sporter contour, rather than varmint profiled. The outside diameter at the receiver is 1.14in (2.89cm) tapering down to 0.598 (1.519cm) diameter at the muzzle. With the barrel being 22in (55cm), the Titan has a sleek, light, yet highly pointable feeling to it, ideally suited to stalking or foxing on the move.

The stock does not reflect the same quality,

being a hard, black plastic moulded unit with pressed-in checkering at the fore-end and pistol grip. It is nicely contoured, ambidextrous and very slim in the fore-end section, and with no cheekpiece to the butt section. However, the thin and almost hollow fore-end lacks rigidity and is easily twisted, which is never really conducive to good group sizes when the rifle is shot.

When tested, the Norma 40-grain ballistic Tip ammunition grouped at 0.5in (13mm) at 100yd and would make a super fox round. With this level of accuracy, foxes at 200yd (183m) and corvids beyond that yardage were no problem, and the Night force scope also offers extreme light gathering and precision optics.

As a complete package with threaded muzzle and synthetic materials the Titan is a robust, well put together and thought-out rifle, and accuracy was really good despite the flimsy fore-end.

The Remington LVSF

The Remington Model 700 series of rifles has become an industry standard as far as reliability and accuracy are concerned, and continues to evolve in various guises. The latest of these is the Light Varmint Stainless Fluted (LVSF), which blends the weather-resistant nature of the stainless action and barrel, yet takes the form of a

The epitome of a classic 'walking' fox rifle, the Remington LVSF is both lightweight and short, and available in some good fox calibres.

For those requiring a heavier, more static fox rifle, a varmint-profiled Remington SPS with synthetic stock and heavy contoured barrel is ideal.

mid-weight varmint rifle that is lightweight and highly manoeuvrable.

The LVSF has been designed around Remingtons ADL blind box magazine system; it is rather fiddly to load, but you get a strong stock with fewer cut-outs to give a better bedding surface. It is the stock that really catches the eye, with the LVSF lighter, sleeker design profile. Overall black in colour, it has a nice speckled finish that gives a degree of grip to it, whilst the pistol grip is very long raked, positioning the hand perfectly for trigger control. There is a low comb to the butt with an integrated cheekpiece to the right, although you can shoot the LVSF left-handed with no problems, giving a good degree of flexibility.

Bedding of the action comes in the form of pillar columns to the stock screw recesses to stop material compression, and the recoil lug's rear face beds against an alloy block. Remington have opted not to free-float the barrel; instead it is bedded near the front of the barrel channel in the stock. The action is the Model 700 small length with a 2.4in (6cm) ejection port opening. It is constructed from stainless steel, and one of the great advantages of the 700 action is its round configuration and great inherent strength. The bolt, too, has two large forward-lugging lugs that make for a precise and strong lock-up.

The trigger unit is factory pre-set at 5lb (2.27kg); it can be adjusted, but requires the stock to be removed. It may be a little heavy, but it breaks clean enough.

At only 22in (55cm) long with a muzzle diameter of 0.65in (1.65cm), it makes the LVSF a very solid, slick-handling little rifle. The 6.7lb (3kg) weight is not really compromised when a scope is added, and having the barrel screw cut for a moderator would not make this rifle any heavier than some standard-weight rifles in its class. This is why as an all-round fox and deer (where legal) rifle, it really comes into its own.

50-grain Winchester Ballistic tips in .223 Remington with a velocity of 3327fps and 1229ft/lb energy would be a good all-round load with only a minus 2.2in (5.5cm) drop at 200yd (183m) from 100yd zero, making it deadly against foxes.

For any fox shooter wanting a quality rifle in a tough weather-resistant format, the LVSF is very hard to better.

The Remington SPS

Think of this as the bigger brother to the LVSF Remington. Remington offered two versions of their renowned Model 700 rifle, namely the ADL and BDL formats. Gone is the old ADL model, and in its place is the new SPS (special purpose synthetic) range that offers great performance at a reasonable price.

Strikingly, the varmint model sports a long 26in (65cm) barrel to eke every last drop of velocity from the ammunition, and the stock has had a complete revamp. The profile of the barrel is pure varmint, offering the blend between heavyweight and usability, finished off in a well crowned muzzle. Finish is aka ADL, which means a coarse, flat black-blue, almost parker-ized. It will not win any awards for beauty, but actually it is highly practical on a sporting arm, offering a non-reflective surface and capable of taking the rigours of everyday abuse without wearing unduly.

Moulded synthetic stocks save money, but actually offer benefits to the shooter in terms of weather resistance; however, many people feel walnut still looks nicer. The SPS has nice inset cast stippled grip areas to the pistol grip and fore-end, distinguishing this model – although gone is the R3 recoil pad, and in comes a solid black rubber unit. There is a low comb to the butt stock with a low-sited cheekpiece that is classic in design but lacks real shooter benefits. The fore-end is much better, because past the stippled grip area just forward of the magazine well the girth swells to give a semi-beaver tail fore-end profile. There are three vented cuts each side of the fore-end, which help in cooling the barrel and also give the SPS varmint a radical and modern look.

With a vastly improved trigger pull, Remington calls this the new X-Mark Pro Trigger, which is essentially a 'tweaked' assembly. There is meant to be an overall 40 per cent reduction in weight of pull, coupled with minimal creep and far superior adjustments. This is refreshing, because we come out from that 'politically correct trigger pull' thinking we have all suffered from USA rifles.

Chambered in .22-250 calibre, the SPS is an all-round varmint/fox calibre if ever there was one, and is accurate with a good variety of both factory and reloads.

Reloads range from 40-grain Noslers travelling at 4038fps with a charge of 38.8 grains Varget powder – these are deadly on hooded crows, although a mild load with a 55-grain Sierra Blitz King of 37.25 grains H414 powder will produce 3618fps and 1599ft/lb.

CUSTOM RIFLES

Venom Custom .17 AK Hornet

If you are in the market for a short range – that is, below 200yd (183m) – fox and crow round that would be reloadable, small calibre, thrifty

For the more adventurous, the .17 Ackley Hornet calibre has to rank as the most efficient little fox calibre available, here shown chambered in a Sako 78 sporter by Venom Arms.

on powder, low on noise and recoil, and above all accurate with enough energy to get the job done without overkill, then the .17 Ackley Hornet is it. It's a Wildcat round based on the .22 Hornet necked down to .17 calibre, and then fire formed to give the old Hornet's tapered case shape a significant case capacity increase with parallel walls and sharp shoulder angle. For its size, it is a beautifully proportioned case that translates into a highly efficient engine room. There is zero recoil, so all shots can be seen connecting with the target, a great benefit if you miss! This also means it is easily moderated to the point that the muzzle report is that of a .22lr target round, and with the small payload, it is economical to shoot.

A suitable donor .22 Hornet project rifle such as an old Sako Model 78, an early forerunner to the modern Finnfire rifle with a detachable magazine, would make a fine lightweight walking varmint tool.

This is a relatively easy and less costly Wildcat

rifle using Pac-Nor Super Match Grade stainless-steel barrels, which have always served me well. The twist rate of the rifling is of paramount importance, to achieve peak performance in velocity and accuracy in conjunction with being able to stabilize a wide range of weights of bullets. Luckily the .17 Hornet uses at best a range of 15- to 25-grain projectiles, and makes at least a one-in-ten twist rate necessary. There is no reason that a faster twist, such as a one-in-nine, be used to stabilize a 30-grain pill, but this is a bit heavy for the Hornet and compromises its function.

The stock was an STD Sako sporter affair, which had hydrographic in real tree hardwoods HD to complete the custom and effect look and practicality.

To reload the .17 Ackley Hornet you will need several forming and case trimming dies, as well as all the usual precision-loading techniques. It's rather fiddly, but well worth it.

I will detail the loads in the cartridge chapters, but you can expect velocities of 3778fps from a load of 11.5 grain Vit N120 powder — just dynamite on rabbits, crows and foxes up to 200yd (183m).

Where the .17 Ackley Hornet wins over other .17 or .22 small cases is in its tremendous efficiency in powder burn and velocity gain. It is accurate and cheap, and admittedly rather finicky to reload, but the rewards are there. My .17 Hornet is without doubt my favourite varmint cartridge. I have faster and snazzier cartridges, but that little Ackley serves me well for 90 per cent of all my needs up to 200yd (183m).

Steve Bowers .20 PPC

Most riflemen or women are happy with the offerings from a myriad of commercial manufacturers when choosing a rifle for fox work. However, there will come a time when some will want to upgrade their equipment, or they hanker after something just that little bit special. Steve Bowers is a very talented precision engineer from Cheltenham, and his custom rifles are superb.

To achieve the best possible tolerances in build, and therefore potential accuracy advantage, means going for a custom action. Choice here usually resides with many Benchrest target actions that also lend themselves very well to hunting use. Action makers such as Stolle, Stiller, Nesika, Hall, Viper and RPA are equally good, but this project used the BAT action from the USA. This is a stainless-steel action with extremely close tolerance, which combines extreme accuracy with good looks.

Again faced with a choice of some of the best barrel makers available, including Border, Shilen, Hart, Krieger, Walther and Douglas, Steve decided on a Pac-Nor from Oregon USA, as he has achieved excellent results with this premium barrel maker. A super match-grade

The ultimate fox rifle: a Steve Bowers custom .20 PPC on a BAT action and radical laminated stock design. Fully silenced, this rifle can humanely dispatch a fox at any range where the operator has confidence in their ability.

stainless-steel varmint-profile barrel would achieve a blend of excellent accuracy combined with a rigid barrel profile. Steve was to fit one of his super-efficient slim-line sound moderators, and a barrel length of 22in (55cm) achieved ample velocity and suitability for moderator use.

As important as the barrel maker is calibre choice. When ordering a custom rifle, why not get a little adventurous and have a calibre that reflects a bullet of the moment, or one of the many wildcat designs? In this I mean a modified parent case to eke out every last drop of accuracy and velocity potential. Calibre of choice was then the extremely efficient .20 PPC round. This is a necked-down version of the popular 6mm PPC round that started life as a target round, and migrated to the game fields because of its inherent accuracy and knock-down performance. This offers lightning-fast flat-shooting velocities, great for the longer-range fox, all in a bullet diameter that is less wind sensitive than a .172 calibre and not as pedestrian as the .224 calibres.

The Pac-Nor barrel was ordered as a three rifling groove one-in-eleven twist format so as to stabilize the lightweight 32-grain and heavier 39- or 40-grain .204 projectiles.

Steve has cleverly utilized an integral sound suppression system that outwardly changes little to the appearance of the rifle, yet offers good noise reduction.

The barrel is shortened to 22in (55cm), and the weight saved here is complemented by the addition of the sound moderator, so the rifle stays perfectly balanced. The shroud is made of high grade aircraft-quality stainless steel, and remains 1in (2.5cm) in diameter regardless of barrel contour. The rear section of the unit is secured via a dual high pressure 'o'-ring gas seal, and depending on barrel girth at this point, the corresponding amount of steel from the barrel is removed to achieve a gas-tight fit and overall custom contour.

Forward of the dual 'o'-ring seal, the front 1.5in (4cm) of barrel is profusely ported to release a primary jet of gases that are uniquely redirected via a bleed gas valve, down and rearward into the cavernous rear section of the moderator. As the bullet enters the primary and substantial baffles it effectively closes off the moderator to the atmosphere, and so maximum gas coolant of the powder gases is achieved. A further six baffles, all crafted from stainless steel, do a good job of noise reduction and eliminate muzzle flash.

Many a good custom rifle can live or die on the standard of stock it wears, and whether the design is up for the task of all-round fox use. At first appearance the stock does look large and ungainly, but believe me, every last inch and contour has a direct purpose to achieve balance and comfort when shooting in any position. For best weather resistance and unshifting zero, a laminated stock of midnight black colours was ordered, and this was crafted into a surprisingly light ventilated fore-end and height-adjustable rear stock configuration.

The sum of all the parts is only as good as the marriage between them, and a close symbiotic union between each unit achieves the best possible platform from which to launch a perfectly placed bullet. As such, all the metalwork – that is, action – is painstakingly bedded to the stock by Steve using a weatherproof synthetic compound called Devcon to ensure there is no shifting from zero in any weather conditions. The external metal surfaces were also coated with a mil-spec epoxy resin compound that is acid, waterproof and non-reflecting, perfect for outwitting old Charlie.

Being an unusual calibre, one has to form the brass before loading can commence. This is easily done, and Steve can advise as necessary. Sierra 39-grain Blitz King bullets, when loaded with 28 grains of Vit N133 and Federal Gold primer, achieve just under 4000fps velocity and 1385ft/lb energy.

This translates into an incredibly flat trajectory, perfect for fox work. When zeroed at 260yd (238m) you are only low by 0.8in (2cm) at 100yd (90m), and a minuscule minus 1.2in (3cm) at 300yd (274m), which means aiming dead on to 300yd. This is perfect if lamping when a quick shot may be necessary with little time for working out trajectory drops.

Accuracy margins from this rifle are tiny: one enlarged hole at 100yd, and very tight groups even out to 300yd and beyond – serious fox or vermin medicine.

Chapter 5
Deer Rifles

There is increasingly a trend for rifles to perform a dual role with regard to deer and fox duties, and in the Blaser rimfire conversion even combining rabbits. This is due to the industry's recent fascination for switch barrel modular rifles that can be converted quickly within calibre groups to perform many tasks. Sportspeople are therefore offered a more diverse rifle to suit their needs, whilst manufacturers save costs by using a common donor rifle. This is not to say that tradition and fine quality are not still sought after: they are, and there are still many fine traditional rifles on offer in enough configurations to keep shooters happy.

The majority of deer are shot at 100yd (90m) or below, especially in wooded areas, with longer shots on the hill of 250yd (230m), so any of the deer rifles on the market, even with factory ammunition, are usually capable of printing 1–2in (25–50mm) three-shot groups at 100yd – which is more than adequate for deer work where a heart/lung shot is taken. However, we all aspire to better accuracy, and this is the crux of the matter, because the difference in each

The Blaser K95 is a true gentleman's stalking rifle, but also offers a very light rifle for arduous hill climbs.

Respect for any game you shoot is of paramount importance, especially so with deer, which provide not just good sport, but superb food for the table; harvest only what needs to be culled, in this case an old roe buck.

deer rifle lies more in the styling and feel, while accuracy can never really be guaranteed until you take possession. If you take the issue of accuracy out of the equation and concentrate on whether you want traditional styling and materials, such as blued steel and walnut stocks, or whether your rifle is going to be used in bad weather, then a synthetic-stocked option with stainless-steel fittings may be more appropriate. Again, weight is very important, and while an occasional stalker may not worry too much about a rifle's weight if he doesn't use it very often, if you are carrying a heavy rifle in the Highlands you soon notice every ounce!

This brings us to the materials used. Many manufacturers have opted for aluminium actions, where weight saving is the bonus for using this light, high-strength alloy. The bolts lock directly into the barrel so integral strength

is still maintained. Barrel length is also related, and influences velocity; handling and overall length may be determined on whether a sound moderator is being fitted. Furthermore if you use one rifle for many tasks and wish to switch ammunition load or types quickly, a detachable magazine may be your best choice.

More important is the reliable feeding of cartridge from magazine to barrel; all too often a crooked cartridge or ill-positioned or damaged magazine can cause problems. If you dislike detachables, then a fixed floor-plate model allows an integral design; you won't lose magazines, but you do need to load the cartridges through the top of the action, which can be a little awkward on some models. A compromise is used on Browning A-Bolt designs, which have a convenient box magazine that detaches from a hinged floor plate.

Action lengths to accommodate varying sized cartridges may also influence your choice, as longer or magnum-sized actions are heavier, and a short action may be more suitable if overall weight is a concern.

One of the real changes within the industry is the trend towards switch-barrel rifle designs, primarily amongst rifles at the higher end of the market, which gives a good degree of flexibility in choice. Not only can the barrels be changed to differing calibres, but stock design, materials and compact storage for travelling are all possible. Although not a new idea, European manufacturers seem to have embraced it, and Blaser, Sauer, Merkel, Mauser and Krico all offer a modular system.

Regardless of styling, the primary choice of shooters is the type of action your deer rifle should have. Legal issues with centrefires in this country dictate that only single shot, bolt action, straight pull, double rifles or lever action rifles can be used, and some grip-cocking designs also.

Some designs are more suitable than others, so here I shall discuss only the most popular and those most readily available on the British market today. Most important is that you choose the rifle that suits your needs and fits you and your requirements, not that of a colleague. Your quarry, whether rabbit, rat, fox or deer, cares little for the style of rifle you use – a well placed shot is all they worry about!

SINGLE SHOT RIFLES

Single shots still have a place in the stalking genre, although some shooters may baulk at the lack of a swift follow-up shot. In truth, a single shot is all you need, and this sort of rifle makes an accurate and reliable stalking partner and in the right hands is very easy to reload quickly if the need arises. In fact having just one shot to hand really concentrates the mind on your field-craft and stalking abilities, and making the one shot count. Many single shot rifles also have the useful advantage of barrel changes for length, profile and calibre, and most are light and highly manoeuvrable rifles.

Again, Blaser and Merkel make superb examples of single shot rifles for the wealthy British stalker with their K95 and K1 models respectively, whilst BRNO and Baikal cater for the person who wants performance and not looks. The T/C G2 or Encore rifles are, however, more widely available; the Encore is just the big brother to the G2 carbine, being able to handle higher pressure cases such as the .308 and .30-06, whilst the Ruger No. 1 is a more traditional single shot.

The Ruger No. 1

The Ruger No. 1 rifle is one gun with an obvious nineteenth-century single shot design. It possesses a falling block action that gives a very strong lock-up, and its clean lines and great handling qualities make for an unusual yet failsafe stalking rifle. It was introduced in 1967 when Bill Ruger, the owner of Strum Ruger Inc., saw a gap in the market for a quality single shot rifle, just when most manufacturers were pushing the bolt action rifle as 'the' design to have.

Like most good designs, the No. 1 is simple with clean lines to its profile. The entire trigger, sear and safety mechanism is contained within the tang section at the rear of the action, rather like a shotgun. The mainspring is outside the action on a welded section to the front of the receiver; this not only houses the ejector spring but also serves as an attachment base for the fore-end. The only visible external screw is the pivot pin that secures the Farquharson-style lever. This finger lever latches directly on to the trigger guard, which therefore prevents you being able to wedge your finger between the trigger and the lever, as in other systems. To open the breech the lever is moved downwards, thereby unlatching it from the guard, and there begins the downward movement of the breech block. When it is level with the exposed rear end of the barrel, the final downward movement of the lever works the extraction of a spent case, with the last few degrees of movement initiating an off-set toggle that hits the extractor and thereby kicks the case to the rear and so clear of

The timeless beauty of the Ruger No. 1 rifle appeals to many shooters, and its single shot action should not be viewed as a negative.

the action. There is small screw on the fore-end bridge that can vary the force of the extraction process, so reloaders don't have to fumble around in the mud after precious brass. Because of the design of the action, the extraction system is strong enough to cope with modern high intensity rounds.

Keeping to the traditional lines of the gun, there is an old-style express quarter rib on top of the barrel, which acts as a scope mount base to receive Ruger's own scope rings that are supplied with the rifle. Another good feature is that because there is no bolt-operating system, the Ruger's short receiver allows 26in (65cm) barrels to be fitted and the overall length is still 2.5in (6.3cm) shorter than that of the other 24in (60cm) model. Overall handling is therefore very favourable as the generous rounded fore-end and stock without cheekpiece allows a very speedy mounting procedure, with excellent pointing characteristics. It feels very natural in the hand, and despite the high left-handed wall of the receiver, is equally at home in the right or the left shoulder. Wood quality is also very good: usually No. 1s come with a better grade of wood than other models in the range.

The accuracy of these guns can be excellent, and also annoyingly contrary. Any problems that people have with these guns – and this is rare – come from the fact that the forearm exerts a good amount of upward pressure against the barrel, thereby affecting the bedding and consistency of the gun's performance. This can be rectified in two ways: either glass bed the forearm to the fore-end hanger and then free-float the barrel so it vibrates consistently after every shot; or review the amount of torque exerted on the fore-end screw as this can really affect the gun's accuracy (group size and point of aim).

BOLT ACTION RIFLES

Bolt action rifles are by far the most popular in each category, and there is plenty of choice. This type of rifle utilizes the most reliable and probably the strongest of designs, with a bolt being operated by a side-mounted handle that chambers and unchambers a round with the reciprocating movement. The bolt is secured within the action via locking lugs at the front of the bolt, which recess either into the receiver walls or directly into the barrel. Some bolts have twin opposing lugs, some have smaller multi lugs in series, and some have three or four opposing lugs. All perform the same task of a secure lock-up, but the smaller multi-numbered type usually has a shorter bolt lift.

Custom actions such as Stiller, Borden, BAT, Nesika, Barnard and McMillan offer a degree of precision fit and tight tolerances not seen on standard factory rifles, and form the basis of

Callum Ferguson from Scotland still produces superb stalking rifles, made to the customer's requirements and Callum's exacting standards.

Clean, elegant lines and good wood-to-metal fit describe the Sako 85 well; any deer stalker would be proud to own such a rifle.

some superbly accurate rifles. Rifles built with these actions can produce stalking rifles of unerring accuracy that will outlast even the most ardent shooter. However, many a good standard rifle can be rebarrelled or bedded to achieve optimum performance. Some manufacturers produce rifles classed as semi-custom: commonly Cooper, Kimber, RPA and HS Precision all offer British shooters a class of rifle just that little bit special.

Because so many manufacturers offer a bolt action in such an array of styles, stock designs and materials, and because it is usually a one-piece stock design and capable of handling calibres from vermin to dangerous game, all this makes the bolt action rifle by far the best choice. The difference between each bolt action is not that great, but these small nuances prevail more as a marketing edge than anything else.

Sako Rifles

Sako of Finland have reincarnated the 75 model into the new 85 rifle. Unlike the Sako's stable block brother the Tikka T3, the 85 action is available in calibre-specific sizes, matching cartridge length to overall size of action. Not only does this look far nicer, it also means the length of bolt travel directly corresponds to the effort needed to cycle a particular overall cartridge length, unlike the T3 where one size fits all.

Beautifully finished with a deep satin, non-reflective finish, the Sako's action is a well constructed unit with integral scope rails on top. The bolt is where a few changes occur: first, the superfluous safety key system, that very few owners actually used, has been replaced by a smart sculptured bolt shroud, purely cosmetic but still a nice touch. The bolt body is the same reliable three locking lug system to enhance the lock-up into the receiver ring, but the bolt glides on five raceways, making the 85's action really smooth and precise, so there is no binding in operation. There is the familiar claw extractor recessed into the bolt face, which is excellent, and the bottom of the bolt has a slot cut so that ejection is simultaneous with contact on the ejector spur at the rear of the action body as the bolt and cartridge is withdrawn. One important feature is the controlled round feed design to the bolt, so there is direct engagement of the cartridge rim as it is plucked from the magazine lips. This allows precise lower angle feeding and control on the round at all times, and improves reliability. The bolt handle is amply proportioned and well executed with a tear-drop bolt knob that has a clean low profile lift, therefore easily avoiding snagging any scope's eyepiece.

The Tikka T3 combines value for money with very good workmanship; designed in Finland, the T3 will keep going when you have given up.

Available in varmint, synthetic and laminate, the Hunter model wears a beautiful traditional sporter walnut stock. Instantly appealing, Sako have opted for a finely crafted classic English stock design that incorporates well cut distinctive checkering patterns to both fore-end and pistol grip, and an overall oiled finish. There is a comfortable straight-line comb without any cast, very similar to older model classic Sakos, which not only looks good but certainly helps to comfortably redirect the felt recoil. The dropped cheekpiece is perfectly shaped for a good head angle, and finished off with a shadow line rim.

Sako triggers are always good, available as a single stage as standard, or as an optional extra as a set trigger. The single stage is as set at the factory at 3lb (1.36kg), although you can adjust the weight from 2–4lb (0.9–1.8kg) via a small Allen key if desired, placed through the back of the magazine well. Another unique feature on this model is the magazine release system: Sako have redesigned this area and dubbed it the 'total control' latch, and it is designed to stop any accidental premature release of the magazine.

In keeping with other sporting rifles, the profile and length of the Sako 85 is 42.25in (1.07m) overall, with a 22in (55cm) barrel capable of 1in (2.5cm) groups at 100yd (90m).

While for a practical stalking rifle the use of synthetics and stainless steel has its merits, with its classic lines in walnut trim the Sako 85 is one of the best-looking stalking rifles on the market.

Tikka Rifles

Tikka, also of Finland, continues to get the balance just right by providing dependable rifles at realistic prices. The important thing is that all Tikkas shoot really well straight from the box. I have owned a Tikka LSA 55 .308 since I was seventeen. Tikka's T3 now comes factory threaded to accept sound moderators, which is a very good idea for the British market.

Tikka T3 rifles now share one common action size, the main reasons being that manufacturing time and the costs of retooling are reduced, where most rifles have at least a short- or a long-action version to accommodate differing calibres. Tikka T3 rifles now come only as a long-action design, with the differing calibres being catered for by changes to the magazine and the action. This gives a good strong action, but it can add unwanted weight to the rifles shooting smaller calibres, as well as meaning a longer-than-normal bolt travel. In reality this is no problem, and you hardly notice the extra travel needed on a rifle in .308 calibre.

The solid one-piece machined steel action has the characteristic Tikka integral scope rails of 0.67in (17mm) diameter running its full length, although it is drilled and tapped if you wish to fit other bases. Sako/Tikka Opti-lok mounts give a secure and non-damaging scope-mounting system with their synthetic tube-clamping system.

The bolt is long, and has forward-mounted

semi-coned twin-locking lugs that track beautifully smoothly in the action rails, another Tikka trait. The bolt lift, too, is very shallow, allowing a fast, effortless operation.

Due to the one-size-fits-all action, in order to accommodate all calibre sizes within the magazine and maintain reliable feeding, Tikka use the same size magazine construction but with a filler block at the rear, enabling all the calibres' overall lengths to work. The magazine is an all-polymer construction item which is strong, light and waterproof but may not be to everyone's taste.

I have found the triggers on Tikkas to be good. The T3 utilizes a single stage adjustable unit. However, Jackson Rifles offer the superb CG Universal two-stage replacement trigger that is worth its weight in gold.

The overall finish of the metal parts is subdued satin stainless steel for action and barrel, which is hard-wearing enough for most stalking conditions, and non-reflective.

The barrel has a slim sporter contour of 20in (50cm), and in .308 calibre has a rifling twist rate of 1-in-11in, enabling it to stabilize all but the very heaviest bullets. The cold hammer-forged construction is concentric, and the barrel is fully free floating as far back to the section of the barrel profile that starts to taper, which is good for accuracy, but better still is the threaded barrel. Having a muzzle threaded at the factory for sound moderator use takes away all the hassle of having to get the rifle recut here in Britain, so the stalker can fit a moderator straight out of the box.

Tikka T3 rifles can be sourced as walnut stock, laminate or synthetics to cater for all situations. The stainless-steel version has a black plastic synthetic stock with ambidextrous layout; it is called a glass-reinforced copolymer, and is indeed better than most synthetic stocks as this model is stiff enough in all the right bedding areas. There is no cheekpiece; although the straight comb is sufficiently high, there is a good thick black rubber recoil pad that can have spacers inserted to increase the length of pull from 13.5in (34cm) to suit your own preference; sling swivels are fitted as standard.

For a standard factory gun with no tuning the Tikka T3 has a very good performance, which is actually what most Tikka owners expect from their rifles. It is also why today the T3 Tikka is one of the best-selling factory rifles, and certainly offers great value for money.

Remington Rifles

If ever there was a 'most popular' award, the Remington model 700 bolt action would have to win it. Offered in many forms, from entry level SPS grades through the laminated or synthetic varmint models to lightweight mountain rifles or classic CDL stalking guns, it would be very difficult not to like at least one model. Remington upgraded their triggers to the X-Mark Pro, which gives the shooter a far better pull without tinkering. The Model Seven is a more compact version of the Model 700 based on the XP-100 pistol action, and is available in some very useful light and fast-handling rifle configurations. The newer Model 710 and now 770 range are both aimed at the entry level shooter on a budget, but still have a detachable magazine and synthetic stock.

Model 700 actions are often the favourite of custom rifle builders due to their strong design, but I like the Model 700 LSS mountain rifle as a great go-anywhere stalking rifle. However, there can be problems to the above approach in that if you make a rifle too light the recoil increases, and reduce the barrel weight too much and it will heat up very rapidly, destroying accuracy in a trice.

The mountain rifle is a perfect blend of weight and size reduction, to give a useful rifle that weighs in at only 6.5lb (2.9kg). Sensibly Remington still use the tried and tested model 700 action as the cornerstone from which the other variants stem from, and have saved weight by shortening and slimming the barrel profile and offering a slightly more slender stock design.

The action has become an industry standard for accuracy potential and strength, and utilizes a jewelled bolt with characteristic two forward-locking lugs that cam securely into the recesses of the forward receiver ring. The bolt handle is semi-dog legged in gait with a checkered flat face to both sides, and affords good camming action to lock and unlock the action.

The hinged floor plate indicative of this model is finished in a painted silver to match the stainless-steel action and barrel. On this model the capacity was four, which is more than ample for any stalking exploit.

With an all-weather stainless finish, this rifle desires a similarly made stock. The LSS model actually stands for 'laminated stainless steel', and so it wears a brown laminated stock designed to be as weatherproof as possible, and offers a stable platform for all the metal work. Anyone who has owned a standard wood stock and used it in bad weather can tell you how the stock can warp and swell if not properly sealed. Not so in the LSS mountain rifle, where rigidity and strength are very good. Its looks may not suit everyone, but it does fend off the worst of the British climate.

The crux of the mountain rifle ethos lies within the barrel profile, to achieve best weight without losing functionality: too short and the muzzle blast increases, too long and slender and the barrel acts like a whip, certainly detrimental to accuracy. But there is a good compromise, and the conclusion to any stalk is that the first shot really counts. Therefore by keeping the barrel reasonably long and slender to reduce weight, accuracy is not impaired due to heat build-up, certainly not for the first two or three shots anyway. The Remington's barrel is 22in

(55cm) long and has a very aggressive taper towards the barrel's muzzle, starting from 1.18in (3cm) at the receiver and reducing to 0.56in (1.4cm) at the muzzle, no larger than the width of the little finger.

The Remington LSS offers the stalker a great 'go anywhere' rifle in a practical and accurate format, and with the first shot being the most important, the fact that slim barrels heat up quickly is of little consequence in a stalking situation.

The Browning Rifle

The A-Bolt rifle, a design of long standing from the late 1980s, is a strong, accurate rifle concept available in wood or synthetic formats. As the Miroku shotguns, they are made in Japan, which keeps the cost down whilst maintaining very good quality control.

I have owned two A-Bolts before, and operation of the bolt, design of the safety and overall finish are very good. It is quite small and compact, with a 22in (55cm) barrel and overall length of only 40.75in (1.03m), and weighing only 6.4lb (2.9kg) without scope, making it a practical, lightweight stalking gun.

The action has a standard small-diameter bolt with three large front-located locking lugs. These cam into the recesses of the receiver ring

Mountain rifles such as this Remington LSS are designed to get that first shot on target precisely where you aim it, without any added weight that will leave you fatigued after a lengthy hill climb.

With short bolt lift and unique magazine system, the Browning A-Bolt is available in walnut/blued finish or synthetic styles; either are fine stalking arms.

on lock-up to make a very strong closure, good for both safety and potential accuracy. Viewed from the front it looks like the letter A, hence A-Bolt. The bolt body has a three-fluted rotating casing that helps stop bolt twisting at the extremes of bolt throw, and allows the base of the bolt to ride smoothly over the magazine well. The bolt lift is only a scant 60 degrees elevation, and extraction is accomplished by a small, spring-loaded claw-type extractor group in the right locking lug. Final ejection is accomplished by a strong plunger type set in the bolt face.

An interesting feature of all A-Bolts is the magazine construction. It is dubbed a detachable magazine design, but actually, rather than a button-release mechanism as most rifles of this genre, Browning have their magazine sitting in the bottom of the floor plate. If a shooter wants, they can refill the magazine at any time by simply adding cartridges from the top through the receiver cut away if they wish. It is a good system, enabling a spare magazine to be carried or stored away for safety reasons.

The barrels on the sporter models are slim, sporter-weight profiles of 22in (55cm), and have either a good deep even blued finish for the Medallion models, or tough non-reflective black on the synthetic models. The stock has a classic sporter design without cheekpiece, and is therefore quite ambidextrous as there is no palm swell to the pistol grip. The stock finish is very thick and highly polished with lacquer that is very weatherproof, but the sun can reflect quite badly off it. Synthetic models have a really nice synthetic black sporter stock with almost a nap to the finish, and have a solid, not a hollow feel.

Sauer

Think of a classic, elegant stalking rifle, and the Sauer 202 model has to be right up there at the top of the list. Its enviable build quality and versatile barrel- and stock-change facility have endeared it to many shooters wanting a vermin/fox and deer rifle with an option to upgrade with larger calibres or wood quality as

Quality rifles such as this Sauer 202 in 6.5 × 57mm shoot as good as they look. The ability to change stocks, barrels, actions and triggers makes the 202 a very versatile 'one gun for many uses' rifle.

one sees fit. Indeed, a synthetic stock option or target/varmint style stock allows even greater versatility.

Typically the Sauer 202 model is a classic stalking rifle with varying grades of walnut wood, and deep, even bluing to the metalwork. Choice is limitless as there are ten differing grades of wood with five varying fore-end and stock profiles. Add to this twenty-three differing calibres with various contours and lengths and you have a great platform to base the exact rifle to match *your* requirements.

The Sauer uses a two-piece stock arrangement that secures to the action body via long-threaded bolts accessed through the butt stock or fore-end. This has two obvious advantages: first, the rifle can be stripped down to a very small overall length for safe and convenient storage or when travelling abroad; and second, in order to gain access to the barrel-retaining bolts and exchange barrels.

At the heart of the 202 Select rifle is the all-steel action that combines strength and precise engineering – although if you are weight conscious then an alloy action is an option.

It is manufactured from a single piece of steel, giving a strength that is further enhanced due to the fact that the bolt locks directly into the chamber end of the barrel. This one-piece design forms the 'modular' heart of the Sauer rifle, from which barrels, triggers, bolts and magazines all interchange. The barrel is retained by three cross-bolts that transverse the front of

the receiver and securely clamp it in place around its chamber end with the aid of a locating peg. It is not as fast a barrel change as, say, the Mauser or Blaser rifles, but it does offer a very secure option. Due to the precision engineering involved, no loss in head space is apparent, and accuracy between calibre change is maintained, although you with obviously need to re-zero your scope or have a quick-change scope mount for each barrel.

The bolt has a solid body with six forward-locking lugs; it locks directly into the barrel and has a supported head. Extraction is via a single claw extractor on the right side, and ejection is by a sprung plunger that gives an efficient expulsion of fired cases from the rifle.

Such practical details set the Sauer 202 aside from its competitors, as does the single set trigger mechanism that comes as standard. With light and positive let-off in normal mode, the trigger can also be significantly lightened in pull weight by pushing the blade forwards 0.5in (13mm) to the set position, where only a few ounces of pressure will trip the trigger sear.

The Sauer Select is a true 'old world' stalking rifle, but with all the modern features required to make it desirable and, more importantly, functional, accurate and reliable in the field, where it really performs. I love the flexibility for a swift yet solid barrel-change facility, and appreciate the many calibres and stock options to allow you to achieve that unique and very personalized stalking rifle.

The Mauser

Mauser can trace their history back to 1898 and their model M98, the action of which has undeniably formed the basis of the modern bolt action rifle. Today Mauser have a new action, the new M03, a totally different stalking rifle that transforms the old style into a very stylish and practical stalking arm.

The M03 is the elegant yet full-bodied build of the rifle. This is largely attributable to the stock, which possesses clean, classic lines fashioned from a good grade of walnut, available in many grades and all having a hand-rubbed finish. There is a high, straight comb, perfect for good scope-to-eye alignment, and the fore-end is nicely finished off with a black ebony cap in standard form or a silver engraved insert on the de luxe model.

There is only one action size, and it handles the small calibres from .222 right up to .375 H&H; this makes the receiver long and thus contributes to some of the heft of the M03.

There are no scope rails or grooves, but instead an integral three-sided quick-release arrangement that necessitates the use of a one-piece scope mount. This is a necessary item on this switch-barrel rifle, because the barrel cannot be removed without the scope being disengaged. The mount locates very snugly as the three-lugged rotor drops into the receiver cutouts, and all you need do to tighten it into place is to push forwards on both locking levers.

The bolt is enormous, and accounts for 14.11oz (400g) of the overall weight; it is beautifully engineered. There are several interesting design features. First, because the bolt locks directly into the back of the barrel, it has to be long to transcend the short front receiver bridge; nevertheless the best effort has been made to keep strength whilst shedding a few ounces yet keeping an attractive design. The receiver bridge is very open; there is no side wall on the left-hand side, which allows good access in the event of a stuck cartridge, and the bolt being faceted on four edges gives the Mauser M03 rifle a unique appearance.

The bolt lift is short at about 55 degrees travel, leaving the open bolt at a 90-degree angle to the receiver wall, thus allowing maximum room to operate the bolt without fear of snagging on a scope.

The safety lever forms part of the bolt shroud at the rear, which actually decocks the M03 and locks the bolt down. This can be very useful, as the rifle can be carried with a chambered round and allows a stalker to silently cock the M03 only when a beast is spotted and a shot is necessary. It is a quick, simple and foolproof system.

The special feature of this barrel is not only the very precise cut rifled interior: at the chamber end below the barrel are two threaded studs rather like the Blaser design, and this allows the barrel to be dropped vertically into position within the fore-end to marry up with two corresponding locking nuts. With this system a fox rifle can be converted into a deer gun or African rifle in minutes, with the coinciding change of

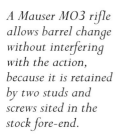

A Mauser M03 rifle allows barrel change without interfering with the action, because it is retained by two studs and screws sited in the stock fore-end.

appropriate bolt head and magazine. You do, however, have to remove the scope first, and this is where that quick-release scope mount is mandatory.

The Mauser MO3 series of stalking rifles is really worthy of serious consideration as an alternative to similar operating marques.

Ruger

Ruger offers the British shooter an array of rugged rifle types to suit vermin, fox or stalkers alike. Their original Ruger M77Mk1 bolt action rifle was based, as were so many at the time, on the inspiring Mauser action design. Twin locking lugs up front, large full length external extractor and solid action, the new Hawkeye is the result of years of honing a good idea.

'Old reliable' best describes the Hawkeye action. The bolt is 6.75in (17cm) long and forms a substantial spine for the M77 action, and the two locking lugs provide a large surface area and cam smoothly into the receiver with good overall engagement to ensure a strong lock-up. The large extractor allows a controlled round feed, which ensures positive loading and extraction from the magazine to barrel, and vice versa.

The receiver incorporates the integral scope mount bases at the top of the action, which I really like, made even better with the inclusion of a set of 1in (2.5cm) scope rings that have a unique locking system to the rifle's action. The magazine is the tried and tested internal box type with a floor plate arrangement that is loaded from the top through the receiver and supported by a blued metal cage and follower. In .22-250 calibre the capacity is four rounds.

A good choice would be the All Weather model. It is stainless steel for both barrel and action, which is undoubtedly weather repellent, and the textured finish is much finer and subdued, almost grey in appearance, which on a sporting arm is an advantage. Hammer-forged barrels ensure a good degree of precision in their accuracy and concentricity. The barrel is non-floated, and pressure is exerted at the fore-end and then all along the sides until it meets the receiver ring. Not my first preference, but the Hawkeye still shoots nice groups for a sporting arm.

The trigger is another area where the Hawkeye model has had a make-over. Dubbed the LC6 system, Ruger have offered a much better and more usable trigger pressure that will find favour with most shooters. American rifles all had heavy trigger pulls. Savage started the ball rolling with their Accu-trigger, and then Remington with their X-Pro model. This Ruger LC6 is indeed smooth, and is set up as a single-stage pull with an immediate sear let-off that is totally predictable, and a nice surprise for all the right reasons.

With the Ruger in .22-250 calibre the stalker has the option on more than one species: a flat-shooting calibre for foxes, or a heavier bullet for roe in Scotland or muntjac and CWD south of the border.

The CZ Rifle

Offering possibly the best Mauser 98 derivative, CZ rifles from the Czech Republic are solid and reliable, and give real 'old world' manufacturing techniques.

If ever there was a classic, pure stalking rifle, then the CZ 550 has to be it. Staying true to its ability for getting the job done, it may not be the newest, but it offers reliable, consistent accuracy and function from a century of design and at a price that is very hard to beat — and the reality of life is that at the ranges most deer are harvested, all you need is a reliable and safe firearm.

The stock represents that European layout with short, slender fore-end with checkered grip, all hand applied with a shallow draft to the butt stock, but possessing a generous grip area, again with hand checkering applied. The comb of the stock is low, aka open sight application, but the hog's back design suits the CZ, and when a scope is mounted low enough, it does not really hinder the use of the rifle/scope combination.

Weighing in at nearly 3lb (1.36kg), this is a solid forged action made from a strong alloy steel; it is certainly no lightweight, but is well finished and nicely blued.

The bolt has large twin locking lugs that ensure an all-important solid lock-up on loading, and the large exterior sprung extractor claw design has shown itself to be reliable in any situation. The non-rotating extractor really

The CZ 550 is one of those timeless rifles made when plastics were unheard of, and as such makes a sturdy and utterly reliable stalking partner.

gives a positive, controlled round feed, and ejection is also brisk.

Although a detachable magazine is available on a similar model, the four shot, hinged floor plate design will suffice.

The trigger is a single set stage affair, similar to their small action 527 model, which can be set to a very light hair setting if desired. The factory trigger pull of just over 2.5lb (1.1kg) cannot be considered unduly heavy. The overall length of the barrel is nearly 24in (60cm), and with a diameter of 0.825in (2cm) at the receiver tapering to 0.625in (1.6cm) at the muzzle, allows a reasonably good, stiff yet manageable overall taper-to-length ratio. Finish is the typical CZ deep bluing, and it is furnished with a set of open sights. Most will discard these in preference for scope mounting via the receiver, which is achieved by integral dovetails on top of a flat-topped, same height receiver platform.

This rifle thrives on adversity, putting the onus on the stalker to achieve a successful result; in some ways this gives the deer a very fair chance, which in my book is no bad thing.

The Krico

Krico's Model 902 is another German design now made in Italy by Marocchi, and which incorporates a switch-barrel system. Very Germanic in styling, the Krico uses an alloy action as the backbone from which the two-piece stock is held and the barrel-change facility is secured. There is a tang-mounted safety catch and three-shot detachable magazine, and the bolt has a nice short lift due to the arrangement of three locking lugs. Take-down is easily managed.

For a stalker who likes a rifle to be a bit different, then the Krico offers that distinction.

The Merkel

Merkel offer a high grade stalking rifle called the KR1, a solid rifle with that undeniable heft that speaks of quality components crafted from the best grade steels and timber. The stock reflects the German style, and has the traditional hog's back profile favoured by the Europeans. The quality of walnut is good, even on the standard grades.

Interestingly, the Merkel's receiver mechanism is an integral part of the bolt system, and shuttles back and forth along guide rails allowing access to the barrel, very similar to a Blaser. The one big difference is that unlike the straight pull Blaser rifle, the Merkel has a more traditional turn bolt arrangement. Compared to a more normal bolt rifle, the difference is that the entire bolt is encapsulated within the receiver casing, making for a strong design that is further

On the Merkel KR1 rifle the top half of the action moves with the bolt operation, and so makes quite a unique arm for those who like to be different.

enhanced by the locking arrangement of the bolt lugs directly into the rear of the barrel.

This allows a speedy transition of bolt manipulation, like a straight pull, but has that added feeling of security on lock-up because the lugs cam into the barrel's recesses and are not pushed home, as on a straight pull. The bolt's lugs offer a comprehensive lock-up with twin rows of three locks, ensuring safety and correct cartridge alignment in the chamber, and this contributes to the shorter 65 degree or thereabouts bolt lift from the nicely contoured butter-knife bolt handle. Extraction is positively done by a large extractor claw recessed into the side of the bolt, and the lively ejector takes care of cartridge expulsion via a bolt-mounted plunger type.

The Merkel has a quick, simple barrel-change facility very similar to a Blaser in that two threaded studs protrude beneath the barrel and locate into the lower receiver section; they are tightened using two captive nuts from under the stock, the rear one being actually under the floor plate. The bolt head is detachable, allowing a change of calibre groups depending on the size of the cartridge head, and because the action is offered only in the long length specifications, all that is needed to complete the calibre change is to replace the magazine.

The Thompson Center (T/C) Icon

T/C are more commonly known for their Contender carbines, but now there is a new bolt action rifle with detachable magazine designed to reflect all the best bits that current stalking rifles have to offer. There are certainly similarities to the bolt from an RWS and stock checkering panels from a Sako, and the integral bedding block is reminiscence of the H-S Precision system.

Outwardly it is a conventional-looking steel action with a satin-finished black sheen, but there are several good innovations. First, the Icon comes with integral weaver-style bases built into the bridge of the receiver. This is a common mounting system with a wide range of scope rings that fit, and so makes good sense. Also the ejection port is generous, despite the receiver strap covering the top of the action; this adds to the strength, but does not impede cartridge manipulation due to the Icon's detachable magazine facility.

This one-piece, CNC-machined solid receiver has one more interesting feature – in fact three features in the guise of the integral recoil lugs that are dispersed along the bottom of the flat action face: one at the front receiver ring, one in the mid-section behind the magazine well, and the third on the rear tang.

Furthermore the Icon has a clever system to maximize accuracy and consistency: it uses a one-piece aluminium bedding block, and the action's three integral recoil lugs, mentioned earlier, sit into this, thereby maintaining a consistent and strong block for uniform bedding.

The stock is well figured walnut with good colour, and is finished in a semi-matt lustre. The contours are pure classic sporter with a low straight line comb and no cheekpiece, topped off with a black, solid rubber recoil pad and sling swivel studs.

The Icon bolt has three locking lugs arranged in the 'T' format, with the bottom lug scooping up the cartridge from the magazine follower, and the other two arranged at the ten and two o'clock positions. They ride smoothly in the action rails, and give a good degree of bolt-face lock-up in the action recesses for strength and cartridge support. Add to this the low bolt lift of only 60 degrees, which is very low, and the ability to change the bolt handles with the supplied bolt-dismantling tool, and you have a versatile, beautifully jewelled bolt indeed.

The trigger is more conventional, but a number of adjustments are offered. Trigger pressure is set just above 3lb (1.36kg), which is fine and safe on a stalking rifle.

The Icon is also available in T/C's new calibre, called the 30 TC. This is a small, efficient case design which emulates the performance of a .30-06 cartridge! It is a good, solid, innovative stalking rifle from a trusted manufacturer.

The Steyr

The ProHunter from Steyr/Mannlicher is a rifle that irrefutably rebukes traditional views of what a stalking rifle should be, with its racy, synthetic stock construction and new safety system. Its first attractions lie in the radical styling of its stock and the hunter-friendly non-glare coating to the metalwork. As an honest, real life stalking rifle it should prove to be a good choice. The stock is moulded from a dense, high-impact polymer that gives the feel of more heft and rigidity, ideal for soaking up any recoil.

The magazine itself is no longer the trademark rotary affair but a more conventional double-stack system, which I prefer, and it holds four rounds. It is very robustly constructed of a black polymer that will not rust and is capable of taking a few knocks.

The bolt on the ProHunter range has four twin-opposed lugs that lock up into the receiver wall, maintaining a stiff encapsulating grip on

The Steyr ProHunter has a futuristic look and some innovative design features such as the safety bolt, and makes a good all-round British deer rifle, especially in .260 calibre.

the rear of the cartridge. This ensures a correct headspace, as well as minimal vibration on firing, which ultimately helps accuracy.

The barrel on a standard model is slightly less than 24in (60cm) long, and on the mountain rifle model it is a much more practical 20in (50cm), which stops you snagging branches, reduces weight, and facilitates a moderator fit without increasing the overall length too much.

The safety is actually an ambidextrous roller system with three positions, fire, loading and safe, identified as follows:

- **Fire**: a red dot is visible, and the rifle can be fired as normal.
- **Loading**: a white dot is visible on the thumb wheel (roller safety), and the trigger safety is on, although the rifle can be loaded and unloaded whilst in this position.
- **Safe**: both a white and grey pop-up catch now become visible. In this state the safety is on and the rifle will not fire and the bolt cannot be opened. Also in this position the bolt handle itself can now be pushed down further, which actually locks the bolt down, with the firing pin totally locked and safe.

Recoil is moderate for a mountain rifle. This would make a great deer/fox combination rifle for smaller shooters, or those who do a lot of hill climbing.

The Weatherby

The Vanguard, as discussed in the fox rifle section, has many good stalking attributes, but the top of the line is the Mark V model. Designed in 1957 by Roy Weatherby, its trademark nine locking lug fluted bolt with three gas escape ports is distinctive. The bolt lift is short at just over 50 degrees, and the whole action is very strong, which is necessary for Weatherby proprietary magnum calibres. Stock configurations range from ornate European styling to classic models or varmint-profiled or sporter-styled synthetics, all of which make the Weatherby Mark V a hard-hitting and working rifle in the right hands. If purchased in .257 Weatherby magnum, you have a lightning-fast fox rifle and a very flat-shooting and hard-hitting deer gun.

Winchester Coyote, RWS Titan and Howa

These models have been discussed in the fox section, and with appropriate deer calibres would also suit a stalker's needs. Although the Winchester Model 70 has a controlled round feed, twin locking lug and floor-plate bolt action, it still remains a traditional stalking rifle with much to offer, especially as it was this rifle that introduced the shooter to the innovative WSM (Winchester short magnum) cartridge range.

The Savage Rifle

Savage rifles from America have always, to my mind, occupied that niche of good value, cheap rifles that actually shoot far better than their price would indicate. The Model 16 is a pure stalking rifle, being synthetically stocked and constructed in stainless steel to endure the worst of the weather.

The stock is made as a two-part injection-moulded synthetic unit that is less than attractive but seriously practical if you are an ardent stalker. But the injection-moulded checkering is actually very sharp and grippy, and the whole stock design is solid and comes fitted with a rubber recoil pad and integral q/d swivel studs as standard.

The barrel is 22in (55cm) in length. Being fully free floated, the Savage offers maximum advantage with regard to changing weather climes and zero point of impact change.

Where the Savage really comes to life is in the action and trigger area. The action is a solid, tubular, single piece of stainless steel of incredible strength, which allows rigidity to achieve optimum accuracy potential.

The bolt has a unique, dual forward-locking lug system. The tandem arrangement allows precise rotational lock-up on operation of the bolt from the foremost lugs, whilst the twin rear sliding lugs act as a guiding locational force to ensure precise lock-up on closing the bolt.

With the Accutrigger system you have a clean, precise, totally predictable trigger let-off with a foolproof safety feature to make it utterly reliable. Unlike most USA-make rifles, the

For those who require a rugged all-weather rifle, the Savage Model 16 is capable of fine accuracy and can beat the worst of the British weather.

Savage trigger can be adjusted by the owner because a unique safety bar or interrupt system ensures that however much the trigger is adjusted, only a safe let-off is ensured. The adjustment range is anything from 1.5lb (0.7kg) to 6lb (2.7kg) weight, allowing customizing to every stalker's preference.

Savage have achieved a value-for-money, accurate, totally reliable and weatherproof rifle.

STRAIGHT PULL RIFLES

Straight pull designs are becoming more popular due to the success of the Blaser R93 rifle. Although still a bolt action system, the Blaser's bolt's operation is not by lifting it, but by pushing the bolt back and forth guided by integral rails to lock and unlock it. This is a very fast action, and other manufacturers such as Heym offer a straight pull SR30 rifle with ball bearings used as a symmetrical locking lug system in contrast.

A variation on the theme is the interesting Lynx rifle from Finland. This has a large side-cocking handle not dissimilar to that of the old Schmidt Rubin design, but has large side-mounted rear-locking lugs that are unusual. It is a very nice-looking rifle.

Blaser

The Blaser has a proven non-rotating bolt operation and is a highly modular rifle; it uses a quick-release barrel system and scope mountings, and comes in many stock options. The Professional version with synthetic stock and tough exterior finish is a good stalking choice.

The Blaser design is far from conventional. The standard receiver design is done away with, because there is an integral action bedded into the stock, with the bolt and housing reciprocating on top. This action is aluminium and is secured within the stock, providing a light yet very strong backbone from which the barrel and bolt assembly can be used. The bolt body, also aluminium, rides on generous rails, allowing the smooth and speedy operation of the bolt – but this is no conventional bolt operation. Instead, all Blasers use their own straight pull system that only needs a rearward pull on the bolt handle to unlock the bolt from the barrel, then a further continuous pull exposes the cartridges that are then fed into the barrel with the bolt closure.

The real ingenuity of the Blaser system is the way the bolt lock-up occurs. To keep rigidity and strength, the bolt locks directly into the

Blaser's R93 straight pull action is superbly fast, and the barrels and stocks can be interchanged to suit your shooting preference and game species.

back of the barrel with a unique bolt head that does away with the opposing locking lug arrangement and has a 360-degree radial lock-up by means of fourteen collets arranged in a ring formation. These L-shaped collets collectively provide a very solid lock-up, which springs out to engage a recess in the barrel as the bolt is closed.

The Professional model has all the tough synthetic characteristics you need; it is a subtle green in colour, and the crucial grip areas are enhanced with soft rubber inserts in black. Not only does the fore-end have side panels, but there is a third sited below the fore-end that gives good addition hold. They are very tactile and transform the stock out in the field.

Barrels are chrome moly, and have a swift calibre change so your fox rifle quickly becomes a deer or African hunter.

With no receiver, the scope is attached directly to the barrel by a quick-release propriety scope mount. The base is one piece in design with the option of 1in (30mm) rings or rail mounts, and swiftly attaches to precision-cut recesses to the barrel.

The Blaser system must be one of the most innovative rifle systems developed today, using a straight pull bolt system and true modular skeleton to provide a very versatile rifle. Admittedly the straight pull is a little quirky, and you will either like it or not.

DOUBLE RIFLES

The Tikka 512

Double rifles are not necessarily considered for deer stalking, but sportspeople choose a double rifle for the very fact that it has double the number of barrels, thus enabling a fast follow-up shot. Most classic double rifles have a traditional side-by-side format, with firms such as Holland and Holland, Purdey, Westley Richards and Rigby all offering exquisite models. European makers offer either side-by-side or over/under barrel configurations, with Krieghoff, Blaser, Merkel and Heym being major manufacturers.

Cheaper models, such as the Tikka 512, also convert to a double 12-gauge and a combination gun with rifle and shotgun tubes. Being a mono bloc construction the barrel-exchange system is strong, with double rifle calibres ranging from .308, .30-06, 7 × 65R, 7 × 57R, 9.3 × 74R, 8 × 57JRS and 7.62 × 53R with the addition of .222R and 6.5 × 55 for the combination rifle and shotgun set.

You may be wondering how you adjust the impact point, as most double rifle barrels are joined by a central rib and regulated at the factory. True, but this Tikka very cleverly has two points of contact for each barrel, one at the muzzle that can be adjusted for windage, whilst a central hanger uses a sliding wedge system that adjusts for vertical bullet impact. This not only means you can self-adjust or fine-tune your rifle to suit factory or reloads, but can regulate your rifle to have both barrels converge shots at whatever range suits you best.

Chambered in the venerable .30-06 cartridge, the Tikka is a practical deer calibre for deer stalking, and provides more flexibility with prudent reloading. For me, the compact, highly pointable, reliable build of this Tikka with open sights proves that shot placement and fieldcraft are the key factors involved in stalking.

LEVER ACTION RIFLES

Lever actions have never really taken off in this country, although models such as the Win 94 in 30-30, Browning BLR aka '81 Lighting in std deer calibres including .243, .308, 7mm-08, .30-06 and hard-hitting 7mm and 300 WSM calibres, or the Marlin 1895 in .45-70 or Marlin 336C in .30-30, have been used in the stalking fields of Britain.

The Marlin has a classic simplicity, but also a sense of purpose that actually endears itself to many a practical stalker not influenced by modern traditions; however, they are seldom seen in the field here. Best of the lot was the old Sako

Finnwolf from Finland; this was a superbly built lever gun, but sadly it cost too much to manufacture and is no longer produced.

CUSTOM RIFLES

There are many superb custom builders in Britain. Callum Ferguson, Steve Bowers and Norman Clark are the chief makers, and a true custom rifle will involve many painstaking hours of work using the best 'ingredients' in order to deliver superb accuracy, fit and reliability. Often all the parts for a custom rifle have to be sourced form differing suppliers to achieve the desired goal.

I like RPA actions and rifles, and these have been the basis for many a project. The Quadlite action is super tough, with a low bolt lift, four locking lug system held to tight tolerances. The action is rounded and beds easily to the stock, and has a large separate recoil lug and very good adjustable trigger. RPA produce these for sporting use in the guise of the Hunter, with either a thumbhole or sporter Robertson synthetic stock.

My own favourite is a Steve Bowers' custom, a switch-barrel RPA Quadlite rifle that I use for

Double rifles are more commonly used for dangerous game, but this old Tikka is quite at home stalking deer in dense woodland.

calibre testing, which is just a matter of a swift barrel replacement to change calibre. This was the basis of my new wildcat cartridge, the 6.5 Rapier based on a shortened and improved 6.5 × 284 case. I wanted to achieve more realistic powder consumption, yet maintain longevity to the barrel and still turn out a cartridge that would send a 120-grain 6.5mm bullet out of that short barrel at 2800fps and develop 2090ft/lb energy.

The barrel was a Walther match-grade stainless-steel make with a varmint Bowers' custom profile – that is, fairly heavy – and total length of 18in (46cm) unchambered and 1-in-8in rifling twist. In this way, with a muzzle diameter of 0.84in (2cm) the weight of the barrel would give stiffness as well as combat overheating and heat drift.

My RPA switch-barrel rifle chambered in the 6.5mm Rapier wildcat round that I designed for deer, works rather well.

I fitted a sporter Sako varmint profile McMillan stock, inletted for the RPA action, and my scope choice was an excellent Kahles CS Multizero scope with BDC turrets.

A series of four forming dies are used to gradually reduce the shoulder and neck junction back of the parent Lapua case to its final position, whilst reforming the shoulder angle and leaving a long neck for trimming.

Reloading ammunition with 39 grains of Vit N540 powder with a 140-grain Interlock bullet yields 2669fps, whilst 40 grains of the same powder gives 2824fps. Staying with my remit of 40 grains per case, I changed to a lighter bullet with a 129-grain SST Hornady, and this resulted in a velocity of 2850fps – and that's for an 18in (46cm) barrel!

Accuracy was good at 0.262in (6.6mm) for three shots centre to centre at 100yd (90m). It was with the heavy bullets, especially the ProHunters and SSTs, that the Rapier shone: with a payload of 40 grains Vit N150 both bullets would harvest roe and muntjac deer with total lethality and minimal carcass damage whilst achieving good penetration and bullet expansion. Nosler Accubond 130-grain bullets also exhibit really good energy transfer on game with controlled expansion.

Thus with a little intervention from a qualified custom gunsmith, your dream deer rifle is actually a reality.

REBARRELLED FACTORY RIFLES

You need not go to the expense of a custom gun: often only a new barrel and custom work is called for with an existing rifle – as my own Tikka Custom .338 BR. The remit for the project was thus: I have come to the opinion that less is more when woodland deer stalking, by which I mean having enough calibre without overkill. The benefits are milder recoil, better placed shots and lower noise, coupled with deer-legal lethality without excessive carcass attrition. Many cartridges fall into this category, but one that instantly springs to mind is the Bench Rest case, or BR, originally designed by Jim Stekl of Remington Arms in the mid-1970s.

The mid-size BR .308 case is good in its many

For close-range deer work, a slow, heavy, large calibre, such as this .338 BR Bowers custom Tikka, is ideal.

forms of wildcatted sizes, starting from .17 all the way up to .35 calibre, for a woodland deer cartridge that would propel a heavy bullet of 250 grains weight at deer-legal energy figures with small powder capacity, light recoil and ease of moderator use, yet exhibiting a humane, clean kill.

Water capacity of a .338 BR case is 40.5 grains with Lapua 6mm BR brass, and so 25 grains of powder would achieve a non-compressed load with a bullet seated. Velocities in the 2200fps range with a 250-grain bullet would be achievable, yet still remain deer-legal in England and Wales. A twist rate of 1-in-8 would easily stabilize up to 250-grain projectiles in any temperature conditions from a short 16in (40cm) barrel.

Being short, the barrel could be fat, and at only 37in (94cm) long without a moderator and 45in (1.14m) with one fitted, it makes a fine close-quarter woodland rifle.

The donor rifle was an old model Tikka M65 Super Sporter, which Steve Bowers, the precision gunsmith, customized with a Border stainless-steel cut rifled barrel, blue-printed action, reworked and honed trigger and a synthetically pillar-bedded stock.

Case forming just involves expanding 6mm BR Lapua or Norma brass up in stages to .338 diameter with K&M mandrels. Lube the necks well until the final stage, where a degree of neck turning is essential to eliminate a bulge forming at the base of the neck. This done, just reload and fire from the brass in the rifle's chamber.

Relatively fast powders of small weights are necessary to launch a bullet to deer-legal 1700ft/lb energy (England and Wales) from only a short 16in (40cm) barrel. Quickload, a computer ballistics program, suggests VIT N120 powder with a charge weight of 26.0 grains maximum to achieve 100.1 per cent load density, 100 per cent burn rate, and the magical 1827fps and 1854ft/lb energy with a Hornady 250-grain, round nose, flat base bullet.

You could load a lighter 180-grain Nosler Ballistic Tip and achieve a fast, flatter trajectory at 2251fps and 2011ft/lb, but its more explosive nature would mostly cause more meat damage on smaller deer, and not what I had initially intended.

In all, the rifle has all the potential to be a superb woodland deer round without excessive noise or meat damage, and using a small powder charge.

Chapter 6
Cartridge Ballistics

The bullet or projectile is the most important piece of the jigsaw with regard to a sporting arm. It is the smallest piece of 'kit' you will use that actually connects with the target, and if you make the wrong choice the results will be less than perfect. Due to the vast diversity of bullet types and cartridges for the species covered in this book I have again organized them into sections relevant to vermin, fox and deer usage, with common and wildcat cartridges along with bullet types and choice. (See Chapter 10 for penetration tests carried out on ballistic media to show bullet performance down range.)

VERMIN CLASS CARTRIDGES

The Rimfire

Shooting with a .22lr rimfire at rats, feral pigeon or the like in the vicinity of farm buildings risks causing too much damage and therefore prohibits its use, even with subsonic ammunition. Furthermore some shots may be pointed skywards, which would prove very dangerous. There is a selection of reduced velocity rimfire ammunition, however, that might be suitable,

ranging from the pipsqueak BB cap to the .22 CB long round (not long rifle (lr)). Compatibility is no problem, but the BB and CB caps should be manually loaded to avoid jams or malfunctions.

The BB and CB caps resemble an lr case cut down to approximately one third its size but still retaining its rimmed base, with the projectile lightly crimped at the top as normal.

The BB cap design is made by RWS and is marked '6mm Ball Breech Caps' on the tin, but although designated as 6mm they are .22 calibre. The round ball projectile weighs in at 15.5gr for an average of five bullets.

At first glance it looks as if it couldn't knock over a tin can, let alone a rat, however from the Anschutz 14in (35cm) barrel this little cartridge leaves the muzzle at an astonishing 887fps, which generates 27.1ft/lb of energy, which is more than enough for any foray after barnyard pests.

Accuracy can be less impressive, about 1.5 to 2in (4 to 5cm) at 20yd (18m), enough to dispatch your quarry cleanly if shot placement were perfect, although in reality 10yd (9m) around farm buildings is a more practical distance.

Reduced charge .22 rimfires are good at close range: left to right, BB cap, CB cap, Super Colibri, CB Long, Zimmer and .22lr subsonic.

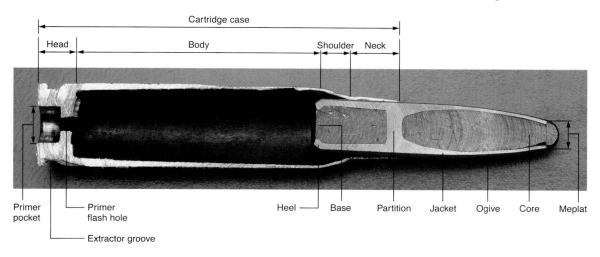

All the relevant parts of a centrefire cartridge and bullet.

An alternative to the BB cap is the similar CB cap, which has identical case dimensions but possesses a conical projectile instead. The RWS CB cap has a sharp, pointed, conical bullet weighting 16.1gr (average of five). Muzzle velocity is a little higher at 959fps, which gives a muzzle energy of 32.9ft/lb, making the CB cap a good choice for close-range vermin control when it is safe to do so.

The conical bullet shape would fair better than the round BB cap projectile with groups of 1.0–1.5in (2.5 to 4cm) at 20yd (18m). This round's effective range, as with the BB caps, is 20yd maximum from the right rifle, but 10yd (9m) is more practical.

Next comes the more conventional-shaped .22 CB longs. These give you enough knock-down power to dispatch a rabbit, and the low velocity makes for very quiet muzzle report without a sound moderator, and it is inaudible with one fitted.

Accuracy is improved due to the more conventional design because there is less bullet jump from cartridge to the start of the rifling in the barrel as compared to the BB and CB caps.

The CB longs shoot a 29gr solid bullet at 705fps and give 32ft/lb energy. They shoot well out to 20yd (18m) with maximum 0.75in (19mm) groups, and 0.5in (13mm) clusters at 15yd (14m). Due to their long case designation they also have the advantage that they can be magazine feed from most rifles.

.22 reduced loads

Type	Bullet / Wt In grains (actual weighed)	Velocity Average of five shots (feet per second)	Energy Ft / lb
BB caps	15.5gr	887fps	27.1
CB caps	16.1gr	959fps	32.9
Super Colibri	19.8gr	612fps	16.5
CB long	29.0gr	705fps	32.0
Eley Zimmer	30.0gr	797fps	42.3
Eley subsonic xtra	40.0gr	1030fps	94.8

Eley and RWS produce a Zimmer (indoor or room) round based on the LR-case configuration. These have a 30gr bullet that speeds across the chronograph at a pedestrian 797fps giving 42.9ft/lb energy.

The bullet is a solid lead projectile and will have a tendency to ricochet on any hard surface, so make sure there is a soft, safe backstop if using these rounds. Accuracy at 20yd (18m) is below 0.5in (13mm), but even at these velocities there will be a marked trajectory curve, so if you intend to shoot them through the same rifle as your 'normal' .22lr ammunition, check the zero at 5, 10 and 20yd (4.5, 9 and 18m) to learn where to hold off or adjust your scope turrets.

Finally a very unusual cartridge is the Super Colibri round from Aquila, manufactured in Mexico. This round utilizes a conical projectile of 19.8gr, weighed average of five, but uses no gunpowder and only relies on propulsion from the primer mixture. An LR case is used, but it is designed to be shot from short barrels. A 14in (35cm) barrel is best, limited to 10yd (9m) around the farmyard, with accuracy of one hole groups at 5yd (4.5m), 0.75 to 1in (19 to 25mm) at 10yd (9m), and nearly 2in (5cm) at 20yd (18m). With an energy of 16.5ft/lb you have more than enough 'oomph' to dispatch vermin, both fur and feathered.

The .22 Rimfire

Short, long and long rifle cartridges in standard, high velocity and magnum configuration, as in the .22 WMR cartridge, are the salt and pepper of the sporting world. The short and long have their uses, but by far the most widely used is the .22 long rifle cartridge (.22lr).

Although high velocity variants abound and can seem enticing, the vast majority of rimfire users in Britain will use .22lr subsonic loads because most rifles will have a sound moderator fitted. High velocity rounds are all right but are too noisy, and actually shed their energy very quickly due to the fact that most achieve these elevated velocities by using a lighter bullet that has a smaller ballistic coefficient (BC).

The .22lr subsonic loads vary enormously between manufacturers and in style, but all have

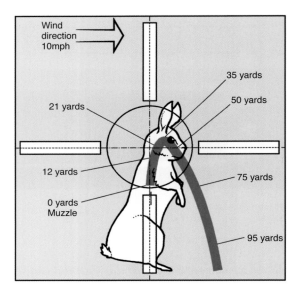

Trajectory of a 40gr .22lr subsonic travelling at 1050fps and the effect of a 10mph (16km/h) wind from 9 o'clock, and the rise and fall above and below the line of sight.

a velocity below the speed of sound at around 1050fps, dependent on climatic conditions.

Most .22lr subsonic cartridges use a lead bullet that weighs in the region of 40gr and has a hollow base design to allow expansion and grip into the rifling on firing, and some sort of lubrication to ease the passage up the bore. A hollow-point tip enables the lead to expand on impact and thus release sufficient energy to dispatch your game. Some super-heavy rounds, such as the Aquila SSS, use a 60gr lubricated lead bullet, a real thumper but sensitive to rifling twist.

Performance can vary dramatically, especially with regard to terminal ballistics, as this is determined by the design and composition of the bullet itself. (For a complete performance test, see Chapter 10.)

The standard .22lr round is approximately 0.61 in length, although the hyper-velocity Stinger load has a 0.70 case length and uses a 32gr bullet at a velocity of 1640fps. Most cases are brass and non reloadable, as the priming mixture is contained in the rim and not a separate primer. When the firing pin strikes the case's rim, the primer mixture is squashed and thus ignites. This is crucial to consistent powder burn and velocities, as any inconsistencies here will result in poor accuracy down range.

Powder content is usually a flake type, with charge weights of 1.0gr for subsonic loads or 2.5gr for HV loads. When you think about it, that is an efficient cartridge to launch a 40gr bullet to over 1000fps with only 1gr of propellant!

Typical external ballistics of a subsonic round, such as an Eley 40gr with a bullet ballistic coefficient (BC) of 0.14 and a high velocity Stinger with a 32gr bullet, BC of 0.0997 travelling at 1640fps, has a trajectory that can be compared in the chart below.

Look how the lighter, less efficient Stinger bullet sheds its energy over range, ending up with near-identical ft/lb energy figures at 150yd (137m).

Although a high velocity round may be tempting, some meat damage at close range will render a rabbit useless – although head shots should always be attempted, which is why a slow, quieter, subsonic .22lr round to the head or neck works far better, in my view, for British sportspersons.

Note that the BC figure is gained from a standard G1 form table used to calculate BC values; if you use an RO4 table, then the Eley BC figure is more like 0.112. This is why I always say shoot your own rifle at the ranges you intend shooting over, and map out your individual rifle's trajectory, not a theoretical one.

The .22WMR (Winchester Magnum Rimfire)

The humble .22 magnum was a natural progression of the venerable .22 long rifle case, and served to satisfy the desire for bigger and better from the shooting public. The WMR's case length is 1.35in (3.4cm) as compared to that of a .22lr case of 1in (2.5cm). Usually sporting a 40gr bullet as STD and capable of 1900fps, it bridges the gap between .22lr and .22 Hornet. I know of several people who swear by the diminutive round as an excellent fox round at 150yd (137m).

Performance from a Remington 40gr pointed soft point at 1711fps/260.1ft/lb gives 50yd (45m) groups of 0.75 to 1in (19 to 25mm).

CCI-Maxi-Mag 40gr jacketed hollow points will run a healthy 1851fps/304.4ft/lb, and feature a totally copper-washed finish to the bullet with a reasonably large hollow cavity. It is quite a hard bullet, which is better for fox use.

Winchester also offer a 40gr jacketed hollow point with copper-washed bullet producing 1886fps/316.0ft/lb out of a 24in (60cm) barrel. It offers mid-range performance with better than average groups at 100yd (90m), probably due to the 40gr weight as opposed to some 30gr.

Federal Premiums feature an excellent Sierra 30gr jacketed hollow-point construction with a large cavity for controlled expansion, zipping over the chronograph at an average of 204.3fps/278.1ft/lb.

Comparison of velocity and trajectory between an Eley subsonic and CCI Stinger high velocity .22 rimfire round

Eley Subsonic 40gr bullet

Range in yards (m)	0	25 (23)	30 (27)	50 (46)	75 (68)	100 (90)	125 (114)	150 (137)
Trajectory	-1.5	0	0	-0.7	-3.8	-9.2	-17.4	-28.4
Velocity fps	1050	1004	996	966	932	902	875	849
Energy ft/lb	98	90	88	83	77	72	68	64

CCI Stinger 32gr bullet

Trajectory	-1.5	-0.2	0	+0.2	-0.7	-3.0	-7.0	-13.0
Velocity fps	1640	1481	1451	1340	1219	1123	1051	995
Energy ft/lb	191	156	150	128	106	90	78	70

The top of the tree with regard to velocity is the CCI Maxi-Mags V with a 30gr JHP bullet that screams at 2333fps/362.7ft/lb.

There is certainly excellent killing power from any of the cartridges listed. At 50yd (45m) we know it can perform, but when conditions are windy the .22 WMR struggles to group at less than 1.5in (4cm) at 100yd (90m). Heavier bullets buck the wind better, and you will have to experiment with your own gun. However, a fox will not stand in a windless corridor for you, so it illustrates the limitations in my mind on the effective range on the cartridge. Under ideal conditions, I would say 150yd (137m) absolute maximum, if they do not come any closer than that, do not shoot, or get a different calibre rifle.

.17 Mach 2 and .17 HMR Cartridges

There is no denying that the Hornady .17 HMR has found its niche in the shooting marketplace and shooters' repertoire that requires a safe, fast, flat-shooting, small calibre for dispatching vermin – and small wonder that its inception has sparked an entirely new interest amongst shooters in small calibre rifles. By the same token it was inevitable that the .22lr case would undergo a similar miniaturization, as did the .22 WMR. The result was the new .17 Mach 2 case that actually uses a .22 rimfire Stinger case from CCI and launches a 17gr V-Max bullet, as does the HMR, but at 2100fps and not 2500fps.

Eley, CCI, Hornady and Remington all produce .17 Mach 2 ammunition. The Eley averages a staggering 2167fps/177ft/lb from a 20in (50cm) barrel; this is 67fps above the advertised 2100fps velocity. Hornady shot 2017/154ft/lb, with CCI shooting a good 2085fps/164ft/lb and Remington 2033fps/156ft/lb.

In the real world in terms of trajectory and down range performance, the Eleys start at the muzzle with 2167fps/177ft/lb, at 50yd (45m) you still have 1858fps/130ft/lb and at 100yd (90m) you have 1591fps/96ft/lb. Really the .17 Mach 2 is a 100yd cartridge, but at further ranges the results are 1351fps/69ft/lb at 150yd (137m), and 1182fps/53ft/lb at 200yd (182m), a marked decline from the original velocities.

I originally sighted at 50yd and found that compared to a .22lr high velocity round travelling at an average of 1250fps, the Mach 2 had 0.85in (2cm) less drop at 75yd (68m) and nearly 4in (10cm) *less* drop at 100yd (90m)! That is a great advantage. Similarly when compared to a Stinger .22lr round (32gr) of 1640fps, the .17 Mach 2 had 0.5in (13mm) less drop at 75yd but only 1.78in (4.5cm) less drop at 100yd. Not such a difference, but accuracy from the .17 Mach 2 is far superior to the .22lr at that range.

In fact my own personal zero range, to get the best trajectory from the Mach 2 round, would be 75yd (68m). At this range you are −0.28 (7mm) low at 25yd (23m) and 0.19 (5mm) high at 50yd (45m), so dead on in real terms. Zeroed

The .17 calibre rimfires offer a much flatter trajectory than the .22lr round on the left; the three differing .17 Mach 2 rounds are good to 100yd (90m), with the 17 HMR reaching out to 150yd (137m) on a good day.

at 75yd and then at 100yd (90m) you are only 1.02in (2.6cm) low, so that long shot at a rabbit is a tiny elevation compensation. Just for interest, at 125yd (114m) you are −3.1 (7.8cm) and at 150yd (137m) you are −5.9in (14.9cm) low – and beyond that, forget it. As far as performance goes, the .17 Mach 2 is to me an excellent round. It does not pretend to be a long range round – 100yd maximum, in my view. If the wind is blowing, then be sensible and keep the range shorter. A 10mph (16km/h) breeze can blow that 17gr pill 5in (13cm) off course at 100yd!

The .17 HMR (Hornady Magnum Rimfire)

This was originally designed as a flat-shooting varmint round to compensate for the .22 rimfire's failings in terms of rainbow trajectory and ricochet problems. The .17 HMR was really intended for quarry species – not foxes, but the little 17 grain bullet has found a unique place in the shooting community of Great Britain.

Bullet weights are 17gr and 20gr either in polymer tip or hollow-point construction. The 17-grainer was introduced first, but was soon thought of as marginal on fox-sized game, so a tougher 20gr hollow point was introduced.

When fed into a ballistics programme such as the excellent Quickload and Quicktarget, you find that tested Hornady 17gr ammunition at

CCI, Federal, Hornady and Remington, all with 17gr V-Max bullets, with the CCI at farthest right loaded with a 20gr Game Point for foxes.

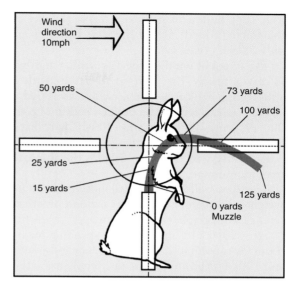

Compared to a .22lr trajectory, that of the 17gr HMR round is much flatter.

2578fps and 251ft/lb energy with a 100yd (90m) zero – at 50yd (45m) the trajectory rises 0.22in (5.5mm) above the sight line, at 100yd you are on zero with a remaining velocity of 1901fps/136ft/lb energy figure. At 150yd (137m) the 17gr bullet had dropped −2.5in (6cm) and was speeding along at 1598fps/96ft/lb, whilst out at 200yd (180m) the trajectory had dropped down −7.25in (18.4cm) and only had 1411fps/75ft/lb energy remaining. As an interim, at 175yd (160m) there was a −4.75in (12cm) drop, and at extreme range at 250yd (228m) the drop was −11.5in (29cm).

What does this tell you? Well, out to 150yd (137m) this round is flat shooting with little need for much trajectory compensation, which is always useful in a situation where there is no time for lengthy considerations. However, out to 200yd (180m) it does fall off markedly, and in a windy situation I would be doubtful about connecting with a target on the first shot. Nevertheless, the 20-gr bullets have a muzzle velocity of 2344fps and 244ft/lb energy, which drops to 1720fps and 132ft/lb at 100yd (90m), and has dropped to below 1300fps at 200yd with only 75ft/lb remaining. There is also a larger trajectory drop at 200yd if the initial zero is 100yd.

The 20gr bullet drops nearly 9.5in (24cm) at this range (200yd), whilst the 17gr bullet drops only 7.25in (18.5cm).

The effect of wind on the 17gr bullet at 50yd (45m) is nearly 1in (2.5cm) deviation with a stiff 10mph (16km/h) wind, whilst at 100yd a similar breeze offsets the bullet's path by up to 3in (7.6cm). At 150 and 200yd you have 7–8in (18–20cm) adjustment and 14in (35cm) respectively, which is why 150yd is the absolute maximum range.

The 20gr bullet fares a little better due to its weight advantage, but there is little in practical terms to discern between the two.

So, 150yd (137m) was the absolute maximum for rabbits and corvids on less windy days, and 100yd (90m) for foxes, preferably using the 20gr bullets.

The revival of the old 5mm Remington magnum may resolve all these problems with a newer 30gr (38gr original) travelling at 2300fps – let's hope so.

Wildcat Cartridges

If you want something exotic then you may well be tempted into having a rifle rebarrelled in the smaller calibres, such as .14, or even .10 or .12! First, however, is a practical small calibre for people who like the 17 HMR but think it is a shame it cannot be reloaded due to its being

a rimfire case. This is the .17 Squirrel, which is a .22 Hornet case shortened to 0.965in (2.45cm) in length, and the neck diameter reduced to accept .17 calibre bullets. It can shoot 15gr Berger bullets at 3500fps with a meagre charge of only 8gr of powder, translating into a really nice, mild, 150yd (137m) vermin rifle.

Next down the calibre scale is the .14 calibre – in fact .144 diameter – where a couple of cartridges shine. The .14-221 is based on a necked-down 221 Fireball case, and is somewhat overkill on such a small bullet, but velocities of 4200fps can be achieved!

Better balanced is the .14 Walker Hornet, a 14-calibre version of the .22 Hornet with improved body taper. A 15gr Genco hollow-point bullet on top of 12gr of Reloder 7 powder achieves a whopping 4003fps velocity and 534 ft/lb energy, enough for any marauding squirrel or rabbit.

If you really want to get silly then the microscopic 10 and 12 calibres, the brainchild of one Bill Eichelberegr from the USA, are available in suitably necked-down cartridges as diverse as the .22 Jet, 30 carbine or even .32 H&R pistol case, to name a few. When you get to this small a size, cleaning rods and equipment become an issue and sourcing reliable accurate expanding ammunition can become problematic, but still great fun.

The Sako Quad in any rimfire calibre is a real performer, again with a fast barrel-exchange system.

Fancy something different? Then why stick to .17 calibres when you can own a .14? Seriously small, fiddly to load and a pain to clean, but they will put a smile back on your face!

FOX CLASS CARTRIDGES

The .17 HMR round has been discussed in the previous section, so let's look at the centrefire fox cartridges available. There are more rounds than I can include here, but I shall run through the most common or useful.

Small, very fast projectiles that shoot flat and have explosive terminal ballistics from a vermin hunter's point are very hard to beat.

The .17 Ackley Hornet

This is a very accurate and mild to shoot cartridge capable of handling the lightest .17 calibre bullets from 15 to 20gr comfortably. It is super efficient to about 250yd, and burns little

powder, spitting out 20gr Bergers at 3800fps by only burning 12.5gr of IMR 4227 powder, or my preference of Vit N120. It also makes little noise and is naturally easily moderated, and will not wear out barrels by throat erosion as in some of the other faster .17s. I personally think the .17 Ackley Hornet has a great future in the British shooting scenario, where safety is an ever-pressing issue.

The .17 Mach IV

One of the best balanced and really classic .17 calibres is the Mach IV. This is based on a .221 Fireball case that has been necked down to .172 calibre. It only needs 18.65gr of Vit 133 to speed a 20gr bullet out of a 24in (60cm) barrel at 4000fps. This has been eclipsed by the Remington .17 Fireball, which is Remington's attempt at legitimizing the old Mach IV round. Factory ammunition shoots 20gr Accutip bullets at 4000fps and generates 710ft/lb of energy. For a lightweight walking vermin rifle that doubles as a competent fox rifle to 250yd (228m), the .17 Fireball is hard to beat. In the right hands, this cartridge is just dynamite on vermin, depositing all of its energy within the body cavity for an instantaneous kill.

The other really big plus for any .17 rifle is that it is virtually ricochet free, making it excellent for use around the farm and suburban areas.

Some of the available .17 calibres: from the left, .17 Mach 2, .17 HMR, .17 AK Hornet, .17 Fireball and .17 Remington.

The .17 Remington

The .17 Remington is a cartridge of over twenty years' vintage, legitimized by Remington by reforming .223 cases. The standard factory loading of a 25gr bullet is advertised to have a velocity of 4030fps, but in the real world I have never been able to achieve much more than 3850fps from a 24in (60cm) barrel. You need to reload to achieve the elusive 4000fps ceiling.

The close range reloads always centre around the excellent Berger bullets that range from the diminutive 15, 18 and 20gr. That also includes the excellent Hornady 20gr V-Max bullet, which is superbly consistent. If I am to shoot feathered vermin such as magpies and crows, then an explosive 15gr or 18gr Berger is ideal. Available as a flat-base design or maximum expansion factor (MEF) bullet, both provide super-fast velocities coupled to a very flat trajectory and sheer on-target energy transfer. Admittedly range is limited, since a very light projectile travelling very fast sheds its velocity at an alarming rate; however, out to 200yd (180m) they are really effective against feathered pests.

The best accuracy comes from the mid-range or all-purpose 20gr V-Maxes and 25-grainers. A 24gr payload of RL15 powder will shoot a 20gr V-Max at 4070fps on a cold day and 4200fps on a hot one from a 24in (60cm) barrel. The V-Maxes are my favourite: they shoot really flat, are accurate, and instantly deadly.

The 30gr Berger bullets give a longer range, and the larger 30-grainer ensures a better ballistic coefficient and as such retains more energy down range. With RL15 powder the 30gr projectile is shy of the 4000fps mark at 3975fps – accuracy is phenomenal, although as with all the seventeen bullets, if you push them too fast, too soon, the high rotational spin in flight can cause the bullet to disintegrate before it reaches the target!

Everyone should have at least one .17 calibre rifle in their collection: they add a very interesting facet to your sporting shots.

The .17 PPC

There are two ways to look at the .17 PPC cartridge: first as a super-fast, flat-shooting, mid-range varmint rifle necessitating bullets in the 15 to 25gr weight range; or with heavier 30 or 37gr bullets for longer range use. The Berger 37gr VLD bullet has a BC of 0.343, better than some 75gr V-Max 0.243-diameter bullets, and the 30gr Wood Chuckden Boat-tail bullet has a BC of 0.270. To put that into context with the .20 calibres, despite their smaller size of a regular .224 varmint bullet, the .17s are lighter and can be driven faster but have a better BC due to their very sleek, long wind-bucking design.

Being a wildcat round you have to form cases. The .17 PPC starts life as a .220 Russian case, then using a two die-forming die set you can reduce the neck diameter from .224 to .172. Be careful to lube the necks correctly – I use Imperial sizing wax. Once formed, you will need to neck-turn the case necks to achieve the correct clearance with that of your rifle's chamber, because the brass gets a bit too thick after the neck reduction. My chamber reamer had a 0.197 chamber neck, and so a loaded round

.17 calibre bullets range from the diminutive Berger 15gr hollow point up to the 30gr Woodchuck Den.

Small calibres can be fun and offer some good wildcat rounds: left to right, .17 Ackley Hornet, .220 Russian case, .17 PPC, 6 PPC, .17 Rem and the .20 BR.

would have to have a neck diameter of 0.195 to give the necessary 0.002 clearance for precise bullet release. All that is needed then is to fire form the brass in the rifle's chamber, and the characteristic PPC case is formed with a beautifully sharp shoulder and tiny neck.

The .17 PPC case likes the medium powder burners such as Varget, Benchmark and Reloder 15, although Vit N135 or H4895 would also perform well. The Hodgdon Benchmark is a starting powder; 24gr pushes the little 20gr V-Max out of the 24in tube at 4437fps, whilst 25gr Bergers and Hornady bullets liked Reloder 15 powder to achieve 4394fps. That is fast, and would be a devastating crow or fox round, delivering more kinetic energy and being a little less wind sensitive than the lighter weights.

The real contenders in my eyes are the 30gr Gold Wood Chuckden bullets. 24gr of Hodgdon`s Benchmark powder gives 3877fps, whilst 25.5gr jumps to 4108fps, so care is needed with small calibres and pressures.

The .20 Vartarg and .20 Tactical

These are the brainchild of the much respected small calibre expert Todd Kindler. The smallest of the two is a modified and necked down .221 Fireball case to accept .204 bullets whilst achieving velocities of 3950fps with a 32gr bullet and nearly 3750fps with a high BC 40gr V-Max – that's some performance. This is a

superb British low noise, 'do anything' cartridge for vermin or foxes, and in a rifle that is moderated it makes a sensible night-time lamping partner. A 20 Vartarg turbo case is bigger than the Vartarg, using a .222 Rem parent case.

Better still, and probably, in my view, the most practical vermin and fox cartridge, is the 20 Tactical, which is a necked down .223 Rem case with longer neck and altered shoulder. With 32 or 40gr bullets, or any of the Berger 30 or 35gr hollow points, the Tactical Twenty – or 20 TAC, as it is known – can outperform most other similar case sizes due to the better BCs of the .204-calibre bullets.

It is reasonable to assume that powders that work well in .223 cartridges will work in the .20. Tactical, Hodgdons 4198, Vit N133, Win 748 or BLC-2 would all be candidates for the lighter .204 bullets, whilst Reloder 10, Benchmark or N135 might better suit the heavier, 40gr V-Maxes.

The 30gr to 40gr bullets will stabilize in a 1-in-12 twist rate barrel. The 45gr likes a faster twist, whilst the 50gr Bergers require a 1-in-9 twist to stabilize them. In fact a 1-in-11 might be better than the 1-in-12, just to be sure of bullet stability.

Vit N 133 powder, which I use in my 6mm PPC, and a load of 24gr will launch a 32gr V-Max at over 3800fps, whilst 26gr will break the 4000fps barrier. In fact if you decide on the 40gr bullet, which I prefer, the V-Max bullet has an astonishingly high 0.275 BC compared to the 0.215 of the 32gr V-Max. Reloder 10 is a very good choice here, with a weight of 25gr as a maximum load for the Hornady 32gr V-Maxes, with a velocity of over 4150fps. The same load with the 40gr V-Maxes gives just over 3975fps and is a very accurate and safe non-barrel-burning load. Speed can be very nice for flat trajectories and explosive on target performance, but you pay for it in accelerated barrel heat-up, mirage and fouling, with ultimately shorter barrel life.

It is in its trajectory that the .20 Tactical shines: frugal powder weights yet high velocities with high ballistic coefficient bullets translates into superior performance when compared with .224 bullet weights.

A 40gr .204 bullet with a BC of 0.275 starting at 4000fps only drops −30in (75cm) at 500yd (457m), whilst the same weight 0.224 bullet with BC of 0.200 will drop −38in (96cm). Similarly, the smaller .204 bullet drifts less in the wind at that range, 24in (60cm) compared to 37in (94cm) for the 0.224 bullet. This is all due to the higher BC values from the smaller, more streamlined twenty calibre as compared to the comparatively fatter, less efficient 0.224 projectile.

The .204 Ruger

Twenty calibre rifles are all the rage these days. Nestling nicely between the .17 (.172) and .22 (.224) calibre centrefire rounds, the .204 or twenty calibre has the benefit of a slimmer projectile diameter blended to an intermediate weight, which translates into more efficient down-range ballistic from either of the former two candidates. The new .204 Ruger is simply a .222 Rem magnum case necked down to accept .204 calibre bullets, and emulates the .20 Terminator wildcat round. Factory ammunition dictates that only 32gr and 40gr projectiles are the most popular, but newer 45gr bullets are now available for more controlled bullet expansion. The 32gr are quoted at producing 4225fps and 1268ft/lb energy, whilst the 40gr bullets produce 3900fps or 1351ft/lb energy.

On the face of it, that is amazingly flat shooting, fast ammunition, and just right for a night's fox control. However, the truth lies in the actual testing, because test barrels and factory quotes do not usually relate to the individual rifles and their idiosyncrasies. Nevertheless, Remington 32-grainers had a velocity of 3987fps and 1129ft/lb energy from a 25in (63cm) CZ barrel with 40gr Hornady ammunition, with velocities and energy figures of 3735fps and 991ft/lb respectively. Regardless of velocity, even at these figures a 32gr bullet when zeroed at 100yd (90m) will still be in the chest cavity of a fox at 275yd (250m), and that in real life is all that matters.

The .20 PPC and .20 BR

The .20 PPC that uses a fire-formed .220 Russian case is discussed in the fox chapter; the .20 BR is similar, but utilizing a larger BR case instead has more potential with heavier weight twenty calibre projectiles. Depending on rifling twist, the .20 BR can push a 32gr bullet from a 1-in-12 twist barrel at nearly 4250fps with a long barrel, and a 39 Blitzking or 40gr V-Max bullet at 4100fps plus. That is a very flat shooting and ultra-explosive projectile, which makes for a safe vermin gun and extremely deadly foxing tool.

The 20 BR performs best with a 50gr Berger Varmint bullet and 1-in-9 twist to stabilize it perfectly to achieve a velocity of 3850fps and 1646ft/lb; with the Berger's BC of 0.295 the retained energy down range is superior to many comparable .224 bullets of the same weight, and even some 6mm calibres. The downside is that you are pushing a small bullet hard down a small bore, and throat erosion will mean a shorter-than-normal barrel life if you are not careful.

The .20 Satan

This is a wildcat I developed over four years ago. I wanted to push as heavy a .20 calibre bullet as fast as I could, but still remain within safe pressure levels and maintain good accuracy. To date, only Berger produce a bullet heavier than 40gr, and this is the 50gr Varmint Boat Tail bullet, which needs a 1-in-9 twist to stabilize it rather than the 1-in-12 common to the lighter .20 projectiles. I wanted to achieve the highest ceiling velocity from the 50gr Berger and still be safe, and had the idea of using the 6 × 47 Swiss match case. This is a match-quality .308 bolt-face cartridge with a cartridge length of 1.85in (47mm) and therefore represents a three-quarter length .243/.308 case capacity.

Forming the brass meant running virgin 6 × 47 SM brass through a .22 BR FL die set with the sizing button removed to initiate the first neck sizing procedure. Next I ran the case through a .20 BR FL die with the button removed to achieve the primary .20 neck calibre diameter. I then trimmed the cases on a Wilson neck trimmer to 1.8215in (46.26mm) to the chamber/reamer spec, and ran each case through a .204 expander mandrel to even out neck concentricity and give enough neck tension to the bullets for fire forming.

The 36.5gr of Reloder 15 achieved 3950fps velocity with a Berger 50gr bullet, and then a rise to 37gr yielded that mythical 4000fps figure of 4016, 4021 and 4012fps with no pressure signs and great accuracy of 0.25in (6.35mm) and a very usual energy figure of 1791ft/lb. The consistency of the velocity with a 15fps variation or less meant an efficient case design.

After some initial testing with a 0.5in (12.7mm) high zero at 100yd (90m) I found I had only a 1.5in (3.8cm) drop at 200yd (180m)

My own contribution to the world of wildcat calibres is the Satan line-up, based on the Swiss Match and newer Lapua 6.5mm × 47 case.

and 3in (7.6cm) at 300yd (274m). That is a fantastically accurate and practical flat trajectory by anyone's standards, and in reality means that if a crow or fox appears at any distance out to 300–350yd (274–320m), you just aim dead on.

As can be seen from the table, starting at the same velocity with the same bullet weight, the more aerodynamic .204 calibre beats the .224 projectile at long range.

The .22 centrefire (.224) has been the main-

Comparison between a 40gr V-Max bullet in .204 and .224 calibre to show the differences in performance

Calibre	Range (yards)	Velocity (fps)	Energy (ft/lb)	Trajectory (inches)	Wind deflection (10mph)
.204	0	4000	1421	-1.8	0
40gr V-Max	100	3541	1114	0	0.8
	200	3129	870	-1.0	3.5
	300	2753	673	-5.6	8.3
	400	2407	515	-14.8	15.6
.224	0	4000	1421	-1.8	0
40gr V-Max	100	3424	1041	0	1.1
	200	2919	757	-1.2	4.6
	300	2466	540	-6.6	11.1
	400	2057	376	-17.8	21.3

.22 centrefire bullets come in all shapes and sizes, from hollow-point boat-tails to flat-base soft points, with a good choice of polymer-tipped bullets such as Ballistic Tips and V-Maxes.

stay of the fox shooter for years, with many excellent cartridges in this section, and some transcend the barriers of small deer cartridges where legal with proper bullets.

The .22 Hornet

One of the most underrated cartridges of all time, the .22 Hornet is all you need for close-range vermin or fox work in Britain if you choose your loads carefully.

Pigeon-holing the Hornet was always the problem, as it was above rimfire velocities yet not as poky as most other .22 centrefires, so as a rabbit gun it had too much energy whilst for anything larger you could be forgiven in passing up the Hornet in favour of, for example, the larger .222 Rem. Indeed, why not have a .17 HMR rimfire? Well, at the same ranges the Hornet shoots a heavier bullet with more authority without going over the top, so one-shot humane kills are far more predictable, and more importantly to me the Hornet is reload-able, enabling a variety of hand loads to be uti-lized. The effective range is however, about 175–200yd (160–180m).

The Hornet has a slow rifling twist, only 1-in-16in. It is unable to stabilize heavier bullets very well, such as the 55-grainers, so it is best to stick to the 35, 40 and 45gr bullets, as these give the best compromise between velocity and energy figures combined with flattest trajectories. At 100yd (90m) zero you are only 0.35in (8.9mm) high at 50yd (45m), very usable at my ranges,

yet –5.8in (14.7cm) low at 200yd (180m) with Berger 45gr bullets travelling at 2600fps.

The Hornady 35gr V-Max bullets, either reloaded or used as a factory-loaded Varmint Extreme ammunition from Hornady, offer the highest velocity and flattest trajectory for short range, with dependable, highly frangible results where a ricochet would be undesirable. The only drawback is that the lighter, stubbier bullet has a lower ballistic coefficient and thus is blown about more by the wind at longer range. The 35gr Hornady V-Max can be sent flying at 3057fps producing 726ft/lb energy with a pal-try powder charge of 11gr VIT N110 with spec-tacular down-range performance.

The .221 Fireball

Originally designed for pistol use, the .221 Fireball has a unique place in the sporting world as being a super-efficient cartridge for fox or vermin work, all from a case that cycles better than a Hornet from the magazine and gives just that bit more thrust.

The 221 Fireball case is a shortened 222 Rem case introduced in 1963, and is only about 150fps velocity behind its big brother despite its 18gr powder capacity.

The 35gr V-max bullets can be pushed at 3700fps with Hodgdon H 4227 powder, which makes a flat rabbit load, or a 40gr bullet with a charge of 18gr VitN120 powder produces 3300fps, and is very good as a fox round. You can, of course, load heavier bullets such as the

55gr V-Max, but velocity drops to around 2800fps. This is still good, but my choice is the 40gr bullet as it offers the best all-round performance.

The .222 Rem

Remington recognized a niche in the line of available cartridges between the Fireball and the Swift in terms of performance, and so the .222 Rem was born, surpassing both in terms of accuracy, ease of reloading and light recoil, yet still possessing enough velocity for foxes at 250yd (228m).

The bullet diameter is .224 and used a 1-in-14 rate of twist to the rifling; this means that bullet weights from 40 to 55gr can be comfortably handled with great accuracy, and the normal 50gr loading is capable of 3200fps generating a useful 1000ft/lb energy. This is useful because it makes it legal in Scotland to cull roe deer with the .222 using a minimum 50gr bullet at a velocity of 2450fps and 1000ft/lb figures. In my opinion this is where the .222 Rem really shines, because in England and Wales it is a great fox, muntjac or CWD round with enough energy to get the job done.

Its demure stature belies its abilities in terms of ballistics. You can push those 40gr bullets out at 3480fps using 21.4gr of H4198, which is remarkable if you consider the small charge of powder used: it's a very efficient little case. Using the same powder, H4198, a 50gr bullet can be launched at 3306fps with 20gr of powder, whilst the 52gr and 55gr projectiles drop to only 3115 and 3051fps using 19.5gr and 19gr of H4198 powder respectively.

Personally for roe I would go for a 55gr soft point bullet travelling at 3095fps from a charge of 25gr Varget giving 1170ft/lb. Factory ammunition is bountiful from most manufacturers.

Out in the field, a 50gr bullet starting off at 3150fps with 1102ft/lb of energy will still have 472ft/lb energy at 250yd (228m), which is more than a Hornet at 200yd (180m). However, zeroed at 100yd (90m) that 50gr bullet will be down to −2.9in (7.4cm) at 200yd and −11.8in (30cm) at 300yd (274m).

To sum up, the .222 Rem has true potential for foxes at 200–250yd and varmints out to 300yd, and with the right legal load can be used for roe in Scotland, and muntjac and CWD deer in England and Wales — and that is about as versatile as it gets.

The .223 Rem

The .223 Remington started life as an experimental military round, but Remington soon launched the sporting version from brass using the same head size as the .222 Remington but with a longer overall length but shorter neck.

The .223 filled a niche between the venerable .222 Remington and the larger .22-250 round, and it would serve as an excellent all-round small game and varmint round. As always, however, the choice of rifling twist is crucial — in fact, where most .22 centerfire rounds utilize a 1-in-12 or 1-in-14 twist for the lighter bullets, the .223, because of its military heritage, can also utilize the heavy bullet weights and tighter twists of 1-in-9, 1-in-8 or even as fast as 1-in-7, thus making it a truly flexible round to reload for.

In a comparison between the .222 and the .223 using the same bullet style and weight of 50gr, the former has a muzzle velocity, on average, of 3200fps whilst the .223 trots along at 3400fps, a 200fps advantage with only a minimal powder increase of 2gr over the .222. In fact the increased .223 case capacity is capable of launching a 40gr bullet at 3800fps, which is great for vermin, a 55gr at 3275fps, which is more than good enough for Scottish roe, and the 75-grainers for longer range pests at nearly 2800fps.

The .223 is a very popular round, and factory ammunition abounds with a good range of bullet weights for any application.

Remington offer their good Accu-Tip bullet in both 50 and 55gr projectiles with a velocity of 3323fps and 3277fps respectively from an RPA rifle with 24in (60cm) barrel. Sako, too, offer a Gamehead bullet in both 50 and 55gr at comparable velocities, which doubles as both a fox or Scottish roe round.

Federal cater for both the fox and roe stalker in that the V-Shok range has a 40gr Nosler ballistic tip that speeds along at over 3744fps (great for foxes), whilst the 55gr weight Sierra Game

King makes a good Scottish roe round or more frangible ballistic tip for longer range foxes. Both have a velocity of nearly 3250fps.

Hornady have an excellent line of .223 ammunition called Varmint Express. The brass and manufacture is first rate, and they have a proprietary 40gr V-Max that travels at 3861fps depending on barrel length, and the larger 55gr V-Max pushes 3277fps and 1312ft/lb energy.

Reloading is where the true potential can be gained, because efficient and prudent loading will achieve a low recoiling, highly accurate round that is easily suppressed and very capable at sensible ranges. With the small case capacity the .223 is suited to powder-burning rates of faster to medium variety, excelling with Reloder 7, Hodgdon Benchmark, Vit N120 or N133, Varget and H322.

Light bullets such as the 40gr V-Max shoot very well when using powders such as Benchmark where a load of 28.75gr produces a velocity of 3843fps and 1312ft/lb energy from a 24in (60cm) barrel.

The 50gr projectiles such as the Ballistic Tip or the Speer TNT and the excellent V-Max like 24.5gr of Vit N133; this gives a velocity of 3448fps and 1320ft/lb energy, making the 50gr Ballistic Tip bullet a good fox round at any distance.

The 55gr and 60gr bullets at 3250fps using a load of 24.25gr Benchmark and 55gr Ballistic Tip produce 1290ft/lb energy and provide a dependable hard-hitting bullet. A Nosler Partition 60gr flat-base can be pushed at nearly 3100fps using a charge of 23gr of H322, but you may need a faster twist such as a 1-in-10 or faster to stabilize it and achieve best accuracy. This load makes a good roe round north of the border, or for muntjac in the South.

Where the .223 wins over the .222 and its larger rival the .22-250 is in superior ballistics with the minimum of powder and maximum efficiency; it is hotter than a .222, but not as hot as a .22-250 so you needn't worry about barrel wear and life.

The .22-250 Rem

In my view the .22/250 is certainly the best of the .22 centrefires in terms of versatility and outright ballistics if you intended to stretch the range a little further. In 1965 Remington legitimized this wildcat, based on the 250 Savage case, into a factory round, and the advantages of the .22/250 over the .222 Remington in terms of velocity are at least 475–650fps.

Starting with the 40gr bullet heads, these are real screamers ballistically, but take care to use bullets with thick jackets and not those for use in .22 Hornet rifles, otherwise the bullets will come apart as the centrifugal force of the rifling imparts its spin. However, the Berger 40gr MEF, Nosler Ballistic Tip and Hornady V-Max are good, and coupled with 36.25gr of Hodgdon Benchmark powder, maximum load will yield a 4021fps velocity from a 24in (60cm) barrel.

Bullets in the 50gr and 52gr range are more like the ideal varminting weight, as 35.75gr of Alliant RL15 generates 3671fps and 3611fps respectively. If you prefer to use a heavier bullet, especially for extended ranges or for roe or muntjac, then I use the 55gr bullets. With a powder weight of 38gr of Hodgdon Varget or Vit N140 it achieves a healthy 3600fps with a 55gr bullet head, and this weight is about ideal in a .22/250 round as it gives predictable accuracy and good wind-bucking properties combined with reliable performance on varmints, foxes or smaller deer where appropriate. A 52gr Hornady A-Max fox bullet travelling at 3700fps when zeroed 0.5in (13mm) high at 100yd (90m) drops -0.9in (2.28cm) at 200yd (183m), -3.1in (7.9cm) at 250yd (228m), and -6.2in (15.7cm) at 300yd (274m) allowing for minimum sight correction.

Shooting a .22-250 does not just mean running at full throttle: sometimes a reduced load becomes useful for those quieter moments, and where the sheer power of the .22/250 is not required, here a load of 18gr of H4198 with a 50gr Sierra Blitz King bullet gives a healthy 2388fps, great for around the farms and with sound moderator use.

The .220 Swift

The origins of the Swift are the wildcatting of a 6mm Lee Navy case to achieve the magical 4000fps velocity with .224 centrefire bullets. At

The venerable .220 Swift, here in a Tikka and old Tasco barrel-mounted scope, is still a good vermin/fox calibre despite the newer .20 calibres becoming available.

first glance the .220 Swift looks more like a deer cartridge than a varmint round. Original Swift cartridge loads were meant to send a 48gr bullet down a 24in (60cm) barrel at 4110fps.

There is the traditional 1-in-14 twist barrel option to stabilize and launch light bullets from 30gr to 55gr at stupid speeds; or by contrast you may elect to opt for the more efficient and long-range contender in the form of a 1-in-9 twist to stabilise 70 to 80gr VLD bullets to exploit some serious down-range performance and eke every last drop of range out of the venerable old Swift.

Commonly a 40gr bullet weight, such as Combined Technologies, Barnes and Hornadies V-Maxes, rate as some of the best. When using 40gr bullets from any maker I usually use Reloader 15 powder; although a little slow, a charge of 43gr gives 4286fps from a 28in (70cm) barrel. Again, Varget powder with a similar load generates about 75fps extra over the RL15 load, whilst powders such as Ramshot TAC and Vit N150 can be used.

The 50gr bullets are where the Swift comes alive. With a 1-in-14 twist barrel you can push them hard, and their increased BC of approximately 0.220 and increased energy values makes this range of bullet weights extremely effective against varmints. A Barnes 50gr VLC in front of either 40gr of either RL15 or Varget and 41gr of Vit N150 can safely produce over the 4000fps velocity ceiling and is flat right out to nearly

300yd (283m). Similarly 52 or 53gr bullets offer the shooter some nice high BC values for a .224 calibre rifle, and some very consistent match-grade bullet heads can be used for optimum accuracy.

If you want a classic varmint rifle, then as far as I am concerned my Swift is just that, classic, but the new .20 calibres are more efficient, and are already making inroads on these shores.

The 5.6 × 50mm and 5.6 × 57mm

These metric cousins of the .22 centrefires can offer the clever varmint shooter an unusual and very effective alternative cartridge. The smaller of the two is the 5.6 × 50mm, which is 0.12in (3mm) longer than a .222 magnum case. Its primary purpose in Europe, where it originates, was to enable the shooting of roe deer, but it is really better suited as a vermin/fox round. With 39gr Blitz Kings, a velocity of 3700fps is achieved, whilst 50gr bullets such as the V-Max delivers 3550fps with BLC-2 powder, producing a lethal fox load.

The 5.6 × 57mm is significantly larger, being based on the 6.5 × 57 cartridge necked down to accept .224 calibre bullets. Developed in the mid-sixties by RWS of Germany, its intended use was against roe deer and chamois. Lighter 50gr bullets travel at 3900fps, and 40gr well above this, and would make a better fox load as they would be too explosive on deer. A better bullet weight would be 55–60gr at 3600fps, or use the factory loading of 74gr RWS bullet designed for deer use with a velocity of 3400fps and muzzle energy of 1900ft/lb. These are interesting choices for people who like something a little different.

Sabots

This is an interesting alternative to using your deer rifle as a fox gun. A sabot, or shoe, is a discarding casing around a smaller projectile that fits your existing calibre rifle, such as a .224-diameter bullet encased in a plastic sabot whose diameter is .308 and so will fire in any .30 calibre rifle.

A typical .30 calibre sabot weighs 6gr, and you can use .224 calibre bullets of any weight dependent on the parent barrel's twist rate in being able to stabilize them. I have used custom-made sabots that use a .308 rifle but are capable of shooting .17, .20 and .243-sized projectiles.

As the cartridge is fired, the bullet and sabot are one piece, but as soon as they leave the barrel, the forward section of the sabot folds open like a flower petal to release the surrogate bullet on its unimpeded way. This method results in much higher velocities than are possible from the standard calibre with lighter bullets – but accuracy can be no better than the original calibre, and fitting a sound moderator is not an option as the sabot will damage it.

Subsonics / Reduced

Reduced velocity bullets, or bullets travelling below the speed of sound (subsonic) in full bore rifles, give a degree of flexibility for the person who owns just one rifle. Note that reducing a load in any cartridge can be dangerous, as with all reloading, so it is essential to consult a good reloading manual first, or let an expert do it.

I use my .308 deer rifle for foxes too, and use both reduced loads with light bullets to effect close-range encounters, and subsonic, heavier bullets for very quiet fox control. A good powder to use is SR4759 from IMR when coupled to, say, a 125gr Nosler ballistic tip or 110gr Berger hollow point. Usually a charge of 15–18gr powder gives a 1500fps–2000fps velocity with correspondingly low noise levels but just as lethal.

Subsonic loads dictate that a very small charge of fast powder is used – commonly Vit N320 in my .308, with a charge weight of between 9–10gr propelling a 200gr Lapua subsonic B416 projectile. You must use a short barrel and a fast rifling twist, usually 1-in-8, to stabilize the bullet. The report with a moderator is inaudible, but only head and neck shots should be used as the bullets will not expand at 1050fps velocity and so ricochets must be avoided – but it is still a very useful fox-only loading.

You can use your .22 centrefires with reduced loads also, but trying to get them to

Sabots, or 'Shoes', offer the chance to shoot lighter bullet weights for the calibre of rifle by using a plastic sabot to hold the sub-calibre bullet.

shoot subsonically means that very small charges of powder due to the light bullet weights and inconsistencies will affect accuracy – besides which most .224 calibre bullets will not expand at subsonic levels.

DEER CLASS CARTRIDGES

There are a great many deer calibres available made suitable to the deer species and range at which you wish to shoot, and to the relevant law that governs the differing deer species. I have chosen the more popular rounds with some newer and very good alternatives, and a few viable wildcats as well.

The 6PPC, 6BR, 6.5 Grendel and 6.5 × 47 Lapua

These can all be classified as intermediate deer cartridges. Each case utilizes a short and rather fat case design for its length, which seems to give that efficient powder burn to achieve good velocities with minimal powder but with great consistency.

The 6PPC and 6.5 Grendel utilize one of the best kept secrets in ballistics, and that is the .220 Russian case expanded at the neck to the required calibre and then fireformed to the new cartridge dimensions. The 6mm BR is nothing more than a stubby .308 case at half size and the 6.5 × 47 Lapua is a three-quarter size .308-length case necked down to accommodate the slim 6.5mm projectiles.

Ballistically the barrels need to be long to achieve deer-legal velocities and energy in many of these calibres, especially with the 6PPC, and barrels should not be less than 24in (60cm). If you shoot north of the border keep in mind also that there is a 100gr minimum bullet weight for larger species of deer.

The 6PPC, an absolute gem, has dominated the bench-rest target game for decades but also has a keen following amongst shooters in this country, a large portion of whom are stalkers or fox shooters. Ballistically this has the minimum capacity, with some of the lighter bullets not making the grade; however, with a suitable barrel with rifling twist to stabilize a

Intermediate cartridges such as the 6mm PPC, 6mm BR, 6.5 Grendel and 6.5 × 47 Lapua, next to a .243 round on right, all give the British deer stalker legal, accurate, non-venison-destroying cartridges.

70gr bullet or larger 1-in-12 or less, the PPC is superb.

The 29gr of Hodgdon H322 powder sends a 70gr bullet out of a custom 24in (60cm) barrel at 3362fps velocity and generates 1756ft/lb energy – just there legally, but its huge advantage is in the very light recoil, and the ease with which you can moderate a rifle and actually spot your shots and suffer no flinching, ensuring far better shot placement than with a heavier recoiling calibre. Similarly, if you need to shoot 100gr bullets, then 28gr RL 15 will be suitable, producing 2743fps and 1754ft/lb. But you need to remember that with bullets of this weight and length, unless the rifle's chamber is throated to accept them, they will have to be seated much further into the case than is practical.

A much better bet in terms of practical calibres is the 6mm BR, which due to the normal or standard .308 size head, unlike the dedicated PPC size, suits far more rifles.

Lapua make cases, so no case forming. A small charge of 29.5gr of either Vit N133 or Hodgdon Benchmark propels a 70gr projectile at over 3362fps from a 24in (60cm) barrel to achieve 1757ft/lb energy. The BR case is better suited to the heavy bullets, as it is often throated thus, and a 100gr Game King can be shot at 2784fps and generate 1807ft/lb energy with a powder charge of 28.5gr RL15. Similarly the same powder but with 32gr dead will push an 80gr bullet at over 3161fps to give 1775ft/lb.

With the 6mm bullets sorted, let us turn to some efficient 6.5mm calibres. Here there have been significant inroads into cartridge efficiency, all led by the target fraternity but still just as useful to us stalkers; only a change of bullet type is necessary.

Two new 6.5s that have become extremely popular are the unusual 6.5 Grendel, which is nothing more than a lengthened 6 PPC case and necked up to accommodate a 6.5mm bullet. A 129gr bullet such as the Hornady SST loads seated rather long, which is good as it feeds well through a standard magazine size with little modification. With a load of 28.5gr, the Hodgdon Varget generates 2551fps velocity and 1864ft/lb energy from a 24in (60cm) barrel.

If you go up to a 140gr bullet, say the Interlock, a good solid deer-proven projectile, then the same load of 28.5gr Varget generates 2473fps and 1902ft/lb – still in safe pressures. With that type of performance, why bother with anything that kicks more and uses more powder at sensible deer ranges?

In the new 6.5 × 47 Lapua, the 47 denotes the case length in millimetres: a .308 is 51mm, so you are between that and a BR cartridge of just over 39mm. A Lapua 6.5mm × 47 will send a 129gr Hornady SST bullet out of a 24in (60cm) barrel with a 1-in-8 twist rifling at 2796fps and 2240ft/lb with only a powder charge of 40gr Hodgdon H380: that is superb. Similarly, switching to a heavier bullet with a 140gr Interlock, also from Hornady, and a charge of 40gr IMR 4831 SC, gives a very healthy 2681fps velocity and 2235ft/lb energy. Easily deer legal in any part of the Great Britain, the 6.5 Lapua is super-efficient with minimum fuss, noise and recoil.

The firearms industry must be realizing the need for these calibres because Hornady have just introduced a shorter, super-efficient 6.5mm called the 'Creedmoor', and Thompson Center have done likewise with the venerable .30 calibre with the 30TC round.

The .243 Winchester

Due to the minimum .240 calibre requirement in England and Wales and 100gr bullet weight in Scotland, the .243 Winchester cartridge is often chosen. It is not too large for muntjac or roe, yet it is powerful enough for fallow and red when using the right bullet. In fact the .243 has a dual personality in that it treads that fine line from being a fine varmint calibre to an excellent mid-range deer round. You do need to choose the right barrel twist, however: a fast 1-in-9in or 1-in-10in twist would stabilize the heavier 100gr class deer loads, whilst the slower 1-in-12 or even 1-in-14 twist rate would achieve peak performance in the light varmint bullet weights.

Ballistically the .243 Winchester is capable of launching a 55gr bullet at nearly 3800fps and a 100gr projectile at 3000fps, and thus covers a broad spectrum of uses in the field. The Nosler Ballistic Tip 55gr bullet is especially designed for varmint/fox shooters. It can be pushed at 3775fps with 49.75gr of H380 powder or 45gr of Varget at 3756fps, and as such offers the shooter a very flat-shooting, explosive cartridge combination. If zeroed at 100yd (90m) the bullet only drops 5.75in (14.6cm) at 300yd (274m); however, the muzzle energy deteriorates from 1740ft/lb to 883ft/lb at that range because of the light bullet weight and lack of momentum at range.

If you want to step up the weight there is a good choice of 70 and 75gr bullets offered by Hornady, Nosler, Barnes, Speer, Berger and Sierra, to name just a few. Typical velocities range from 3550fps for the 70-grainers and 3400fps for the 75gr bullets, with 1959ft/lb energy and 1925ft/lb energy respectively.

The 80gr, 85 and 95gr bullets make excellent deer bullets if not pushed too fast for smaller species of deer at 3225fps, 3175fps and 2950fps respectively with the soft point, spitzer, partition and ballistic tip type of bullets. If placed properly on target, the extra weight penetrates well and delivers a good compromise between kinetic clout and pure hydrostatic shock caused by velocity within the body cavity area (heart/lung).

The last categories are the heaviest 100gr bullets solely used for deer stalking. One of my favourite deer loads for the .243 is 41.5gr of Hodgdons H4350, a shortened extrude powder under a Sierra 100gr Game King. Velocity is 2883fps from a 24in (60cm) barrel, which equates to 1846ft/lb energy and is therefore deer legal. It is mild recoiling, very accurate, and the Game Kings expand very dependably on game with predictable results.

For the seasoned stalker or shooter who wants a rifle to fulfil both roles of a fox and deer rifle, the little .243 is ideal. There is an excellent array of bullet heads powders to suit any situation, and its mild recoil has endeared it to a lot of shooters in this country.

The .260 Rem

The .260 Remington may not be the most popular calibre on the British market but it is fast becoming my favourite all-round calibre. It is simply a .308 case necked down to accept 6.5mm bullets.

There are many instances where people say a .243 is too small and a .308 is too large, but the .260 sits somewhere in the middle and should be ideal. Stalkers have long known the ballistic capabilities of the slender and long 6.5 bullet as a deep, penetrating, accurate projectile, whilst foxers appreciate the down-range performance of the lighter hollow-point designs. The range of bullet weights commonly starts at 85gr and transcends the mid-range weights of 120gr up to 140gr, with some varieties as heavy as 160gr. Performance is a real pleasure as the .260 is a mild kicking round, so it can be used in lighter rifles; it is easily sound moderated and inherently very accurate.

Factory loads of Remington ammunition in 140gr Accu-Tips are designed to expand reliably on deer-sized game and exhibit a muzzle velocity of 2618fps and 2131ft/lb energy from a 22in (55cm) barrel. The 120gr AccuTip is really good as a roe round, expanding dependably and not too rapidly so as to cause carcass damage, with a 2798fps velocity and 2087ft/lb energy. Down-range performance is good. The 6.5mm calibre has high ballistic coefficients (BC), meaning they fly through the air with less deceleration than bullets with lower BCs. Zeroed at 100yd (90m), a 120gr bullet travelling at about 2800fps velocity will be 3.2in (8cm) low at 200yd and 12in (30cm) low at 300yd (274m), compared to a .308 125gr bullet at the same velocity that drops 4.2in (10.6cm) and 14.6in (37cm) respectively.

Reloading is really where the .260 ballistics shine, enabling the reloader to unlock the performance from the .260.

The 85gr Sierra hollow points loaded with 48gr of Hodgdons H4350 powder speed along at 3105fps velocity with 1820ft/lb energy from a 22in (55cm) barrel. This is a great fox load.

The versatile 120gr Nosler Ballistic Tips are good for both fox and deer use. Travelling at 2750fps velocity with 2099ft/lb energy, this load is very flat-shooting and mild-recoiling. My load would be 43.5gr of Alliant RL19 with Federal Match primers.

Another good and hard-hitting bullet is the Hornady 129gr SST. These bullets offer a good blend of ballistics and predictable expansion, and are best used for deer-sized game. Velocities can reach 2650fps with a healthy 2012ft/lb energy, and this is probably my favourite all-round bullet for the .260 calibre. Again, Alliant RL19 is a good choice here, with 43gr achieving that 2650fps velocity from 22in (55cm) barrels.

However, to many the 140gr bullet is the deer load, with most of the major manufacturers producing bullet heads in this weight and achieving at least 2600fps and 2101ft/lb energy. Nosler make a good Partition in this weight, as do Sierra with the accurate 140gr Game King, whilst Hornady offer their dependable SST bullet in this weight. My load is 42.5gr of Alliant RL19 for 2668fps with a 140gr SST bullet.

Despite its relative scarcity, the .260 Remington has a loyal following in Britain amongst many stalkers and varminters.

The 6.5 × 55mm and 7 × 57mm

I have discussed these together, because as with the .260 Rem, these two cartridges are regarded as perfect all-round calibres for the British sportsperson despite being old designs – and I have to agree.

The 6.5 × 55 or 6.5 × 55 Swedish Mauser – not to be confused with the 6.5 × 57mm from RWS – is again a nice cartridge, first produced in 1894 for the Swedish military. By its age alone, this cartridge shows that you cannot put a good cartridge down and, as with so many cartridges, its popularity comes and goes as new shooters rediscover what our predecessors always knew. The 6.5 × 55 is a superb cartridge for all the deer species in Britain today. Loaded with heavier 140 and 160gr bullets with velocities of 2750 and 2450fps respectively, you have a good cartridge to tackle larger red stags and rutting fallow. The 140gr Hornady SST bullet is very good.

You can down size to 100 or 120gr bullets for smaller species, either at reduced velocities, or run full throttle at 3200 and 3000fps using 41gr Vit N150 or 48gr RL19 powder respectively. This also doubles as a load that bucks the wind at longer range for precise fox or vermin work, although the 85gr Sierra has to rank as a superb vermin or fox bullet with its fast-expanding hollow-point design and over 3300fps velocity.

The 7 × 57 is more geared to deer work, but with proper loading also makes a good dual-role fox rifle calibre as well. Again emanating from the late nineteenth century, this old military workhorse has seen favour with hunters worldwide for all species, right up to African game.

Loaded with a Nosler Ballistic Tip bullet of 140gr, which is perfect for the 7mm calibre, travelling at 2800fps and generating 2438ft/lb energy, it is plain to see why this is a favourite. Easy to shoot with milder recoil than some .30 calibres and good BCs to the 7mm bullet form, the 7 × 57mm is a 'one gun for all game' sort of rifle. Rigby choose this cartridge for their .275 Rigby loads in their traditional Mauser-based sporting rifles, but this old vanguard is not out of place in a modern sporting rifle, and has also seen new life for long-range varmint shooting as an Ackley-Improved case and loaded with very wind-slippery 140gr A-Max bullets.

The .308 Winchester

Time has proven the .308 Winchester cartridge to be a solid, reliable, accurate and very flexible cartridge to work with. Its origins lie as a shorter military version of the .30-06 cartridge, so the overall length would allow a rifle design to be shorter and lighter, yet still as deadly as the big –06.

Traditionally I think of a .308 calibre as having 150gr bullets travelling at 2850fps with 2706ft/lb energy as a typical deer load. A

standard twist rate of rifling would be 1-in-12, but 1-in-10 is preferred for heavy bullets.

Firstly the .308 is a very unfussy cartridge to load for, accepting a wide range of powder burning rates to accommodate the differing weight projectiles, from fast powders for lighter bullets such as Reloder-7, to Vit N-150, a slower powder for the heavy stuff.

The Barnes bullet, 110gr XFB, has a ballistic coefficient (BC) of 0.322, which really means that compared to a lighter more conventional .224 50gr varmint bullet, it retains more energy and, more importantly, is less affected by the wind at long range. I have used powders ranging from RL-7 with a maximum charge of 41gr to launch this bullet at near 3350fps from a 26in (65cm) barrel, whereas RL15, a slower burner, uses about 50gr of powder to achieve the same velocity – although some say it does give that all-important, in terms of accuracy, maximum load density where there is little air space between the top of the powder charge and the base of the bullet. Recently I used a Berger 110gr varmint bullet with 40gr H4198, which achieves a velocity of 2871fps from a 14.5in (36.8cm) barrel!

On the flip side to this bullet weight you can equally use the 110gr at a reduced velocity. When IMR SR4759 powder is used, it is transformed into a 1500fps quiet, well moderated, light recoiling yet effective fox gun in settled areas. Even at those slow velocities, the 110gr bullets can still expand enough to give good penetration coupled to good transfer of energy on target. I use a load of 16.25gr of SR 4759 to push this 110gr bullet at 1543fps from an 18in (45.7cm) barrel that is fully suppressed, and it has proved itself to be a great fox load.

You would think the 125gr bullets would be better for light deer species such as roe and muntjac. When driven at 3150fps it is certainly deer legal energy of 2754ft/lb, but meat damage is a concern. I have used this on both species, but instead of utilizing their light weight for higher velocities I have downloaded to 2495fps and still kept it deer legal at 1728ft/lb in England, with better results.

The 150gr bullet is synonymous with the typical deer weight. There is a vast array of bullet types in this weight, all achieving about 2850fps/2706ft/lb. Hodgdons Varget is a good

The .308 Winchester cartridge is a true all-round deer cartridge. With a diverse range of bullet styles and load data you can load this round for vermin, foxes or deer.

choice here, and I often use 42gr to push a 150gr bullet at a leisurely 2545fps, or 47gr to push it to maximum for a blistering 3000fps velocity. Bullet placement and correct choice of bullet type is far more important than sheer velocity.

Probably the best all-round .308 bullet weight is the 165gr; velocities up to 2700fps can be achieved with H335 with 42gr of powder, and Vit N135 using 43gr is nearly the same. This weight is a great choice, both as a larger species deer load for red, sika and fallow, giving good ft/lb energy figures, whilst long-range shooters can benefit from the higher BC in the class of 0.500, which is great for retained energy and wind bucking.

What should be evident is that the .308 spans the whole range of any species of game to be taken in Britain – and what other cartridge offers such versatility, accuracy, handiness, tolerable recoil and flexibility?

The .25-06, .270, .280 and .30-06

This family of cartridges is all derived from the venerable old .30-06 case, being necked down to accept smaller bullet diameters, and by altering the neck and shoulder dimensions.

Another excellent cartridge that can be used

for vermin, foxes or deer with the appropriate bullet weights is the .25-06. Bullet-weight choice is good, ranging from as small as 60gr up to 120gr. The lighter bullets, especially the Hornady hollow points and Nosler ballistic tips, are better suited to fox work, with 75gr V-Max bullets being able to exceed 3600fps from a 24in (55cm) barrel.

For deer I have used the heavier bullet weights of 100, 115 or 120gr. Factory Winchesters' loads of 115gr bullets preformed perfectly well on muntjac deer, with the tougher, heavier jacketed bullet causing little meat damage but humane one-shot kills.

The .270, using .277 diameter bullets, was the mainstay of the Forestry Commission, but it has fallen out of favour due to its perceived harsh recoil and the damage it inflicts to the valuable venison. However, poor bullet choice – that is, relative expanding rates and poor shot placement – has a lot to do with it, and the .270 is a good flat-shooting deer cartridge with 150gr bullets tipping the 2900fps barrier, especially the Hornady SST or newer 140gr Accubond, which have good penetration and expansion characteristics.

Again, the .280 Rem is a 7mm version of the necked-down .30-06, at one time called the 7mm Express Remington. In my opinion this

The Weatherby range of magnum calibres are still popular, however the newer SAUM and WSSM and WSM cartridges are gaining ground fast.

is the best of the lot because it uses better BC bullets than the smaller versions yet delivers tremendous down-range performance; it can also be had as an Ackley improved case with new factory Nosler custom brass.

A 154gr Interbond bullet can reach 2900fps, and when sighted in at 100yd (90m) zero drops -2.7in (6.85cm) at 200yd (183m), and -10.7in (27cm) at 300yd (274m), making it a usable open country or hill cartridge for elusive stags without going the magnum route. Even at 300yd there is 1947ft/lb energy left, which is over the minimum legal ft/lb energy figure to shoot deer; the Ackley version is even better.

The .30-06, like the .308, is an old stalwart of military parentage and the basis of all the preceding cartridges. The .308 can do anything the .30-06 can do, but falls short when bullets heavier than 180gr are necessary. In its Ackley improved form the .30-06 becomes a long-range deer round *par excellence*, and when throated correctly for VLD or other high BC bullets becomes a master at longer range varminting.

Standard loads include a 150gr bullet such as the Remington Swift Sirocco Bonded travelling

at over 2900fps and delivering 2802ft/lb energy, making a tough large species deer load. For those favouring a heavier bullet such as the 180gr, then a velocity of 2700fps is achievable and 200gr bullets such as the good Nosler Partitions can be pushed at 2550fps and give 3177ft/lb.

MAGNUMS, WSSM, WSM, LAZZERONI AND WEATHERBY

There are some very good magnums available to the British shooter, such as the flat-shooting 7mm Rem mag or the .264 Win mag, or if you prefer a bit more velocity then a .300 Win mag or .338 version may suit you better. Personally I would rather use a standard calibre and stalk just that bit closer than suffer the extra recoil, but these do have their place where longer shoots are tricky, or wily stags avoid all other attempts to approach them.

WSM cartridges (Winchester short magnum) from Winchester, and the similar Remington SAUM (short action ultra magnum) cases are an attempt to achieve the same ballistics as the long magnum designs but in a shorter and more squat case design for better efficiency and smaller rifle actions. Take the WSM case: at 2.10in (5.3cm) long, this is available in .270, 7mm, .300 and .323 calibre variants, with the .270 version's ballistics similar to the old .270 Weatherby case but in a smaller package, whilst the .300 WSM duplicates the longer 300 Win mag (2.620in/6.655cm in length) performance.

The WSSM (Winchester super short magnum) case is, in turn, a shortened WSM case that caters for vermin or fox shooters with the .223 WSSM, with velocities comparable to the .220 Swift case. With the .243 WSSM you outshoot the .243 Winchester cartridge, and performance is more like a .243 Ackley improved case design. Time will tell if they become popular here in Britain.

Roy Weatherby designed a whole series of magnum cartridges back in the 1940s, and for many years remained unchallenged as the king of magnum cartridges available to shooters. Small calibre .224 Weatherby magnums offer the fox shooter a flat-shooting 50gr bullet at 3900fps, and the larger .257 case spits out 117gr bullets at 3300fps and so is a good longer range deer cartridge. However, his supremacy has been usurped not just by the WSM and ultra mag cartridges, but also by John Lazzeroni who, like Weatherby, designed a totally new series of cartridges in the 1990s based on his own designed case. These have blistering ballistics to tackle any game, but at a price.

IMPROVED CARTRIDGE DESIGNS

Improving a cartridge usually involves altering the case dimensions to make it more efficient, or changing the calibre, or totally redesigning the case into a new wildcat round. The most famous are the P.O. Ackley improved cases, known simply as 'Ackley Improved', where an existing case, say a .243, has its body taper straightened to gain maximum powder capacity, coupled to a more aggressive shoulder angle, typically 40 degrees, to eliminate case stretching and case rearward thrust.

BULLET SIZES

It is important to remember that cartridge names often do not reflect the actual true size of the bullet being fired. In this I mean a .260 actually shoots a .264 diameter bullet, and this is also correctly called a 6.5mm projectile, whilst a .243 bullet is called a 6mm projectile but is actually 6.17mm in diameter. It is just a way that manufacturers use of naming cartridges differently from their competitors.

BULLET CHOICE

By far the most important consideration to the sportsperson is matching the bullet to the type of game you intend to shoot. Fail to do this and you run the risk of inadequate penetration, poor bullet expansion, or too much expansion causing surface wounds only. I will say it again, you

This .250 Savage shows at left, a standard case, and at right an improved case that has more powder capacity, less bolt thrust and less case lengthening.

can spend a fortune on equipment and clothing, but when that bullet leaves the muzzle you had better be sure you have chosen it not because it is the fastest or most accurate, but because at the end of its trajectory it can be depended upon to perform exactly how it should do to achieve a humane, first-shot kill.

Bullet Types

For all game species a predictable *expanding* bullet is necessary, and legal in the case of deer species, to affect the maximum energy transfer from projectile to the game, ensuring a lethal shot. However, not all expanding bullets perform the same, and what works on a rabbit or fox will not be suitable for larger species, and vice versa.

There is no magic bullet, but with careful thought the correct type can be used to its best capability.

Rabbits

With rabbits when using .22lr ammunition there is little choice. The projectile is made of lead mixed with antimony to varying harnesses. This is important, because although most sporting .22 rimfire ammunition sports a hollow point design, not all bullets expand the same due to differences in composition and depth of

hollow point (see the penetration tests in Chapter 10). .22 rimfire bullets are also notorious for ricocheting off most surfaces, but the ability to expand or fragment will also become a consideration when making your choice, and not just the accuracy.

The .17 Mach 2 and .17 HMR utilize a copper-jacketed bullet with polymer tip so that it expands rapidly on entry into the game, thereby performing two functions: rapid lethality and 'dumping' of energy into the vitals, and any pass-throughs are fragmented enough to be of less ricochet risk than a .22 lead bullet.

The only problem comes when bullet placement is less than perfect and the bullet expands primarily outside the chest cavity or cranium, and in these circumstances a nasty surface and non-fatal wound will result. This is why, with these fast .17 rimfires, the 20gr hollow point was invented, to allow sufficient penetration and then expansion to ensure swift results.

Foxes

In the same vein, bullets used for foxes shot from centrefire rifles not only have to stand up to higher pressures within the barrel, but also to faster rotational speeds as well as faster maximum speeds, and still expect to perform perfectly at the other end. Here you need a bullet's

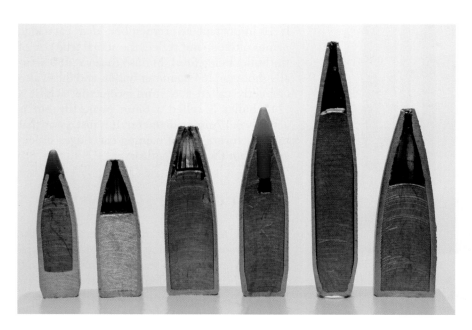

A selection of centrefire varmint bullets sectioned to show the differing internals that can alter their terminal ballistics so dramatically.

A selection of sectioned deer bullets showing the wide range of construction that will alter the way they will expand down range. Choose wisely!

jacket to have sufficient wall thickness to cope with the high velocities. Many smaller bullets designed for Hornet and Jet cartridges stipulate a maximum velocity for good reason: put those in a .22-250 and the bullet will break apart with the extra rotational speed.

All types of bullet are applicable here, and the choice is really yours. Some hollow points are tougher than polymer-tip bullets, such as Ballistic Tips, V-Maxes and Blitz Kings, whilst soft-nose round or flat varieties expand more slowly. Barnes Varmint Grenades use a sintered material instead of a lead core, which is supposed to vaporize on impact. I have had mixed results both with velocity dependency and accuracy.

For long-range fox work do not be put off by the heavier match-type ammunition and VLD format, because although they are designed for target work to glean as much ballistic advantage as possible, they often perform tremendously well at the terminal end with predictable expansion – the bullet test media has proved this to me.

Deer

Deer bullets are different. Whereas a fox round is usually travelling very fast and needs to penetrate a softer body form and then rapidly expand, a deer round needs to penetrate deeper into the body cavity and then expand enough to be lethal, but not cause too much venison damage. This is a tough order, depending on the size of the deer and the range you engage it. Here the ability to reload can be an enormous advantage over factory loads, because you can use one bullet type for all deer but load the velocity to suit the species size.

Factory ammunition will suffice for 90 per cent of all deer work, but careful reloading can yield optimal bullet performance.

When head or neck shooting, a fast, frangible bullet is desirable to instantly disrupt tissue. The classic heart/lung shot, on the other hand, calls for a more slowly expanding bullet that penetrates the hide and possibly rib bones, and then continues to expand, causing internal hydrostatic and mechanical tissue damage by imparting all that stored energy within it, and then exiting, causing an hydraulic effect which is lethal if the bullet is placed correctly.

If the range is no longer than 100–150yd (90–135m) I often choose a heavy bullet that travels more slowly for deer, because I prefer the kinetic shock effect, and there is less meat damage than is caused by the faster ballistic tip varieties. The only problem comes from over-penetration and the risk of ricochets. I have used this to great effect on muntjac and roe with the .338 BR using a 250gr bullet; everything would say this is too much weight for the smaller species, but at the sedate 1900fps and 2000ft/lb at short woodland ranges, its pure knock-down capabilities with little or no meat damage is amazing. Alternatively I use a fast expanding bullet such as a Nosler 125gr B. Tip, but run it at a slower speed, though still with deer-legal velocity and energy to achieve the same results.

Popular Bullet Designs

Most bullets from any manufacturer will follow the same format as below, but will have their own take on what they perceive to be a better design; I have therefore explained a few of the more popular ones here.

Hollow Point
The front section of the bullet is open with a void beneath, thus allowing the copper jacket to rupture, allowing the lead core to expand; how hollow depends on its application and the manufacturer. Berger makes an MEF, or 'maximum expansion effect', hollow point that is dynamite on small vermin.

Soft Nose
Conventional soft point bullets have the lead core exposed at the tip; this starts the bullet expansion and can have the form of either flat, round or spitzer design. For good all-round design, I use a 250gr round-nose bullet for the .338 BR, because the large front sectional area imparts real thump at the other end.

Nosler Ballistic Tips
Nosler have designed a polymer- (polycarbonate-) tipped bullet in both varmint (for rapid expansion) and deer construction (for predictable expansion). The polymer tip, colour coded to match the calibre, resists deformation, retains BC in flight, and starts the initial expansion on impact. The large jacket base drives the bullet forwards, and with no partition the degree of expansion is governed by velocity impact and whether you hit bone or tissue.

Sierra Blitz Kings
Sierra's bullet is very similar to the V-Max bullet in that it has a polymer tip to facilitate rapid expansion, and retains bullet form if knocked. The tips are all green and make very effective vermin control loads.

Hornady V-Max
Hornady's famous all-round vermin and fox bullet uses a polymer tip like the ballistic tip, which is designed to withstand hyper velocities. The tip when in contact with the target forces the thin jacketed wall and the lead core all expand very rapidly thus causing maximum energy transfer and little risk of ricochets. Coupled with often high BCs, a 40gr .20 calibre V-Max is a truly superb crow or fox bullet at any range.

Barnes X, Triple Shock
Barnes has become synonymous with solid copper bullets that penetrate deep and then expand, although they do back conventional lead-cored bullets too. The X bullet is solid copper to eliminate core separation, and the nose section has a hollow cavity to enable expansion. They are sometimes tricky to get shooting because their solid nature can cause fouling in the bore, however the Triple Shock with its three-ribbed bearing surface eliminates this problem.

Nosler Accubond
This is a really good deer bullet that combines a bonded lead core to avoid voids, helping concentricity and integrity on expansion, and a polymer tip to retain ballistic performance and ensure predictable expansion at the end of its trajectory. Accuracy, penetration and expansion from these bullets are excellent. The 120gr 6.5mm Accubond performs superbly in the 6.5 Rapier cartridge on both deer and foxes.

Hornady SST
This is a transition bullet that combines an aerodynamic ogive design for superior flight, but also expands rapidly; it has a thick jacket and an interlock ring to keep the rear lead portion secure to drive the bullet home. This is a great all-round deer bullet.

Speer Grand Slam
This is a more substantial bullet design for larger species of game. The flat base design has a protected soft nose to avoid damage, with the nose section of the jacket possessing thin fluted sections to allow expansion. The inner lead core is bonded to the copper jacket when the molten lead is poured into the bullet, to avoid separation. Grand Slams hit hard and cause minimal meat damage, but they can be pricey.

Fail Safe
The front section is solid copper alloy with a

hollow point to allow deeper penetration and weight retention, whilst the rear steel cup shields the lead core to drive the bullet forwards with minimal deflection.

Nosler Partition

A great bullet from Nosler with an integral partition of copper across its mid-section that allows the front thinner jacket to expand more quickly, whilst the shielded rear bullet section continues to drive forwards unaffected to allow deeper penetration. This is one of my favourites.

Barnes Varmint Grenades

This bullet is Barnes' creation for varmints, utilizing a sintered/granulated mixture of metals compressed within the thin copper-jacketed walls that initiate a violent expansion on impact. In practice you need to get the velocity right and match the seating depth to your rifle for best results.

Sectional Density and Ballistic Coefficients

Many factors influence a bullet's trajectory and terminal ballistics, not least its ability to be aerodynamic or to retain energy.

Sectional Density (SD) is simply the bullet's calibre or diameter in relation to the weight of the projectile. This is obtained by dividing the bullet's weight by the square of its diameter i.e. 150 grains .30 calibre bullet would be 0.226.

SD relates to a bullet's ability to perform on game in relation to its penetrating abilities as all 150 grain .308 calibre bullets have the same SD regardless of shape. But having a high SD is not the whole story as it does not convey the bullet's internal construction and how it will expand on target so you need to choose a bullet suitable for its end use.

Ballistic Coefficient (BC) is really a figure that tells a shooter how "wind slippery" the bullet is i.e. its ability to resist air resistance. Working out a BC is more difficult than SD figures although the two look very similar. A BC multiplied by the bullet's mass divided the square of the diameter figure is derived from a bullet's ability to overcome air resistance when compared to a 1 inch boat tail spitzer artillery shell. This is expressed as a coefficient or Ingalls number which equals the inverse drag of air on a bullet.

You can have a range of 150 grain 30 calibre bullets all with an SD of 0.226 but their BC will all be different due to their differing shapes.

The BC is more related to aerodynamic abil-

Depending on bullet style and internal design and velocities, not all bullets are equal.

Ballistic comparison between several .308 150gr bullets with differing ballistic coefficients

Calibre, Bullet style and BC	Range (yards)	Velocity (fps)	Energy (ft/lb)	Trajectory (inches)	Wind deflection (10mph)
.308	0	2800	2611	-1.8	0
150gr round nose	100	2326	1802	0	1.8
BC of 0.186	200	1900	1203	-4.7	8.0
	300	1531	781	-19.4	20.3
	400	1239	511	-49.4	39.8
.308	0	2800	2611	-1.8	0
150gr soft nose	100	2566	2193	0	0.9
BC of 0.387	200	2344	1830	-3.5	3.5
	300	2133	1516	-13.4	8.3
	400	1933	1245	-30.7	15.2
.308	0	2800	2611	-1.8	0
150gr Ballistic Tip	100	2591	2237	0	0.8
BC of 0.435	200	2392	1906	-3.4	3.0
	300	2202	1615	-12.9	7.3
	400	2020	1360	-29.6	13.4

ities and therefore has more of an influence on trajectory due to the shape of the bullet. It is a comparison between a standard model form to the bullet's deceleration due to air resistance. But it is not a constant figure and is influenced by velocity, changing as the bullet decelerates down range. Most bullet makers give an average BC figure, except Sierra but the PC ballistic program Quick Target will give multiple BC values to give exact trajectory curves for shooters.

Any bullet that has the same BC regardless of calibre that starts at the same velocity will have the same trajectory downrange. However as the BC increases so does the bullet's calibre, weight and length. That is why smaller bullets such as .224 diameter can never get to the figures of larger calibre bullets such as 6.5, 7 mm and .30 calibres as a length to weight ratio becomes impractical, i.e. the length is far too long. You need a good bullet mass coupled with high velocity for a high BC.

The BC goes up with more bullet weight and goes down with increased bullet diameter but the reality is that a high BC may make a bullet's trajectory better but it does not guarantee good accuracy. Always go with the diet your rifle prefers when shooting game.

Chapter 7
Scopes and Mounts

If you cannot see it you cannot hit it.

Although some manufacturers still produce rifles with open sights, it is rare these days that any sportsperson other than close quarter or dangerous game hunters will ever use them, so universal is the trend for using an optical scope. Scopes, although an additional cost, are of real benefit to the shooter in that not only is the target magnified, but a more precise aiming point is achievable with finer adjustments, and, really importantly, images can be resolved even in poor light, which is when most shooters are active.

Quality optics always pay dividends in the end, because not only do you experience better optical quality and image clarity, but colour retention and target recognition are all usually better. The lenses have multi layers of coatings in order to transmit the maximum amount of light, which is a huge advantage at dawn or dusk. Even more importantly, the sight adjustment and reticule type and position have to be totally precise and extremely robust to ensure a guaranteed zero. Add to this a waterproof, shockproof and fog-proof construction and a long-term warranty, and you start to see why scopes can often cost more than the rifles they sit on.

I always maintain that quality will out, but the truth of the matter is that many of us cannot afford the best on offer, and often have to take a more pragmatic route. In fact there are a lot of good, reasonably priced scopes these days, and you should be all right as long as you look carefully at what your shooting needs actually are, and are not swayed by sales jargon.

Never skimp on optics: always buy the best you can afford, and you will not be sorry you did.

Cheap scopes are cheap for a reason: they are mass-produced items with their components and manufacture sourced abroad. Costs are cut by the use of plastics and synthetic materials, and often the quality control is not what it should be. However, most shooting will take place at dawn or dusk in poor quality light, so my advice is to avoid high mag scopes because as soon as you combine high magnification with poor quality optics then you are in for trouble. It does not matter how large that front objective lens is, if the lens is poor without proper coatings for maximum light transmission, then

by the time the image reaches your eye it will seem dim and without clarity.

There is a lot spoken about scopes and their ability to give you that all-important last 30 minutes of light. Certainly this can be important, but what you should be ascertaining is their ability to hold good groups – also good build quality to withstand punishment, as well as to discriminate between quarry and foliage. More importantly as a precise placement device they must be reliable in *not* losing their zero, and in maintaining zero under any harshness of conditions. This is where similarly good optics fall down, as clarity is no trade-off for reliable, unshifting zero performance, especially when aiming at live targets.

When dealing with a wide range of quarry from rabbits to foxes and deer, there is a myriad of choices to suit all budgets; however, most have a common format and construction, and it is worth explaining these features.

CONSTRUCTION

Power, Objective and Tube Size

Tube size can be a contentious issue, as this not only influences the outside diameter of the scope but it also contributes to the lens size and therefore light-gathering abilities as well. Also a scope with a larger tube diameter has the potential to offer more internal adjustment for elevation and windage. The most common are 1in (25.4mm) tubes, as these allow a scope body to be mounted low to the rifle and when coupled with a well coated lens, offer all-round performance. 30mm tube diameters are more common on European scope models, although American, and now lower cost Chinese manufacturers, utilize this size. 30mm allows larger lenses and can be coupled to larger objective lenses to let more available light into the scope. Also the internal adjustment is larger, allowing better range of overall movement – although by their nature they are usually heavier depending on whether steel or aluminium is used.

1.3in (34mm) tubes are specialized items, but scopes such as the Schmidt and Bender and Zeiss offer a superb adjustment range for both precise and extra long range capabilities with specialized reticules with illumination, but achieve maximum light-gathering properties from which sporting users will benefit. The cost for such items is always high, as are the mounting systems to enable such a large scope to be fitted to your rifle.

Cheaper does not have to mean poorer, and there are some very good optics from the Far East capable of good work on vermin class rifles – the Lightstream is particularly good.

Whether compact, fixed power, variable or illuminated reticules, the choice is endless; these high end Swarovski scopes offer superb image quality and accurate adjustments not found on cheaper models.

There are two figures that one needs to understand when looking at a potential scope purchase: one is the magnification, and the other is the objective lens size. Their correlation is important if you are to achieve a clear image, even in poor light.

Scopes are described as 6×42, 7×50 and 8×56, or 3-9×40 and 3-12×50, where the first number is the magnification, either a single value or range, and the second is the objective or front lens. If the lens quality were the same, then a lower magnification and the largest objective size would allow the most light through the scope and therefore give the brightest image. However, although the image may be bright, it would be small, so more magnification is needed – but as this increases, if the objective size remains constant, then the image would become darker.

Obviously there is a trade-off here, as there are practical issues on maximum size with regard to costs and maintaining a practical mounting height to a rifle. Some prefer a fixed magnification, which uses fewer moving internal parts that are less liable to failure, although variable magnification scopes offer a good degree of flexibility; however, they have to be good quality in order to maintain zero throughout the entire zoom range.

TYPES OF SCOPE

Fixed Scopes

Fixed magnification scopes are suitable for all types of sporting shots where the user requires a straightforward, sturdy scope. However, prices can range from as little as £20 to over £700, depending on the quality of the optics and if illumination is included. For the beginner or small vermin shooter the cheaper scopes offer an entry level at a good price but you get what you pay for, although there are some bargains to be had. Typically fixed scopes are available as 2.5×32, 4×32, 6×42, 7×50, 7×56, 8×50, 8×56 and 10×42, but each hold a unique place for the sports shooter.

2.5×32 and 4×32 types give a greater field of view and instinctive point-and-shoot technique, and also double as good close-range rat scopes on rimfires, but for general day use a higher magnification version is preferable.

The 6×42, the stalker's classic, is one of the most versatile scopes you can own, offering more than good enough power for shooting at sensible ranges with an adequate objective lens size. Not only is it a one-scope stalker's favourite, but in reality is a straightforward and reliable rabbit or vermin scope, although you may want a little more power for fox work.

The humble 6×42 scope design is by far the favourite stalker's choice.

7×50 and 7×56 scopes are my favourite, as they have transitional qualities of magnification and an objective lens, which boost the power over the 6×42 and give more light-gathering abilities with the larger 50 or 56mm lens. The only problem is as the objective lens gets larger, so does the height you have to mount the scope, and this can affect proper scope-to-eye alignment.

10× plus magnification can be a tempting option offering a larger image and more precise aiming, but at the expense of more susceptibility to shake, and unless you have a quality lens and a larger objective lens size, the image will be less clear.

Variable Power

If fixed power reliability does not suit your shooting niche, then a variable power scope may well be a good option. More than anything the relevance of lens and build quality is even more paramount with variable scopes, as they have to work a lot harder optically and mechanically than their fixed power stable mates. Power range is dependent on application. Lower power variables such as the 1.1-4 or 1.5-5× values are really intended for fast target acquisition at running game, but they also work superbly well as super bright lightweight options for vermin or deer in woodland settings.

Probably a more practical power range has always been the traditional 3-9×40 scopes that blend good fields of view at the lower magnifications whilst still offering chances at longer range at maximum power. Variations on this theme include 1.5-6, 2.5-10, 3-12, 4-16 – in fact they are endless; again, set at the lowest magnification they allow a shot if a deer steps out on a ride at close range, or you call in a fox and it appears right in front of you. Then once settled in a high seat or resting on a bipod, you have time to change to a higher magnification if required. If you start on a high magnification and a deer jumps you, all you will see is brown pelage in the scope, and the chance is gone.

Long-range varmints and some fox shooters often require specialized high power scopes such as Nightforce's excellent NXS range with illuminated reticules, Schmidt and Bender's long-range 4-16×50 scope with graduated long-range varmint dot reticule, which works superbly, Leopold's 8-25×50 VX range of dedicated scopes with Varmint hunter reticules for precise long-range shot placement, and Zeiss's enormous 6-24×72T scope with good mag range and stupendous light-gathering qualities with that huge 72mm objective lens.

FIELD OF VIEW AND EYE RELIEF

Field of view is a major concern, especially for close-quarter woodland scenarios where maximum field of view is beneficial to give a safe and clearer picture of the surrounding environment for the shot. The lower the magnification the wider the field of view; however, this is not always practical, and whereas at higher magnification the detail is more resolved, you have a far narrower field of view and can easily lose a target. Many European scopes have large eyepiece optics that help, whilst Swarovski have gone one further in their new Z6 range of scopes. These push the boundaries of scope technology, particularly in respect of wider fields of view for variable scopes, which has always been an issue.

Eye relief is best maintained for any changing magnification, especially on a heavily recoiling rifle, otherwise contact with the forehead will occur, especially when taking awkwardly angled shots. A minimum of 3in (7.5cm) is practical, and check the scope at all power settings because if it is a variable then at higher magnifications eye relief becomes critical to gain a complete sight picture.

EXIT PUPIL, RELATIVE BRIGHTNESS AND TWILIGHT FACTOR

Exit Pupil

An often touted figure to describe the performance of rifle scopes is the exit pupil. This can be a blessing or not, and does not really give the whole picture with regard to scope performance, as many other factors influence this. Exit pupil is simply the objective size of a scope divided by the magnification, therefore a fixed power 6×42 or 8×56 scope has a figure of 7mm, whilst a variable power scope of 2-10×50 has a value range between 25 and 5.

What does this actually tell you? The human eye is capable of a pupil dilation of a maximum of 7mm, so anything above this is wasted, and below it is not optimal. However, in reality image quality is very dependent on the quality of the lens and coatings used.

Relative Brightness (RB)

This is a scope's capability to transmit light from the image seen to the human eye which can resolve 1in at 100yd or 1min of angle, and the factors that affect a scope's performance are objective lens and power. RB is the square of the exit pupil figure; with a 6×42 compared to a 4-12×40 scope of the same manufacture set at 12 power, the smaller objective lens gives a value of 49 whereas the larger power 12× has a value of 10.9 to give a dimmer image.

But this is only a numerical figure in relation

to the scope's exit pupil, and must be taken in relationship with the twilight factor figures to get a balanced view of the overall picture. The problem comes when you compare, say, a 1.5-5 ×20 scope set at 1.5 magnification that has a 13.3 exit pupil and a RB of 176.9, with that of a 8×56 scope with an exit pupil of 7 but RB of 49: the image from the 8×56 scope of a target at range will always look clearer. This is mainly because the human pupil never exceeds 7mm so it cannot accommodate the larger light beam of the 1.5× magnification; however, it does help with a greater field of view.

The Twilight Factor

With this in mind another useful figure is the twilight factor (TF), where a figure is given for the intensity of light transmitted by the relationship between the magnification and objective size and thus exit pupil; this is stated as the square root of the magnification × objective. The eye does not always have an exit pupil of 7mm: that is the maximum dilation under the worst lighting conditions to allow in maximum light. On a bright day the human pupil can be at 2mm dilation, so a scope with an exit pupil of 7mm under poor lighting conditions will always be best.

Therefore an 8×56 scope would have a twilight factor of 21.2, whilst a 6×42 scope has a value of 15.9, despite having the same RB value of 49. The image of the 8 power will be brighter and relates to the ability to distinguish the target with more clarity, whereas a 2.5-10×56 scope set at 2.5 has a fantastic 501.8 RB but a low 11.8 TF value, so the image is no clearer at distance. Why is that?

Light intensity is the reason, because the farther away your quarry is from the scope, the more the intensity of light changes inversely to the square of that distance. It sounds complicated but it is relevant. The factor here is not the sectional area of light reaching the eye (that is, 7mm in the dark) but the intensity or luminescence of the light within that beam and how it changes with distance through the intervening space.

Therefore a deer at 100yd (90m) has 1/10,000th of the intensity of light as compared

LEFT: *As regards twilight factors, the huge Zeiss 72mm objective lens is amazing in its capability to gather light and resolve an image under the worst lighting situations.*

OPPOSITE: *Scopes have come a long way from the barrel mounted scopes of yesteryear.*

with a deer at 10yd (9m) that has 1/100th (the inverse of the square of the distances). Which is why distance quarry vanishes in poor light, whilst closer game can be seen more readily. But how does the scope's magnification alter things? If you take the exit pupil maximum of 7mm and therefore RB value of 49 for both the 6×42 and 8×56 scopes, then a deer that steps out of a wood at 200yd (182m) has a viewed range of only 33.3yd (30.4m) by the 6 power scope, whilst the 8 power scope reduces that range to 25yd (22.8m). If you square the two values and inverse them, you have 1/1,109th and 1/625th

for the 6 and 8 powers respectively, showing that the 8×56 is the better choice in bad light as it gives an intensity 1.8 times better than that viewed through the 6×42 scope, although both have the same exit pupil size.

ADJUSTMENTS

Scope adjustments are critical in order to align precisely the bullet's point of impact with the scope's reticule. Today all adjustments take place within the scope's body, but the first scopes

Common scopes with the exit pupil, relative brightness and twilight factor values calculated for comparison

Scope specification	Exit pupil	Relative brightness	Twilight factor
1.5-5×20	13.3-4	176.9-16	5.5-10
4×32	8	64	11.3
6×42	7	49	15.9
7×50	7.1	50.4	18.7
8×50	6.25	39.1	20
8×56	7	49	21.2
4-12×40	10-3.3	100-10.9	12.7-21.9
4-12×50	12.5-4.2	156.3-17.6	14.1-24.5
2.5-10×56	22.4-5.6	501.8-31.4	11.8-23.7
5.5-22×56	10.2-2.6	104-6.8	17.6-35.1
6-24×72	12.0-3	144-9	20.8-41.6

often had external adjustment dials rather like vernier gauges such as the old Fecker, Unertl, Lyman and even the first Tasco scopes.

Scopes can have covered adjustment turrets (Hunter style) that you adjust, then leave set, or target turrets that are larger and offer instant adjustment without removing a cover. Each adjustment is made by a rotating dial with audible or felt clicks per interval, and the value for each click and the maximum number of clicks per elevation and windage varies according to each scope manufacturer.

Most commonly one click represents a ¼in (7mm) movement of the reticule at 100yd (90m) distance, and therefore four clicks is 1in (25mm), and most scopes are thus marked. If the zero range is closer, say 50yd (45m), then twice the number of clicks is necessary to move the reticule the same amount (that is, eight clicks as one click now only represents ⅛in/3mm of travel). Conversely at a longer range, say 200yd (182m), one click will represent ½in (13mm) movement.

Most scopes have ¼in (7mm) adjustment dials, which is fine for coinciding bullet impact with reticule, however especially on higher magnification scopes used at longer ranges for foxes or varmints on small targets, a finer adjustment per click can be desirable. Target models and varmint scopes often come with one-eighth clicks, giving finer adjustments, and have tall target turrets that are more visible and suitably marked to allow a fast and precise elevation or windage change when the range and wind conditions change.

Swarovski scope owners have ⅙in (4mm) adjustments, which is hedging your bets, and many German scopes such as Schmidt and Bender have metric adjustments of one click for 1cm movement.

For most shooters ¼in (7mm) are fine enough; what really matters is that each adjustment is exactly what it states it is, and on cheaper models this may not be the case. As a rule I always test a new scope on the range before venturing out into the field for live game by 'shooting the box', carrying out a variable magnification test and ascertaining maximum adjustment travel.

'Shooting the box' involves checking two aspects of proper scope function. Firstly it tells the shooter if the scope is vertically aligned to the bore axis, which is crucial to avoid canting the rifle. The other is to check that the scope's adjustment clicks are the same for each click, thus allowing confidence and precise bullet placement. The procedure is easy, and best accomplished off a bench rest at a distance of 50yd (45m) for rimfires and 100yd (90m) for fullbore rifles.

Shoot a three-shot group to the centre of the target where the cross hairs bisect. Now adjust the windage by turning the turret thirty-two clicks to the right, which will shift the bullet's impact right by 8in (20cm) at 100yd for a ¼in (7mm) click scope or 4in (10cm) at 50yd. Keep the same zero, and shoot three more shots. Now adjust the elevation turret the same amount and shoot three more shots, and then adjust the scope thirty-two clicks left and shoot three more shots. Finally adjust the elevation turret thirty-two clicks down, and the final three shots should group exactly with the original group shot. If they do not, the scope does not 'track' accurately, or it skips a few adjustments, or moves impact-differing amounts per click.

Reticule adjustment for windage, elevation, parallax or illumination can vary from one scope to the next, so learn your own scope's adjustment range, and you will shoot better for this.

Also study the squareness of the box formed: if the sides are not perpendicular to one another and to the axis of the target, then the scope is incorrectly fitted and on a cant.

The most cause for concern with regard to variable power scopes is their ability to maintain zero throughout the scope's full magnification range. It is no good having a good lens if the scope changes zero at differing power settings. So the next step is the variable magnification test. Again, shoot from a steady rest at the range suitable for the calibre of rifle, and shoot either a single shot or three-shot group at each power setting on the scope, and check the point of impact for each shot. If all the shots group together without any outliers, then your scope has sufficient reliable performance to take it out shooting – if it does not, dump it.

Another aspect to correct scope use is to check the total travel of both elevation and windage adjustments, as the turret may be turning but is the impact shifting? It's amazing how many people take it as read that the turret's segmentation gives the full adjustment. First, click each adjuster to maximum 'in' and maximum 'out' adjustment, and take note of the number of turns plus clicks. Halve this number for both turrets, and adjust back to this value so the scope's internals should be optically centred within the main tube. Now shoot a group at 50yd (45m). It will not correspond to the cross hairs, but no matter. Use a large white target bisected into 1in (2.5cm) squares; now adjust up the same quantity of clicks, say sixteen at a time, and shoot a shot, then a further sixteen clicks until you notice no further elevation to the shot. Repeat this for the down adjustment, and left and right windage. It is time-consuming, but worth doing to get the exact and entire range.

PARALLAX

An often misunderstood problem with scopes is called 'parallax error', where the reticule seems to shift its point of aim on a target as you move your eye left or right looking through the scope. This is why shooting technique and exact scope-to-eye alignment must remain the same for each

Diagram to show how a scope mounted with a canted angle can adversely affect your trajectory; the 'shooting the box' method to check alignment eliminates this.

shot. Most scopes designed for full-bore rifles are parallax free at 100yd, thus even some eye movement results in minimal parallax error, whilst rimfire scopes used at shorter ranges have a parallax set for 50yd (45m).

To allow more flexibility, some scopes, especially higher magnification and variable scopes, have an adjustable parallax ring either on the objective bell or side-mounted on the adjustment bowl. This can be used to eliminate parallax at any range, which is very handy, whilst still maintaining focus at closer ranges even on the highest magnification. The better quality models can also be used to reasonably estimate range if set on the highest magnification and then when the focus is crisp, the range can be read off the scale on the parallax ring.

RETICULES

Types of Reticule

The first scopes had a simple, fine cross-hair reticule and were not optically centred, which meant that as the elevation or windage was adjusted, the cross hairs would move in the field

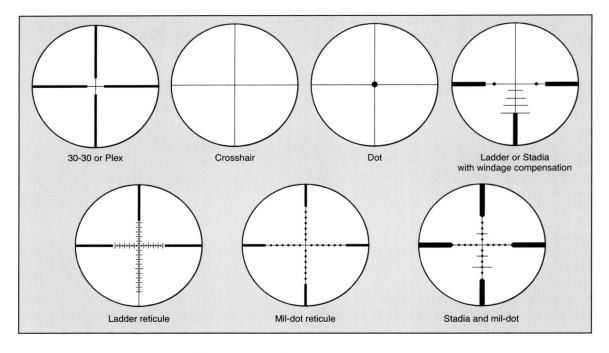

Diagram to show the wide choice of reticule styles, from cross hairs to trajectory-compensating stadia designs.

of view accordingly. Today optically centred reticules maintain the same reticule image regardless of maximum adjustment, and are available in a refreshing variety.

Choice is really a personal issue, but you need to be practical. Too fine a reticule on a rabbit gun and it will be impossible to see in dark conditions or against foliage, although it may be advantageous for a long-range varmint scope used for more precise bullet placement in better light. Conversely too thick a reticule and you run the risk of covering too much of the quarry and not being able to accurately place a shot, especially when using a deer scope on a rabbit rifle.

The most common reticule is the 30/30, which has four thick outer posts with a finer inner cross hair. In this way you have a good central aiming mark but with highly visible outer sections that show up in darker situations and lead your eye to the central portion. Variations on this theme abound, with differing thickness of stadia line and without top posts for less coverage of game. Common in Europe were the

post reticules that have a central point post with two converging side posts. This type of reticule is good for close-range use with fast target acquisition, but is less popular than the crosshair types.

More elaborate reticules used for range finding or bullet drop compensation can be a real advantage, as the stadia lines are well spaced and not overly complicated. Most manufacturers offer a scope so configured, utilizing both stadia lines with or without additional dots for elevation as well as windage compensation.

Scopes such as the larger varmint scopes from Nightforce have a good range of diverse reticules, from Mil dot to some very fancy stadia and dot designs such as the NP1-RR that utilizes stadia, dots and range-finding circles, and the NP-R2 ladder design that allows trajectory and wind adjustment at extreme range when the bullet's path is calculated and relevant reference stadia have been identified. All these make, for example, engaging small crows at long range more precise. S&B have some very good military PM-11 scopes, but the one I like is the 4-16×50 long-range model that sports a fine dot reticule and see-through posts so as not to obscure the quarry. The dots are placed on the bottom vertical posts at intervals, and with the aid of the Quickload ballistics program you can tailor-make a range drop card for most calibres to correspond to each dot.

Zeiss has external turreted click-adjustable or bullet-compensating turrets for specific calibres, and when coupled to their superb optics, offer excellent varmint, fox or deer scopes. Leupold, too, offer trajectory-compensating reticules for deer stalkers with the Bone and Crockett design and a similar finer reticule for varmint shooting. Leupold and Zeiss also offer a retro-fit turret conversion to calibrate your factory or reloaded ammunition to correspond to exact divisions on target-style turrets. Swarovski utilize a TDS ladder-style reticule system, again suitable for engaging targets at longer range, with the addition of useful windage dots to compensate for wind. Kahles on some scopes have a ladder reticule, but also the very good CS multi-drop turret system that uses an infinitely variable trajectory compensation elevation turret with moveable rings as a visual marker for scope adjustments at differing ranges; this is fast and very accurate.

First or Second Focal Plane

Simply put this in the position in which the reticule is placed within the scope, and how it relates to the actual image you see at varying magnifications.

First focal plane scopes have reticules set up in the adjustment bowl of the scope, and in a variable scope as the magnification is changed, so does the size of the reticule. In second focal plane scopes the reticule remains the same size at any magnification range, with the reticule sited in the eyepiece section of the scope.

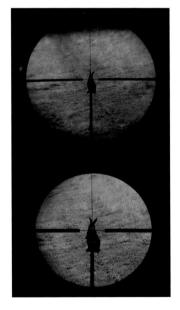

1st focal plane
Relationship of reticule stays constant with regard to the rabbit at any magnification setting.

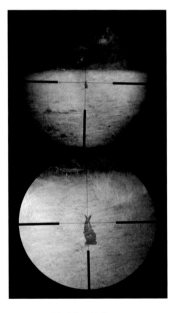

2nd focal plane
As magnification increases (bottom frame), so does the relationship of between reticule and rabbit. At low magnification (top) the thick line is a long way from the rabbit, but not at high magnification (bottom).

The first two images show the first focal plane reticule, where there is a constant reticule relationship to the rabbit at any magnification. The second focal plane scope with changing magnification will shift the reticule placement on the rabbit — see the second of the two pictures.

There are advantages and disadvantages to both types. First focal plane scopes always keep the same relationship between the reticule position and the target position, regardless of zooming between the magnifications. This means that on a reticule with more than just a cross hair and having many stadia lines, each line remains in perfect relationship to the target and thus is very useable for trajectory compensating. On the down side, on a variable power scope the reticule size will increase in size within your vision, which means that on the highest mag the reticule may be too thick and will cover a small target such as a rabbit or crow.

A second focal plane variable scope's reticule remains the same size at any magnification, but on a stadia reticule only the central cross hairs remain in the same relationship to the target, as the magnification is varied. This means you have to memorize or write down a bullet's trajectory compensation for each magnification setting, which is tedious. However, the reticule does not enlarge and cover too much of what you are shooting at.

Fixed power scopes are unaffected by the above.

Illumination

Popular today are scopes with illuminated reticules. Once only available on the most expensive scopes, cheap electronics means that scopes from the Far East invariably have some form of illumination as standard. All illumination is not the same, however, and the cheap variants invariably illuminate the whole reticule, with poor control on brightness, and can cause nasty glare at night. Scopes such as Swarovski, Zeiss, Kahles and Schmidt and Bender use a partially illuminated system typically with very low / dim settings, which is what you want as a night illumination, just enough to see the finer section of the central reticule without destroying your night vision.

The new Swarovski Z6 series have a dedicated day and night switch operation for a very precise illuminated reticule for any poor light shooting. In reality you may never use the illuminated option much, but when that stag disappears into the dark canopy of the pine trees and you lose that reticule among the foliage and branches you may just curse the fact that you did not pay the extra for that illuminated option.

LASER RANGE-FINDER SCOPES

No matter what you think about the increased reliance on technological gadgetry, it is here to stay, and no one item epitomizes this ethos more than the new wave of rifle scopes that incorporate an integral laser range-finding device. Stalkers and foxers have found the benefits of hand-held ranging devices for decades now, and

Illuminated reticules give a scope diversity for dawn and dusk use when the reticule may become unclear. The new Z6 scope from Swarovski allows night and day illumination settings.

they have become a common sight in the game fields. Their ability to accurately determine the range to your target affords the benefit of enabling you to place a shot precisely, which has to be an advantage in terms of a humane shot. The problem comes when the laser is abused by the shooter taking a shot at too far a distance, in which he is not proficient.

Two of the laser scopes are very similar. The Burris 4-12×42 and the Bushnell Yardage Pro 4-12×42 share the same magnification range, whilst the Zeiss has a 2.5-10×50 model from the Victory range called the Diarange. You get what you pay for, and cheaper options are susceptible to weather and temperature extremes.

Bushnell Yardage Pro

Despite its bulky look, this scope's 25oz (708g) weight and 13in (33cm) length is actually no problem, and is no more than some large varmint scopes. It sits very easily to your rifle via an integral rail mount system with weaver-style mounting bases.

The turret is segregated into four clicks per interval, and there are twelve numbered segments giving 12in (30cm) adjustments per turn at 100yd (90m). This applies to the windage turrets, but the Bushnell also comes with a series of removable bullet-drop compensating turrets as standard. In this way, by referring to the data in the manual or supplied cd, you can choose the best fit turret to match the trajectory of your load. Activation of the laser is conveniently operated by a static rubber button on the main tube, which has a dual purpose. Press the top section and the setting for yards or metres is activated, and it is nice to have an option whilst the main section is used to work the laser. The range is displayed above the line of sight so as not to obscure your target, and appears on a faint blue band that is hardly noticeable.

There is no illuminated reticule, but the Mil-dot design allows a useful bullet-drop compensation if you did not want to use the turrets or just needed a faster target acquisition. There is also no parallax adjustment, so on full magnification (twelve) at shorter ranges the image reticule will seem blurred, so just turn down the mag.

Laser scopes give the shooter an instant range readout within the scope's field of view; top to bottom: Bushnell, Burris and the Zeiss.

Burris Laser Scope

Although initially appearing to be very similar to the Bushnell, the Burris differs in several ways. Cosmetically the whole scope body has a small profile change, but all the main features are in the same place as the Bushnell. Only the objective, turrets, reticule and mounting system differ significantly. The Burris has the proviso for a sunshade fitment, which is supplied. The mounts are the simplest of the lot and allow a very low scope-mounting profile, and incorporate a single weaver-style cross-bolt securing unit. The magnification ring is subtly different and much smoother on this model, although the same battery compartment is utilized. The turrets on the Burris are a more conventional layout, and with the caps removed the fixed turrets are low profile – so once you zero the scope return the protective caps and leave well alone. So how can you compensate for range? Well, the Burris relies on a range-compensating reticule, naming their patent Ballistic Plex, although a Mil-dot system is now offered.

The Zeiss laser range-finding scope is designed to give accurate readings coupled with superb optics that will perform in any weather scenario.

Zeiss Diarange

At nearly £2,000, the Zeiss is the most expense of the scopes but does not come with a remote, sunshade or mounts. However, all but the sunshade are available as extras. The mounting system is the integral Zeiss rail running the entire length of the underneath of the scope body. The length of this model is a scant 13.5in (34cm), and takes up no more room than a conventional hunting scope, although the weight is 32.5oz (920g).

The laser is externally mounted on the left side, and is rated to 999m maximum range; it is powered by a single CR123 battery located directly behind the laser. Operation is from a convenient push button sited at the base left of the body by your supporting hand; a remote can be purchased as an extra, but this is hard wired.

Talking of reticules, there is a good choice from Zeiss. This model had the number sixty, which is a 4a type with a floating centre dot that is illuminated. Only the Zeiss has this feature, which makes sense on a sporting scope to allow precise shot placement as the light fades. Furthermore the magnification range of 2.5 to 10 is just about perfect, and the 50mm objective is more than big enough for superior light gathering; so for optical quality the Zeiss wins hands down.

NIGHT VISION

Popular among rabbiters and fox shooters, night vision scopes are becoming more popular, but the expense and, more importantly, sourcing a good, reputable and sustainable supplier has always been the Achilles heel for these types of optics.

Many units have generic body shells as a stand-alone unit only for night use, or there are day and night optics that can be switched, and also the option of attaching a light-intensifying unit to the front or rear of an existing scope. I have used all types, and have found that unless you spend thousands of pounds, their use can be problematical.

The real problem is that mounting systems vary, and can be too high to be used comfortably, or the IR tube blocks the use of the bolt, or both – but by far the worst problem is the choice of intensifier tube.

The main part of the night sight is the removable intensifier tube, and the Gen 1 or Gen 2 models, with many varying sub categories, are the choice, with differing levels of image brightness, quality, manufacturers and price. But remember quality costs. The Centaur 165 is a dedicated night sight, self-contained, and with an XR-5 tube fitted and 6× power lens it offers a good 200yd (182m) fox scope, with the ability to see far beyond: this is very important so that a safe background can be observed before the shot. However, at the time of writing it costs the best part of £5,000!

MOUNTS

Types and Styles

Rimfires and some of the smaller centrefires produce light recoil, and so mounting a scope is not as problematic as with larger calibres. However, it is never wise to skimp on the scope's mounting system, as this can be the weakest link in the rifle set-up, and to avoid spending money in this area can be foolhardy. Many rimfires have integral dovetail scope rails, which then only need a set of one-piece mounts to be fitted accurately. Be careful to choose mounts that have perfectly square/flat bottoms to the base, otherwise the mount will tilt to one side when secured and thus cause a canting problem. Mounts such as Sports Match, Sako and BKL all offer strong, precise and lightweight mounts in varying heights.

Others use drilled and tapped tops to the receiver bridge, and allow you to decide on the make and style of mount you wish to purchase. The spacing between the two fixture screws can be the same for many models or makes of rifles, but the top bridge may be of differing heights. Leupold, Burris, Hillver, Warne and Apel, to name but a few, make bases and rings to suit most modern and some obscure sporting rifles.

Rail Mounts

There are proprietary brand scopes such as Zeiss, Swarovski, Kahles and Schmidt and Bender, which instead of using a ring system to clamp the scope body to the mount, have a one-piece rail integrally fitted to the base of the scope tube. This gives an extremely strong, positive and multi-positional mounting system to any rifle, although it seems more popular in Europe than any other country.

Quick Detachable (QD) Mounts

The ability to interchange scopes between rifles is not a new concept, and indeed it has its benefits as well as determents. By a swift change of optics the same rifle can become a long-range fox gun, or a hill rifle, or a close-quarter woodsman, negating the need for two types of rifle if the calibre were correct. If damage were incurred on a stalking trip, a spare scope could be confidently and easily replaced with a pre-zeroed substitute. Or just as a precautionary measure whilst travelling, the scope can be safely stowed away from the rifle, free from knocks and scratches.

The problem arises in that to be able to achieve this, the scope rings and mounts have to be very well made to ensure an absolute non-shifting zero when they are removed and then remounted.

The most common mounting system,

A dedicated night vision scope such as this Centaur 165 with high grade XR-5 intensifier tube can spot foxes at 200yd (183m) with no problems.

generically called a 'Weaver' base, allows the scope rings to fit not only their own bases but also most other Weaver-type systems. At the base of each ring set is a cross-bolt configuration that slots precisely into the base unit attached to the rifle, and thus helps to ensure a more uniform alignment. Picatinny rails are very similar, although some copies, such as IOR from Romania, have differing slot widths and may not suit all ring types.

Manufacturers such as Leupold, Conetrol and Sako have their own Q/D mount systems, with Warne producing some dedicated mounts from specific rifles such as the 30mm Maxima rings for the Tikka; these proved very accurate, returning to zero after removal and reattachment of the scope. Because these rings fit directly to the rifle's own receiver it is important to position the scope and mounts to the same position or positive stop each time in order to achieve maximum accuracy. Also, keep the grooves or dovetails clean of debris between scope mounting, otherwise this will interfere with your zero.

EAW / Apel mounts are among the best Q/D mounts in the world, and they make high quality units for most makes of rifle, and most scopes ever made. Their swing-off return to zero rings and bases for tube or rail scopes are beautifully made, and rather than lift off and up from the base mount (although claw types are available), they detach from the rear base with a simple lever action and then swing right side from the action to rotate and disengage a tapered foot on the front mount. They are adjustable and do not lose zero.

As a convenient way to store, change roles or clean your rifle, the Q/D scope mount system from any manufacturer certainly makes for a more confident and versatile shooting arrangement.

Fitting a Scope

Often when you fit a scope if the mounts or rings, or indeed the dovetails are not lined up with the bore axis perfectly, an optically centred scope can require a lot of adjustments to zero the rifle. At these extreme maximum adjustments you are not looking through the scope's best optical centre and thus aberrations or vignetting can occur, as well as limited scope adjustment. If you want to adjust for elevation at longer ranges, you may be running on full adjustment. One way to avoid this stressing on the scope (and yourself) is to purchase a scope mounting set that has some form of adjustment to the bases or rings, so all the coarse adjustments to zero the rifle are taken up with their

Quick-release mounts mean that a rifle can change from a long range to a close-quarter rifle in a trice if desired.

Apel swing-off mounts return to zero precisely and allow a shooter to fit one or more scopes to the same rifle, or to keep a scope safe for storage.

movement, and the scope's internal adjustments are then only used for fine tuning.

Millet offer mounts that have Allen key slotted bolts securing clamps to either side of the mount base, and can independently adjust the scope for left or right bias, rather like the old Sako design.

Burris offer their Signature range of scope mounts that have rings in either 1in or 30mm sizes, with a separate plastic circular collar that fits around the scope tube and then in the scope rings. This allows the scope's tube to position itself correctly when the ring top screws are tightened, avoiding stresses to the scope body, very much like the Sako Optilok system. However, Burris have a clever design feature that allows differing plastic collars with sloped internal edges to allow a scope to tilt down at varying degrees to compensate for lack of scope adjustment within the scope's internal adjustments, or just by keeping the scope optically centred for maximum internal adjustment.

Apel mounts are famous for their swing-off and return to zero manufacture, and many of them also have provision in the rear mount to adjust for windage as desired.

Bases – either one-piece or two-piece sets – can benefit from some form of built-in forward slope that allows the scope to tilt downwards, and thus allows more elevation adjustment for

longer-range shooting, especially if you have a fine one-eighth adjustment scope with limited internal travel. Often called MOA (minute of angle) compensation mounts, they are usually designated by the amount of compensation they offer: thus 10 MOA or more commonly 20 MOA allows a shooter to gain 20in (50cm) more of adjustment at 100yd (90m) range. One minute of angle equates approximately to 1in (2.5cm) at 100yd. Ken Farrel from the USA makes some of the best for the more popular rifle makes, in either one- or two-piece designs.

Some scope mounts offer a degree of flexibility in scope mounting options.

Chapter 8
Sound Moderators

Until recently moderators were not a common sight in the British countryside, except for the humble .22 rimfire variety that was used on many a rabbit rifle. Sound moderators for larger calibres were scarce due to the limited number of manufacturers producing them, besides which obtaining the necessary authority to own one in the first place was also a problem. Thankfully the sportsperson in Britain now enjoys a more relaxed attitude to moderator ownership, and there has been considerable advancement in sound moderator growth and design.

Choice between full bore moderators was easy in days gone by, there being only a few options of old-fashioned yet very effective muzzle-mounted cans. Vaime in the 1980s, and later Vaimeco from Finland were the industry standards. Then shooters began to require ever more efficient sound moderators with less overall length, leading to the development of 'over the barrel' mounted moderators. New Health at Work safety decibel levels, and fears of litigation from professionals and sportspersons who used firearms each day, accelerated the use of these short, highly efficient sound moderators.

The new over-barrel design first appeared on these shores as the PES and the Reflex, the PES originally for sporting use and the Reflex as a military unit, but soon both were embraced by the sporting market because they enabled a shooter to fire a full bore rifle without ear defenders, and to enjoy total flash elimination and less recoil – the benefits were therefore palpable and most welcome. Since then the whole suppressor industry has rapidly developed here in the UK, and the British shooter now has a bewildering array of small and full bore moderators to choose from, some good and others not so good.

The sound moderator has become an essential item in Britain, offering benefits with regard to noise and recoil reduction and muzzle blast elimination, all of which helps you shoot more accurately.

DEFINITION AND BENEFITS

So what is a sound moderator, and what are its benefits to the shooter? It is a device that slows and cools the rapidly expanding gases as they exit the barrel's muzzle in order to reduce the noise signature. It is usually cylindrical in shape and possesses a series of internal baffles that progressively retard the forward motion of these gases, thus reducing their energy/heat and therefore noise level, usually expressed as decibels (dB). There are many designs and shapes, but all are trying to achieve maximum noise reduction and thereby stealth in usage, not only to lower the shooter's profile in the presence of other humans, but also so as not to disturb other wildlife.

There are other immediate benefits that are often not appreciated: first, up to 40 per cent of the rifle's recoil is reduced when a moderator is fitted, greatly enhancing the user's comfort and his ability to shoot the rifle accurately. Second, bulky ear protection need not be worn, so the hunter is less impeded; and often the barrel harmonics are damped down by the additional weight thereby further increasing the accuracy potential of the rifle. No wonder the sound moderator market is so popular in Britain today, as the benefits far outweigh the initial cost of purchase.

Sound moderators can be sourced for any calibre now commonly available to the shooter, from the diminutive .22 rimfire, to the higher velocity fox calibres such as the .22-250, and on to the venerable deer calibres such as the .243 .308 and .30-06. The only difference is size and the materials used in their construction, and it is important to consider this when choosing what type is suitable for your calibre: some people are convinced that the largest moderator is going to be the best in terms of noise reduction, but this is not always the case, and it is the deadening quality and the longevity of the materials used that have become a greater deciding factor amongst the more perspicacious sporting fraternity.

It is a myth that a moderator can make a rifle's report be totally silent, especially when using supersonic velocity ammunition, where a bullet breaks the sound barrier at 1050fps depending

ABOVE: Choice for the shooter is growing daily, with muzzle-mounted and over-barrel designs manufactured in all manner of materials.

on temperature and so incurs the sonic boom. This phenomenon cannot be reduced in noise; only the expanding propellant gases or muzzle blast can be extinguished or reduced on entry to the atmosphere after passage through the moderator. This means that subsonic ammunition – below the speed of sound, as in .22lr loads or some specialized centrefire ammunition – *can* be truly 'silent' because there is no supersonic boom, and all the gases can be suppressed so any noise exiting the moderator is minimal.

TYPES OF MODERATOR

There are three main types of sound moderator or suppressor, and they are directly distinguished according to the way they are secured to the rifle's barrel: they are known as muzzle-

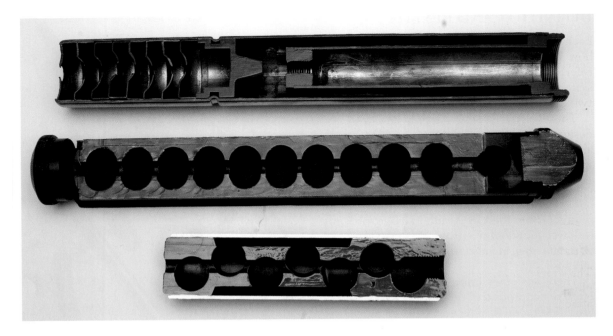

ABOVE: *Top: a sectioned PES T12 showing the fitment of the barrel up inside the moderator, with rear expansion chamber and minimal length in front of the muzzle. Middle: the Vaime shows a typical muzzle-mounted moderator where the barrel attaches to the rear with all the baffles in front of the muzzle. Bottom: a SAK rimfire muzzle can, for comparison.*

LEFT: *Selection of baffles used in full bore moderators offered to the British shooter.*

mounted, over-the-barrel or fully suppressed. Each design has its benefits or not, depending on how it is used. Further problems occur when referring to single- or dual-point mounting systems, where the moderator has a single- or two-point contact with the barrel.

There is an eclectic mix of old and new designs, of baffle and non-baffle systems available to the British sportsperson today, with all manner of materials on offer. It is up to the end user to choose, according to their own particular set of circumstances and needs; below is described a selection of the best that is available.

Muzzle-Mounted Suppressors

The simplest mounting system, often called single-point mounting, is where the suppressor is attached directly to the muzzle of the barrel via a threaded section, and is thus held secure and aligned. The threaded section size depends on the diameter and calibre of the barrel, and can be in imperial or metric measurement. Whichever is the case, the thread must be undercut to allow the moderator to sit squarely to the bore's axis so the bullet can pass freely.

With this system all the moderator's effectiveness is forward of the muzzle, and as such increases the overall length of the rifle quite considerably. This is the one drawback of a muzzle-mounted moderator; nevertheless it can be a very efficient and cost-effective system despite this.

Full Bore Types

The PES 32mm and 38mm: Amongst the best designs are the PES 32mm or 38mm diameter moderators from New Zealand; these are constructed from stainless steel for longevity and strength, and represent excellent decibel reduction for sporting use. The differing diameters can be matched to any barrel profile, and internal volume can be chosen to suit any sportsperson's calibre requirements for maximum effectiveness.

It is important to match the calibre of the moderator to that of the barrel as best as possible; with a moderator whose internal volume best matches and retards the same volume of gas, the differing amounts of propellant gas burnt, and thus the heat generated by the expanding gases, can be most effectively restricted. The PES uses a threaded end cap section to attach to the barrel, and is a sealed unit design, with the rear section incorporating a large primary chamber for the expansion and cooling of the gases as they leave the barrel.

Under enormous pressure the bullet continues through the moderator and the gases are squeezed through the first series of baffles that act as barriers. The PES has a large blast baffle of stainless steel that traps all the force of the gases initially, and then filters them through a labyrinth of curved and dished baffles for the rest of the moderator's length. When the bullet exits and the gases emerge from the moderator they are sufficiently cooled by all that

The PES 32mm muzzle can is small and compact but superbly quiet and tough, being made from stainless steel.

interference travelling around the baffles that they make far less noise as they enter the atmosphere. I use PES cans on most of my rifles, from a .17 Ackley Hornet fox rifle, right up to my .308 Tikka stalking rifle; they have had over ten years' hard use and they all work flawlessly.

Other permutations: Naturally there are many permutations of this system, with other manufacturers offering shorter, longer, takedown, lightweight and differing baffle designs – but they all work on the same principle. One firm that stands out from Finland, called ASE Utra, offers a series of compact muzzle cans as well as a super-short 4.5in (115mm) but heavy stainless-steel moderator called S5. Sadly the old firm of Vaimeco, also from Finland, is no longer producing moderators, as theirs offered both rimfire and fullbore shooters a great muzzle can. However, the JLS Stalker from Britain is similar in design: it uses a strippable aluminium construction with 'o'-ring seals, and a one-piece pierced baffle stack that effectively reduces noise. It represents good value for money.

The ASE Utra Jet-Z: This is another efficient muzzle-mounted design, thus called because the baffle sections are welded into a 'z', taking up the whole internal volume; this maximizes the surface area the gases make contact with, and so retards their passage through the moderator. This is a neat little unit, and as with the PES, it is sealed and requires little attention because the

pressure within the suppressor is often sufficient to blow out any debris that might clog it up.

There are two models, depending on the calibre of your rifle. The Compact adds only 6in (150mm) to the length of your rifle, weighs 20oz (560g), and can be used right up to 300 Win mag calibre; whilst the CQB is best used on .22 centrefire rifles – it is 1.5in (40mm) in diameter, as is the Compact, but is 18oz (520g) in weight, and adds 5in (125mm) to the overall length.

Ultra-compact, robust, super-efficient but pricey, the Jet-Z design offers great decibel reductions.

The Law Enforcement International (LEI): This is a strippable moderator and is offered in three lengths, 12.8in (325mm), 9.8in (250mm) and 7.3in (185mm); the diameter of 1.8in (45mm) remains the same in all three. Although this is an old muzzle-mounted design, its sheer size and internal volume really cools the expanding gases and thus reduces the muzzle report to an astonishing level. There is a thick external tube made from aluminium, and the internal baffle stack comprises a series of stainless-steel spacers and dished individual baffles that effectively reduce noise and are tested to withstand 10,000 rounds of use. Admittedly it increases the overall length of your rifle but where noise reduction is a major concern and length is not an issue, the LEI is very good, and the ability to be field stripped will appeal to some users.

Superbly efficient and compact, the Jet-Z design from ASE-Utra is a sealed, low maintenance, muzzle-mounted moderator.

Rimfire Models

Both .22lr and .17 rimfires are almost exclusively in this class of muzzle-mounted moderators, as the size and diameter necessary to suppress the report of a rimfire is much less than that of a full bore. Again, PES and ASE Utra offer stainless steel, all steel or aluminium cans with removable baffles to allow proper cleaning. JLS Stalker, Husher, Sirocco, Sound Biter, Sako, Wildcat Cub, Parker Hale, Logun, A-Tec and Swift Precision Rifles, as well as some custom items from John Bowkett and V-Tech, all offer different degrees of effectiveness.

The Sirocco SM11: This design is fairly typical, with a light aluminium chassis with a removable end cap so the five conical baffles can be easily removed. There is a small expansion chamber, and noise reduction is excellent with both .22 subsonics and .17 Mach 2 rounds.

The SAK: This is a simple one-piece aluminium baffle stack with a series of chambers within the core and an outer sleeve to seal the unit. It is very simple, easy to clean, and quite effective on .22lr class rifles.

The 32mm and 38mm PES: More efficient are the PES muzzle cans in 32mm or 38mm diameters, again in stainless steel, and these offer the best noise reduction for .17 rimfire users. The Mighty Mouse is a small, efficient aluminium moderator that blends to the external diameter of most rimfire barrels and suppresses the muzzle report very well.

John Bowkett and V-Tech: Some of the most efficient muzzle can .22 rimfire moderators are those from custom houses, the best of which are John Bowkett and V-Tech. The Bowkett design is a solid steel unit with a threaded end cap that allows the aluminium baffles and energy-absorbing springs to be removed. The placement and density of the design makes this one of the best rimfire moderators on the market for both .17 and .22lr rimfire users.

The V-Tech is again solid steel and dense for noise absorption; it is slim-line yet super-efficient, with a series of symmetrical baffles and the all importantly placed primary expansion

Selection of rimfire moderators showing the diversity of design.

chamber. Beautifully blued and made to order, the V-Tech can be sourced to match the exact contour of your own rifle's barrel for a seamless join.

Over-Barrel Designs

This system utilizes a moderator whose length is not all forward of the muzzle; instead the moderator sleeves down over the barrel with only a baffle section in front of the muzzle. This can also be called a two-point mounting system because the moderator attaches to the barrel by the muzzle thread section and is also secured by a further rear bush to keep the rear section aligned with the bore axis. The advantage of this design is that the overall length of the rifle is greatly reduced as compared to a muzzle-mounted can. Also the internal area can be increased by the addition of a larger rear section that sits effectively over the barrel portion

The T12 over-barrel moderator from PES of New Zealand offers excellent noise reduction coupled with stainless steel construction for long life, and hard-wearing Mil spec non-glare coatings.

and forms a large initial expansion area to cool the gases before they travel through the baffle section.

Full Bore Types

Again there are many full bore variations, with manufacturers such as PES, Reflex, B&T and Wildcat all offering over-barrel designs.

The PES moderator: PES offer a T12 over-barrel design with a semi take-down facility so the rear section can be cleaned. The inner sleeve covers the external barrel surface, with the outer section of the moderator forming an enclosed design. The initial turbulence of hot gases is redirected via a solid blast baffle rearwards into the expansion chamber to cool, and then swirled around to travel back up the moderator through the series of baffles. This directed and redirected gas flow is what cools the gases and reduces the muzzle blast signature to very low levels.

Models in the range are all stainless steel in construction, and can be sourced as full length or Scout versions with 32 or 38mm diameter sizes. Their external surfaces are all Mil spec, coated in black to reduce glare and to achieve maximum robustness for use in the field.

The A-Tec: A relative newcomer is the A-Tec moderator from Norway: it relies on the same principle, but is totally strippable. In fact it is more of a hybrid muzzle and over-barrel design in that there is a larger area forward of the muzzle 6.5in (165mm) and 4.5in (115mm) in the smaller rear expansion tube. Aluminium is used in construction for lightness, with a stack of five aluminium baffles, but the primary baffle is constructed from stainless steel to take the violent hot gases that first emanate from the bore. Noise reduction is good. This moderator can be totally stripped, allowing cleaning after the recommended 200 rounds.

Rimfire Types

The over-barrel moderator design is primarily associated with full bore rifles, although there are a few rimfire models, chiefly the PES 'o' ring, the Wildcat Growler and the A7 from TWSG. The PES takes the form of a scaled-down T12 unit that does away with the rear securing bush in favour of two gas-sealing 'o' rings, super quiet and very well made. The Growler has a single one-piece baffle stack of aluminium with vented fins, whilst the A7 uses a series of removable stainless curved baffles. Both sleeve down the barrel but are really overkill on a rimfire, and the muzzle cans are usually a more efficient design. This is why you don't see many over-barrel designs specifically for rimfires, unless used as a fully suppressed model.

Fully Suppressed Moderators

This term describes a rifle that has been modified in such a way as to achieve maximum noise reduction for both supersonic and subsonic ammunition. It usually involves a totally shrouded barrel system and some form of porting to the barrel itself to bleed off hot gases before they exit the muzzle, but not always.

Law Enforcement International (LEI) produce silenced rifles based on Remington 700 actions, as shown, or Sako TRG tactical rifles.

Both the overall length and the weight of the rifle are kept to a minimum, and this provides the 'stealthiest' rifle possible.

Often the design is a sealed unit causing issues with cleaning, and even with a strippable design often the burnt powder residue is redirected within the barrel shroud directly on to the external barrel surface, causing corrosion problems. However, because of their unique and quite often stunning noise reduction levels their foibles are worth putting up with.

Designs such as LEI, Sako, Swift, Bowers and PES incorporate rimfire and full bore designs; they make use of alloy materials or even carbon fibre to keep the weight down, and often have very short barrels. The LEI (Law Enforcement International) has its origins with the military and the police, but their suppressed .308 Remington design has found favour with many hunters. The 14.5in (36.8cm) barrel is stainless steel with a chromed exterior to prevent fouling and corrosion, and is encapsulated by a large, thick-walled aluminium tube for its entire length, with the addition of twenty stainless baffles forward of the muzzle to enhance suppression. This can be unscrewed to facilitate cleaning, which is necessary for this design. Noise reduction is nothing short of astonishing.

Similarly the Sako SSR rifle, in both .22 rimfire and .308, offers extreme noise sup-

pression in a lightweight, short rifle package. The .22lr version is a sealed unit with an aluminium tube running the length of a standard barrel profile – 24in (60cm) – but covers a 12in (30cm) barrel with a transfer port cut through it just forward of the chamber, and thus bleeds off the gases to the outer

RIGHT: Sako made two versions of their fully suppressed moderators to fit both .22lr and .308 calibres. The SSR models here with custom stocks are frighteningly quiet.

Rimfire users can opt for a fully suppressed design such as this PES ported and fully barrel-shrouded 10/22 model, just perfect for lamping rabbits in noise-sensitive areas.

expansion chamber, then into a primary expansion chamber, and finally through a series of modular baffle sections. The result is a .22 rimfire rifle whose signature note is not much louder than the drop of the firing pin: a superb vermin rifle indeed. The .308 version is the same, but it has no barrel porting and is designed to perform best with subsonic ammunition with 180–200gr projectiles travelling at 1050fps for very quiet operation.

PES, too, offer a fully ported and shrouded barrel for the popular Ruger 10/22 and CZ rimfire rifles, and can custom build to fit many other makes; depending on the position of the porting to the proximity of the chamber, the use of either subsonic or supersonic loads is maximized. This is a great tool for the serious pest controller and vermin shooter who want maximum noise suppression and quality.

TYPICAL NOISE REDUCTION IN DECIBELS

Noise reduction tests are notoriously difficult to conduct without expensive sound-metering equipment and the knowledge to use it correctly. To gain some insight into the amount of noise reduction one can expect to achieve from any rimfire or full bore moderator there is a simple table of the decibel ratings you can expect to gain from a rimfire and full bore rifle

Subsonic rounds are best used in moderated rifles; here a .308 Sako SSR shoots good groups with proper hand loading.

with differing loads. For these purposes noise is measured in decibels (dB): commonly if silence is measured at 0dB – that is, the threshold of one's hearing – then at an increasing level, an ambient office environment noise will be 55dB, a lawn mower is about 86dB and a chainsaw is 105dB, whilst an air rifle report is 110dB. Beyond this level the use of some hearing defence is advised, because sustained exposure in a day can cause some form of hearing damage; thus a .22lr rimfire in a rifle is 135–140dB, whilst a full bore rifle is commonly above 160dB, depending on calibre.

A good moderator can reduce the dB levels to one where prolonged exposure is less likely to cause permanent hearing loss to the shooter. For example, a good moderator will comply to the latest personal noise exposure limit set by the European Directive 2003/10/EC, which is 137dB (C), about the level of an unsilenced .22 rimfire. That is why, when a full bore moderator is suppressed, the noise level is likened to that of the report from a high velocity .22 rimfire.

Decibel reduction can often be misleading, as the dB reduction is quoted not only in dB values but also as net or overall dB reduction. Depending on the type and make of moderator, of which there is a huge number, a net reduction of 30dB is regarded as good on a full bore rifle, with 20dB being good on a rimfire.

MATERIALS IN MANUFACTURE

Just as important as internal design are the materials used to construct the moderators. It is important to realize that the pressures and shearing forces generated by the escaping gases from the muzzle are enormous, and would quickly erode and corrode the moderator fitted. In their quest for the perfect moderator many have tried lighter designs, but this is to their peril, as these will not last as long as the heavy designs. Whereas rimfire ammunition can cope with lighter, smaller designs, full bore moderators must retain very fast, hot expanding gases and thus must have a build integrity that can withstand this hostile environment.

Material type is also an important consideration for deadening the vibrational noise on firing the rifle; if it is too thin there is a distinct echo or ring to the moderator, and making the walls and baffles thicker does reduce internal noise from components and is certainly beneficial. Some designs use 'o'-rings and plastics, which can be problematic as over-extended use may cause seizure, or they can be compromised by the use of unsuitable cleaning solvents.

Stainless Steel

Stainless steel is a good material for moderators because its structural integrity is good, as is its

Decibel reduction in rimfires			
Moderator Type	*High Velocity*	*Subsonic*	*CB Longs*
None	140	135	128
Muzzle Can	125	120	110

Decibel reduction in fullbores			
Moderator Type	*.223 High Velocity*	*.308 High Velocity*	*.308 Subsonic*
None	160	165	154
Muzzle Can	126	132	118

resistant nature to corrosive gases. Its longevity is certainly its main attraction, not only in its resilience against corrosion from the outside, the result of abuse and foul weather, but also against the harsh corrosive and eroding properties of the propellant gases inside.

The only down side from a hunter's point of view is its shiny reflective quality, which may scare the quarry, so some form of cover or external surface treatment is advisable.

Aluminium

Aluminium is an appealing material because it offers strength and lightness; however, in a moderator it is less than effective if it is too thin. The threads on an aluminium moderator will often gall and seize up in a very short time, and the metal itself has a tendency to be flame-cut by the advancing hot gases, and soon becomes eroded. Even with hard anodized or treated surfaces, aluminium has a finite life as a moderator material unless it is as thick as a stainless steel unit, with a similar life expectancy – but then the weight difference will be negligible, and any benefit that the aluminium can had will be lost.

On a small rimfire rifle an aluminium moderator makes sense, but you must still maintain it properly and disassemble it for cleaning, because the incredible amount of dirt, wax and unburnt powder that is deposited into rimfire cans will eventually impede the bullet's passage.

Aluminium may seem tempting for lightness, but unless the baffles and wall thicknesses are large you will encounter flame erosion by the hot propellant gases sooner rather than latter.

Steel

Carbon steel is cheap and strong, but will corrode a lot more quickly than a stainless steel moderator if the components are lightweight in construction. Coating with Mil spec paints and Teflons can help, but to increase the life expectancy of these units the walls and baffles are usually made thick to withstand the flame-cutting blast and the harsh environment that a full bore moderator must endure.

Carbon Fibre

The carbon-fibre moderator models, such as the muzzle can or fully moderated version from Swift Precision rifles, are only suitable for rimfire use. They are incredibly light in comparison to steel equivalent models and so add little to the overall weight of the rifle, but offer similar noise reduction capabilities. However, by the nature of their make-up they are sealed units and so cleaning can become an issue when shooting waxy 22lr ammunition through them.

Titanium

Although strong and light in structure, the use of titanium can be problematic in that all titanium-constructed moderators suffer from galling of the threaded sections, and thus in time become increasingly difficult to take apart. Also the price of the materials makes the unit unrealistic as a stock item, and it can only be offered as a custom moderator.

Manufacturers will often use a blend of materials to achieve strength where needed – blast baffles – and to cut weight on the outer casings and baffles furthest from the initial gas flow. However, the different metals heat up at different rates, and this can cause problems with effective sealing and unit integrity.

What Happens when the Shot is Fired?

Firearms expel an incredibly hot and corrosive mixture of gas and chemicals on ignition from the powder charge, which can cause problems of corrosion not only to the inside of the rifle's bore, but also within the moderator itself. An appreciable amount of water is also present, and this can be disastrous in terms of moderator life, especially if the unit is steel, or you have ali to ali thread locks. Moderators can corrode, erode, and simply fall apart with neglect, and a moderator that was strippable can easily seize up beyond repair in a very short period if certain safeguards are not taken.

The gas consists of carbon monoxide, water, carbon dioxide and nitrogen, which is a deadly concoction. Also important is the fact that different materials heat up at differing temperatures, and so a moderator constructed of two materials can actually expand and contract at differing rates, and this can cause a shift in the rifle's point of zero, and the internal threads and components may be damaged or seize up.

Heat haze from a hot moderator is also a concern; not normally a problem from a low velocity rimfire, it can become an issue from a long range, full bore varmint rig that has shot many tens of rounds in quick succession. The subsequent vertical boiling heat mirage can affect the shooter's view through a scope and cause the image to twist and bend out of focus. This is particularly apparent in thin-walled aluminium moderators: although these are light, they suffer from this problem, and from faster erosion of component parts by the accelerating flame-cutting gases.

POINT OF IMPACT SHIFT

It is very important to understand that when your rifle has been zeroed or sighted in at a particular range with your favourite ammunition, the addition of a moderator will change your point of impact. This is because any addition of weight on the rifle's barrel will upset its fine tuning and harmonic resonance on firing. Think of it as a tuning fork that has perfect pitch: if you add a blob of bubble gum to one of its arms, will it still be so melodic? By the same token the barrel will resonate at a different pitch, and thus as the bullet exits the barrel there will be a small but perceivable difference in barrel position that will cause the bullet's trajectory to be slightly off the pre-zeroed criteria. As range increases, the zero shifts even more, and so at 100yd (90m)

where once the rifle shot where the cross hairs pointed, now it shoots at an entirely different point of aim.

The degree of the shift is related to the weight and resonating qualities of the materials used in the moderator construction, and the centre of gravity of the moderator. Adding a moderator can shift bullet impact both up, down or left and right; nevertheless, one widely recognized constant is that accuracy can actually be enhanced with a sound moderator fitted. There is no direct effect on the bullet itself, but the dampening harmonic effect of the extra mass of the moderator serves to smooth the barrel vibrations, allowing the bullet to exit the barrel's muzzle crown at a more consistent level, and thus increase accuracy.

THE EFFECTS OF TEMPERATURE CHANGE

It is also important to remember that not only do the materials used in the moderator design affect noise reduction, so too do the climatic conditions. They will affect the cartridge's velocity, and will increase or reduce the level at which the speed of sound or sonic boom is heard; thus shooting on a hot summer's day will be different from that on a cold winter's morning.

Thus with a temperature of 0°C (32°F), a typical speed of sound is 1087fps, which is above the threshold of most subsonic ammunition so no supersonic crack will be heard. However, if the temperature drops to, say, −10°C (14°F), the speed of sound drops to 1067fps, which is now just about the same as some subsonic ammunition velocity and so a sonic crack will be heard if the ammunition's velocity exceeds this. The converse is true when the temperature increases, when you can shoot slightly higher velocity ammunition and still remain below the speed of sound. Typically at a temperature of 25°C (77°F) the velocity for the speed of sound increases to 1136fps, some 69fps different from that of the −10°C reading.

The chances are that most shooters will use their subsonic ammunition in average conditions, but the knowledge of the shift in temperature and its effect on the speed of sound may influence your choice of ammunition, or explain why sometimes your rifle ammunition combination becomes noisier with differing weather patterns.

MAINTENANCE

In order for any moderator to perform at its intended best you must fit it correctly, and establish a cleaning regime that suits your shooting frequency. If not you will have a potentially dangerous moderator, and it will risk failure long before its sell-by date.

Fitting a Moderator Correctly

Do not be dissuaded from having a proper threading job done just because you cannot afford it: most cheap threading jobs risk leaving your silencer insecure and misaligned, which is potentially dangerous and certainly detrimental to accuracy.

To achieve a correct thread on a barrel muzzle the moderator must be aligned with the bore axis, and not the outside diameter of the barrel. Most rifle bores do not run exactly true through the barrel, so if a thread is cut square to the outside diameter the silencer is often canted off in one direction. Like this, on exiting the bore a bullet is more likely to contact one of the internal baffles, with disastrous consequences. I have seen bullets exiting sideways, smashing through most or all of the baffles, exiting the muzzle cap of the can sideways, and in one instance the can parted company with the rifle! This is particularly relevant with the new trend for tighter baffle dimensions, where the apertures through which the bullet passes are smaller in order to maximize noise reduction.

It is also important that the thread is undercut at its base, allowing the moderator to sit square to the face of the barrel with proper and equal contact; if not, the moderator will have a tendency to lean or tension to one side, again with potentially dangerous consequences.

Also check that the gunsmith cuts the thread size to match your own moderator. There are many thread size options, but I always choose

Depending on barrel diameter and moderator style, muzzle threads vary accordingly – but one thing remains the same: get a competent gunsmith to cut them.

the largest that can be cut on the barrel diameter whilst still maintaining enough shoulder for the can to butt up to. It makes no difference whether the thread sizes are metric or imperial, just choose the size that will allow as much metal between the bore and the bottom of the threads.

Once cut, ask to have the newly threaded sections reblued, otherwise corrosion will start sooner than you think; and when the thread is done, have a cap made to protect the threads when the moderator is not fitted. I often use an extended cap that protrudes forward of the muzzle like a mini brake, as this protects the threads and keeps the all-important crown out of harm's way.

A thread should have a snug fit to the moderator, and should not be so tight that you exert any real force; it should engage the first section and glide down the threads using a single hand. If it is cut square, its contact with the muzzle shoulders is enough to keep it from unscrewing, and ensures perfect alignment to the bore.

This factor is just as important for a muzzle-mounted moderator as it is for an over-barrel model. With moderators that sleeve down the barrel, the rear supporting bush can also be a contentious issue. If you fit an over-the-barrel moderator to your rifle and look at the rear of the moderator with the bush removed, you should see a perfect, concentric gap of equal diameter between it and the outside diameter of the bore. If you do not, then the thread is on the skew, and when you fit the rear bush and tighten the moderator fully, the barrel will be tensioned between the muzzle and the rear bush as the moderator tries to straighten the misalignment. This is not good for the rifle and is certainly detrimental to accuracy. If there *is* proper alignment, then a tight rear bush is beneficial; if there is not, then it would be better to give a couple of thou clearance.

Preventing Corrosion / Erosion

It is essential to take your moderator off after a day's shooting, and not put it straight back in the gun cabinet. More problems are caused to rifle bores from not taking off the moderator than most other damage.

When you shoot the rifle, all that burnt powder and very corrosive gas residue are left in the moderator either stuck to the baffles or loose in the body. The main products from combustion are carbon monoxide, water, carbon dioxide and nitrogen; this forms a corrosive cocktail that starts to corrode the moderator from the inside out, and if the can is left on the rifle and put away standing upright, the moisture and corrosive mixture can, and will, migrate down into the first section of the barrel. If the rifle is left there for a while unshot, the internal surface of the bore will become pitted and rusty; obviously this is not good, and will certainly affect the accuracy of the rifle.

I have seen some rifles that externally are in excellent condition but whose internal bore surface is terrible, because the moderator was not removed after shooting. The muzzle thread will also corrode, as will the crown, and sometimes the situation is so bad that a moderator and barrel become fused together by corrosion. Also, take the moderator off before you put a cleaning brush or patch down your rifle, otherwise pieces of fabric can, and will, get stuck in the can and be contacted by a passing bullet.

Maintenance Procedures

After every shooting session take the moderator off the rifle when you get home prior to cleaning. I always remove the can and let the rifle and moderator come to the same equilibrium or

The A-Tec design, more muzzle can than over-barrel, with baffles of aluminium excepting the first one which is made of stainless steel to take the initial very hot muzzle blast.

temperature as the room you are cleaning it in, otherwise condensation will form on the components and just exacerbate the corrosion problems. At room temperature wipe off any external water, muck and burnt gases/powder. If the moderator is a sealed unit it can be gently knocked on a table top to loosen any residue debris, but more importantly, before you put it away or back on a rifle, oil the interior surfaces to help eliminate corrosion. You can use a light gun oil, which leaves a fine protective film residue; the first couple of shots will smoke, but better that than a rotten moderator.

If the threads are lightly lubricated with a molybdenum grease and then reassembled, a moderator should serve you well. Problems come from reassembling moderators with separate baffles in the wrong order, which can change the weight distribution after the muzzle and thus influence the barrel vibrations and impact. Problems can also occur if the moderator is screwed on at a different tension – though this only really happens if the thread is not under cut and there is no obvious stop to the tightening process, or if the thread has become damaged, or muck stops the moderator sitting properly on the muzzle face. It is a good idea to scribe a reference mark on the barrel and silencer to check the correct alignment, as any discrepancies will then become immediately obvious.

The actual material used in the construction of the silencer can reduce or greatly increase any corrosion problems. Aluminium-constructed cans, although very light in weight, can suffer from gas- and flame-cutting, resulting in erosion of the baffle edges and therefore loss of effectiveness. Also aluminium on aluminium joints can fuse together and make disassembly almost impossible in some cases. Similarly, a light steel-skinned moderator can be prone to rusting internally and externally.

If nothing else, next time you shoot your rifle and moderator combination, take it off after use, which will at least help stop corrosion starting at the crown and prevent rifling of the barrel. But if you spend a little time and effort in silencer care, then your rifle/moderator outfit should give you years of trouble-free service.

CONCLUSIONS

Nearly thirty years of mud, rain, wind and abuse out in the field has led me to believe that simple is often best. If a design has been selling for over thirty years, then it is probably a good one. Parker Hale .22lr cans are still very good moderators, and with subtle changes to design and materials used, have reduced the decibels to a level that cannot be improved upon, except in the realms of ported and full suppression models.

Full bore moderators continue to shuffle for pole position in the noise reduction stakes, but increasingly people are forgetting that of the issues that make a good moderator, light weight and shortness are not two of them. Muzzle cans still continue to exert a strong pull to shooters in terms of robust, cheap, and very effective noise reduction, the only proviso being increased overall rifle length. PES 32 and 38mm or ASE Utra Jet-Z moderators are the best in this respect, and the new PES Extreme is the quietest moderator I have ever tested in twenty years.

Nevertheless people always strive for new ways to achieve the same thing, and the over-barrel designs, although heavier and more expensive than the muzzle-mounted cans, still maintain a firm hold in the market place due to the desire among hunters to achieve a short overall length of rifle with a moderator fitted. My premise here is, choose your calibre carefully, reduce the length of the barrel as not to impede the bullet's performance too much, and then fit the largest muzzle can you can live with. My RPA 6.5 Rapier custom is a case in point, and sports an 18in (45cm) barrel and a PES Extreme muzzle can, which is quieter than any other full bore supersonic rifle I have shot.

Chapter 9
Reloading

Shooters can be divided into two categories with regard to their ammunition preferences: either you reload, or you do not, and there rarely seems to be any middle ground. For many, the use of factory ammunition will suffice for their style of shooting or level of interest, and indeed there is such a variety that the rifleman has a very good choice. Sometimes you are lucky and find a factory load that your rifle likes, and the question then is, what is the advantage of using reloads? Well, other than financial reasons – usually reloads work out cheaper, though not always – the desire to eke out every last drop of accuracy or velocity potential from your rifle will lure many shooters, and I am certainly one.

Personally it has become more than just a need to save money, and now I enjoy the process of combining a variety of components to maximize one's expectations. But be warned: once hooked, you will be found murmuring to yourself in the small hours about charge weights and ballistic coefficients. There are certain legal requirements, and the list is long and varied; quite simply my advice is, always consult your firearms liaison officer as they are best placed to give you their constabulary's exact requirements.

So what advantages can you expect? Well, even with the basic equipment the goal is consistency to each round, trying to replicate the same formulae each time to gain the same result each time.

Reloading can be a time-consuming yet rewarding pastime aimed at achieving the best from your rifle.

The basic equipment includes reloading press, dies, priming tool, scales, lube and powder funnel, and these can be purchased separately or as a starter pack from many manufacturers. Personally I would mix and match equipment to achieve the best of each design, and tailor make your reloading bench to suit your needs. Most gunsmiths will have home loading equipment, so don't be afraid to test their knowledge.

I still use as one of my presses, a very cheap RCBS Partner design that I have mounted to a cradle and which I take out varminting with me so I can reload in the field on load-testing trips and long-range forays. Despite over twenty-five years of use it still turns out great reloads. I have other larger presses for large cases and reforming brass, but the point is, basic kit need not be thought of as inferior.

Areas where I would spend more money is on a good set of scales, whether electronic or manual, and an accurate powder delivery system. You are trying to achieve low shot-to-shot variations that hopefully will translate to good accuracy, and a low variation in charge weights of powder is a good starting place. So too is the use of correct primers to ignite the powder consistently. Reloading books give advice on std or magnum primer use, but not make, and you will find that a small item such as a primer can make a big difference in the burn rate and performance of a load.

Reloading allows you to take control of your components, and you may well want to reduce loads for fox work but increase the charge for deer and stay deer legal. Determining the burn rate of the powder and matching this to the bullet weight and length of barrel can greatly increase performance, both in accuracy potential and velocity. By achieving a harmony of components you can transform a mediocre rifle's group size into something quite special. To many this is just too much bother, but you will never know what you are missing, literally.

One real advantage to reloading is the variety of bullets you can choose. Manual manipulation of their seating depth is vitally important, not only for accuracy but also for correct grip tension from the brass neck to release in a consistent manner, and very importantly maintains a safe pressure within the case.

One of the best ways of increasing the accuracy from your rifle is to alter the relationship between the bullet and the rifling in the barrel in terms of distance from each other. Most factory ammunition will have bullets seated a fair way into the case to make sure they feed through a magazine correctly, but by seating your bullet out a little further you can lessen that jump between bullet and rifling and hopefully achieve better concentricity and alignment as the bullet enters the rifling. This simple step can be accurately measured with many tools.

Prepping all your cases – that is, weight sorting – will eliminate any duff ones, and then you can true up the primer pockets, and deburr any

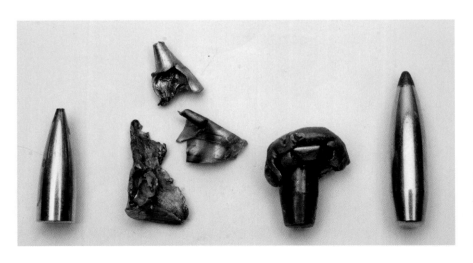

By reloading you can get an insight into how differing bullet types and weights behave.

When you venture into the realms of reloading there is no turning back: it is addictive, and can be as expensive as the quality of equipment deems necessary.

primer flash holes, and inside and out of the case neck. All this will bring you closer to achieving highly accurate loads. It helps to use the same brass that has come from your chamber because it is already fire-formed to specific dimensions. If desired, a simple neck size can make the case reloadable again.

Reloading opens up a great many avenues to the shooter in experimenting with different bullet types, and their construction and shape. You may favour longer range shooting, where a more streamlined and higher ballistic coefficient bullet is desirable; or a more typical or round nose design for woodland stalking at closer ranges. You will find that certain bullets like certain velocities better and perform – expand – on deer in differing ways, and by reloading to maximize the bullet's terminal velocity you will be doing yourself and your quarry a favour. Moreover I have gone beyond reloading just for better loads, and have delved into the world of the wildcatter where you design your own cartridges, involving the bending of brass and annealing, neck turning and bullet swaging.

For safety reasons it is advisable to use a good reloading book and to change only one thing at a time so you can determine what is making a difference, and to keep accurate records. Better still, invest in a ballistics software package such

as the excellent Quick Load and Quick Target, which determines interior and exterior ballistics very accurately.

Before you start, it is imperative that you understand the principles behind reloading technique and the components that go into each cartridge. This includes types of primer, powder choice, bullet seating, pressure issues and how the cartridge is designed to fit certain chambers.

COMPONENTS

Cases

Such a benign thing as a brass case actually has a huge influence on the internal characteristics and ballistics of your rifle. Cases may all look similar within their calibre groups, but differing manufacturing techniques will mean varying weights, affecting internal powder capacity, concentric or out of true necks and shoulders. The worst culprit is the cheap process that just pierces the primer flash hole leaving nasty ragged burrs around the rim, which will affect the primer's performance. Machined flash holes, weight sorted and primer depth uniformity are all areas where a reloader can improve his cases. Buy the best you can afford and spend a little time prepping them by simple sorting

The choice of components is huge, but great care must be taken in using the correct loads for your calibre and rifle.

before attempting to reload, because it will save a lot of heartache later and wasted reloading components.

Powder Type

Every calibre bullet weight and rifle's bore has a preference and a safe use of a certain range of powder types. Powder can be produced in varying forms such as ball, granules, extruded or flake, and there is a type that is manufactured to 'burn' at a given rate, which makes it safe to propel a given bullet type or weight for any given calibre. Reloading manuals or Quick Load must be consulted here to determine correct powder use. Too fast a powder with too heavy a bullet, and the powder does not serve to propel the projectile; instead the pressure rises and may damage you and your rifle. Equally, too slow a powder in a light bulleted case will not ignite properly or completely, giving reduced velocities and erratic results. Actual charge weight has

vastly differing characteristics on the bullet's performance, and overloading is just as dangerous as underloading a charge, with secondary explosive effect (SEE) being a real problem.

It is important to realize that the force needed to move a bullet up the rifle's barrel is all stored within the chemical composition of the powder charge. It is not always the top powder charge that achieves best accuracy, although velocity may be good. It is no good having extreme velocity when accuracy is so poor as not to hit anything! You are actually looking for a compromise: as with all reloading techniques you want the best overall performance, where the powder is consistently ignited within safe pressure so as not to ruin the rifle or case. A load density so that no air spaces exist within the loaded round is preferable, but other factors, such as lot to lot variation, temperature, moisture and accurate weight, all influence consistent powder burn rates.

You are really trying to blend components that achieve maximum performance from their union. This in powder terms means that choosing the right powder and burn rate to the cartridge size and calibre with bullet weight achieves the best velocities. You can achieve this by changing powder types – burn rates which influence the pressure curve either up or down under the bullet. The larger the pressure curve the more contact the bullet has with its

Powders differ depending on the load and weight of bullet they have to propel; some are flake or extruded long and short cut.

Bullet types range from fast-expanding varmint to soft nose or predictable expanding deer loads; you need to try a selection to see what works best in your rifles.

propulsion effects, the more energy transfer and the faster the bullet will go so long as you have a long enough barrel to burn that type of powder. A fast powder gives a quick rise in pressure and then drops sharply, whilst a slow powder burns to the same pressure level but more slowly and maintains that pressure for longer.

Primers

The consistency and quality of the primer cannot be over-emphasized, as it is this tiny and often overlooked reloading component that initiates the whole firing sequence and is responsible for the reliable and consistent ignition of the powder charge. This in turn affects the chamber pressures, the balance of the powder burn and ultimately bullet velocities.

Matching the correct type of primer to the powder within the case is essential to ensure correct and accurate ignition. Reloading manuals will give a guide to the use of either standard or magnum primers, but the actual manufacturer's type will have to be determined by you after trial and error to see which gives the desired velocities for the powder charge weight and burn speed and the accuracy that you expect. Match or bench-rest primers offer consistent and strong ignition plumes of primer mixture gases, and are worth the extra money. Proper seating within the case primer pocket is also critical for dependable, consistent ignition; we will look at this in more detail later.

Bullets

From a sporting point of view it is the bullet that ultimately connects with the game species, and so bullet shape, design exterior and construction are of paramount importance.

Regardless of make, you are looking for as uniform and concentric a bullet as possible with regard to weight, jacket thickness, diameter and symmetrical axis; then there is a sporting chance of having a straight bullet flight. It is then the end game – the species – that will ultimately guide your choice regarding the bullet's internal structure. The varying bullet types and application are covered in Chapter 6. Vermin and fox shooters will require faster expanding bullets for instant and non-ricocheting shots, whilst a deer stalker will require a bullet to penetrate further within a deer before expansion begins, so will demand less frangible bullets, as meat damage of valuable venison can be a concern. Big game hunters require deep penetrating bullets, often of solid construction, to maintain uniformity and to penetrate to the vitals on a thick-skinned game species.

GETTING STARTED

There is a bewildering array of reloading equipment on the market, but loosely speaking it falls into several clear areas, each performing a certain task. There are two very distinct categories of tool necessary to perform any competent reloading job, namely basic and advanced. Due to the potential danger of highly explosive materials, reloading should not be undertaken too lightly. The very best advice is that you define an area that you intend to reload, and build a work surface with clearly marked and defined shelves and drawers so as not to confuse any parts.

Reloading Presses

The most obvious start to any reloading venture is the purchase of the reloading press that manually resizes, deprimes and seats bullets to complete a cartridge.

There are two main types of press, manual and progressive, and this refers to the operation and not the design. Manual presses perform each task one at a time with one pull on the operating handle, whilst progressive presses multi-task the cartridge through each stage, usually on a carousel or by a rotating turret system. The most common are the single stage presses.

Single Stage Presses

Central to all reloading processes is the reloading press that will form the bedrock to your set-up. The typical ⅞in reloading press should still form part of even the most ardent reloader's kit, but you must select a good quality one to keep the unity of the quality reloading procedure. Usually a single stage press is better than a progressive press; however, there are some high quality turret presses now available, such as Hornady, Dillon and Harrell.

The size of the ammunition – case size – is important in choosing the correct size of the

Reloading can be hazardous, and thus an organized and neat reloading desk should be kept.

The RCBS Partner press may be a budget reloading press, but mine is still going strong after some twenty-five years.

Reloading presses come in all sizes; this is the Forster Co-Axial press that produces good quality reloads.

Many reloaders like to use the best kit possible, and this will repay you in smaller group sizes.

press. The RCBS Rockchucker, Redding Ultra Mag and Lyman are good for large cases as well as .308 size ammo, whilst lighter weight presses, such as the RCBS Partner and Redding Boss presses, are used for PPC and BR case sizes. I often use the Partner press in the field as it is small and compact as well as being light and easily transportable.

Most presses operate in the same way. A side-mounted single handle is pulled to provide a lever system that raises a cartridge case on a centralized pedestal before it enters a resizing or bullet-seating die secured within the top bridge. Better quality presses have threads cut into inserts and not the cast press body, so will retain alignment better over time. Some presses, such as the Forster Coaxial press, use a centralized lever and hold the cases in a self-adjusting jaw system and not a dedicated shell holder.

As far as custom presses go, Harrell of USA make an excellent press available in three sizes that is attached to a bench top via a built-in C-clamp, and offers 'on the move' reloading in the field. These are very well made, and ensure perfect alignment between shell holder and dies in operation.

Arbor Presses

An alternative to ⅞in die presses are the Arbor presses that use hand dies, usually from L. E. Wilson or Neil Jones; these come as either neck dies, bullet seaters or full length resizing items. The beauty of these presses is that they are small, and easily carried into the field for on-the-spot reloading, or shoot as you go without the tedium of having to go home and load some more ammo. They have few moving parts and the height is adjustable to accommodate most

Reloading dies: left to right, sizing dies to decap old primer and bring case dimensions back into spec, seater dies to seat bullets, or body dies to size the case's body. These are just some of the many types of die.

cartridge sizes; however, you will find full length resizing difficult to perform on this style of press, so resign that task to the conventional ⅞in die press.

Arbor presses and hand dies offer a much more accurate feel to the reloading process, and will take you that next step towards the extremely accurate rifle. Hand dies are usually all neck-size dies with interchangeable sizing bushes that can be interchanged to suit your own rifle's neck diameters. These neck-sizing dies only size the neck and do not shift the shoulder position on the case, so if after extended use a case starts to feel sticky on extraction, then you will have to resize at full length.

As the neck dies only really have a single depriming probe as a moving part, they are very accurate dies to use and their bushes measure the same as Redding so are interchangeable, which is handy if you use both as I do. These bushes are available in 0.001in size increments, and as such offer the greatest flexibility of choice for the reloader.

In use, the fired case is popped into the neck die on to the deprime probe, and then seated on a compatible base. It is then placed under the Arbor press plunger and the handle moved downwards, which seats the case flush with the die wall. This operation has resized the neck dimensions only so the die is removed, reversed in the base to reveal the depriming probe now stuck out of the top of the die and so another Arbor press stroke depresses the probe simulta-

neously depriming. When the die is removed, the resized deprime case is easily removed. No messy lube and in use very fast and more importantly very accurate resizing, with plenty of 'feel' that aids confidence.

Redding and Hornady also offer bush-style neck-sizing dies for ⅞in presses and are very good and offer an alternative if you prefer. Similarly the hand die Seater that compliments the neck die for Arbor press work is a solid steel or stainless steel piece with the rifle's chamber dimensions accurately reproduced within. The case is placed within a bullet and it is seated accurately via a seater plug that sits on top of the die and is depressed at the stroke of the Arbor press arm. Again, because of the extremely tight tolerances in all hand dies, the case is totally supported and the bullet is seated as concentrically as possible.

Dies and Shellholders

Threaded Dies

By far the most common dies are those that thread directly into the top of the reloading press via a ⅞-14 thread pitch. RCBS, Hornady, Redding, Lyman, Forster and Lee are the most common manufacturers offering dies in full length, neck, and seater die configurations. The die is a hardened steel or stainless steel body with a threaded section at the base, a lock ring and decapping probe with expander ball attached. This die removes the spent primer and resizes the fired case, either full length or just at the neck, dependent on the die purchased. A seating stem (calibre specific) for seater dies replaces the decapping rod and allows a precise bullet placement into the case mouth.

You can upgrade these dies with carbide expander balls, or even opt for the more expensive competition-type dies such as Redding that allow complete case support whilst entering the die, separate neck bushes to adjust neck tension and the portion of neck to be resized without touching the case body. Some seater dies have micrometer adjustments for extremely precise bullet seating, and allow a clear reference point if used for differing loads and bullet types.

Hand Dies

These are really the domain of serious shooters who like to have a hands-on feel to their cartridge prep, and often reload whilst out in the field. The hand dies when used with an Arbor press allow a far greater degree of flexibility in my view, and allow depriming, neck sizing and bullet seater ad hoc whilst out shooting. I use them frequently because I set up a loading table next to me whilst out long-range varminting or testing new wildcats, where I can load on site a small quantity at a time to ascertain the accuracy or velocity; this avoids the problem of travelling to the shoot only to find that the 100 rounds you loaded at home are all poor!

Shellholders

These are essential small metal retaining cups that hold a relevant cartridge secure in the travelling central section of the press, and guide the case into the die and then grip it to remove it again on the down stroke. Some cartridges share a common head size, but it is worth keeping a selection in case you encounter the occasional rimmed or magnum case size. The Forster's Coaxial press does away with this design and has a clamping mechanism built in that accommodates a range of cartridge sizes with one unit.

Shellholders can also be bought or made with varying thickness where they contact the base of a cartridge and thus control headspace and shoulder bump the case to your own rifle's requirements.

Powder Scales

You still have to weigh the thrown powder to establish the correct setting, and I use either a Redding powder scales or an electronic set. The accuracy with which they can repeat a weighed amount, and the ease of use of electronic scales, have really helped reloaders in laborious chores such as case weight separation procedures. Redding, RCBS, Lyman and Dillon all supply very good models, and when combined to a trickler powder dispenser can give very accurate weighing. However, every reloader should also own a balance beam scale set. I use an old Redding scales that can be easily used in the field, are compact and, more importantly, are accurate in use. Again, make sure the surface you weigh your powder on is clean, level and free from air movements or vibrations, otherwise confusing results and potentially dangerous weights will occur.

A powder trickler should be coupled to the scales as an accessory. This allows minute amounts, even individual grains of powder, to be dispensed and weighed at a time. Their use allows the prudent reloader to bring the powder charge weight right up to the expected weight value very slowly and accurately. This is great for all powders and calibres, but particularly useful with small calibre cartridges.

Case Trimmers

Next, some sort of case trimming device is needed in order to keep your cases to safe and recommended overall lengths after firing. This is especially true from hotter cartridges, which will cause a jam fit into the rifle's chamber and can cause pressures to rise alarmingly.

Collet-style trimmers are available from RCBS, Redding and others, and work by using a multi-stepped collet that supports the case head, whilst at the other end a specific calibre pilot supports the case mouth and ensures it is square to the cutter blades.

I use a Wilson case trimmer that holds the case in a tapered case holder that squarely lines up the case against the cutter, whilst an adjustable backstop varies the cutting depth applied by a hand-cranked cutting arm. The case holder is clamped down in twin rails and provides very accurate and square case cutting. It is slower than some cutters, and much slower than powered units, but is still the most accurate, which is what we are ultimately striving for.

I always prefer to manual prep my cases, but motorized trimmers can speed up the process, especially if you have created a weird wildcat round that needs a lot of brass removal. Power attachments for hand drills are available for the Wilson, and especially good are the arrangements of micrometer attachments and differing cutting heads for specific calibres, as well as inside neck deburring tools of varying degrees to suit all types of bullet styles.

Powder Measures

Standard powder measures are numerous with RCBS Uniflow and the Redding series as well as Lyman, Dillon Lee and Hornady models, all of which are good. The Redding 3BR has a change micrometer insert and can accurately throw powder chargers from 5–100 grains with the rifle insert, or 10 grains with the pistol insert, which is great for sub-calibre ammunition and subsonics. The powder is stored in a reservoir above the metering bowl, and a smooth transition from this to case is made with one uniform throw of the operating handle.

For the ultimate in precision two names come to mind, again from the States: Neil Jones and Lynwood Harrell. The differences between their measures and production models are that theirs have machined bodies, very precise click adjustments, lapped measuring drums, removable bottles and variable drop tubes. What you get are the smoothest, most accurate and repeatable powder measures money can buy, and this is a great confidence boaster whilst reloading ammo. I have a Premium model that handles six to 120 grains for regular cartridges, and a Schuetzen for small case capacities such as the .14 and .17 calibres. The click adjustment measure means that I can dial up any known weight from previous measuring and know that the setting will throw that precise amount of powder. The removable powder containers are also useful for changing powder quickly in the field if you are working up loads.

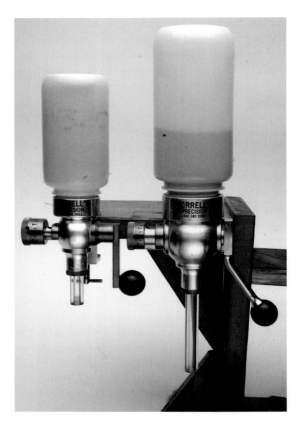

Dispensing powder accurately is paramount for safe and consistent hand loads; these Harrell Culver measures are some of the best.

Priming Tools

Hand-held priming tools can benefit from precision intervention as well. Reloading press-operated priming is all right, but there is a tendency to over-pressurize and crush primers within the pockets. Hand-operated tools have that 'feel' that most precision reloaders want, and products from Lee and Sinclair are all very good. Being able to feel the seating of the primer inspires a bit of confidence, however slow it is compared to more operated procedures. I use a cheap Lee primer that works remarkably well, and with an array of removable shellholders to fit any size rifle case, and two plungers of different sizes to locate small or large primers, your reloading is no chore. Sinclair make a superbly crafted priming tool from stainless steel which has a very concentric and squared axis to allow a very precise single feed of prime into the primer pocket of the case for perfect primer function.

Case Lubrication

Both external and internal case lubrication is essential to proper case preparation. Tasks include full length resizing, case forming, neck turning or sizing and can be sourced as a wax, in an aerosol, on a pad, as a paste or as a dry moly lube for inside neck lubrication.

One of the best, and which seems to last forever, is Imperial sizing wax. Use sparingly for all your reloading tasks, although for tasks involving hundreds of cases it may be better served with a larger pad to roll cases on, or use a spray lube with the cases lined up in a loading tray.

It is essential not to use too much lube as it is not very compressible, and when resizing a case can cause dents in the brass, particularly around the neck area.

Dry lube such as Imperial or Neco is excellent as an inside neck preparation stage, allowing a smooth bullet seating or making sizing tasks and expander balls to move more freely. Forster also make a graphite neck lube, including a range of brushes to reduce friction when neck sizing.

THINGS THAT GO WRONG

Case splitting, bulging/denting, separation, extractor marks and stuck cases are just some of the problems associated with reloading your own ammunition.

Incorrectly set up dies, and lack of, or too much, case lube can be problematic. Neck damage and crushed shoulders can be rectified by using a dummy round set up to use as a guide to correct die settings when that cartridge is due to be reloaded next. Too much lube can cause hydraulic dents to shoulders, and too little will risk stuck cases.

This is all annoying, but worse are split cases and extractor and flat primers, which indicate too high a pressure.

CASE PREPARATION

Specialist Tools

Basic prepping your cases also includes many specialized tools such as expander mandrels that straighten up necks prior to neck turning, also flash hole deburrers and primer pocket uniformers that allow correct setting of all your primers in each case to ensure consistent ignition of your powder charge.

You will also need case mouth deburrers, and neck reamers which reduce internal neck thickness usually after some resizing operation, and again ensure that the bullet is seated concentrically and at an even tension with that of the cartridge case.

This brings me to the concentricity gauges from RCBS, Sinclair or Neco, which all perform similar tasks in as much as they determine the amount of run-out in a cartridge case. This involves revolving a case on its main axis underneath a dial indicator to ascertain the concentricity or uniformity of the loaded round. A round that is slightly out of true will send a bullet slightly off centre into the rifling, and thus upset accuracy potential.

Case Preparation and Maintenance

Of all the consumable reloading components, the case is the only part that we keep and as such needs particular attention as regards quality control, so that we can get rid of any that are faulty. The case is the launch pad from which the bullet is accelerated, and so a properly fitting, consistent, uniform and concentric case that has had some time spent on it, will give that bullet the best start up the rifling of the barrel you can give it.

Case selection and segregation is the first step. Do not skimp on cheap brass: buy the best you can afford – it does matter. I have found Lapua to be excellent, consistent brass, but I have used other makes such as Norma and RWS from time to time for differing calibres.

From a batch of 100 cases you can expect about 20 per cent to have some variation from the mean standard. You are looking initially for obvious visual signs of cracking, buckling neck, rim damage and dents. After this inspection, it is wise to weigh all the saved cases individually to check the variation in overall weight. This is important, because a big difference in weight usually means a difference in the wall or neck thickness of the case, and therefore the internal dimensions can be altered, which would affect powder capacity, burn rate and so on, and this would cause a variation when compared to similar weight cases.

Neck wall thickness can give a good indication of the uniformity of the whole of the case's wall thickness, for possible variance. If you think about it, any extreme variation to neck thickness can result in poor alignment in the rifle's chamber, and as the round is fired the cartridge expands differently to seal the chamber, therefore producing varying pressure and velocity differences.

Usually a variation in weight of between 1 and 2 per cent is acceptable, which means that on a .308 case, if the variation between cases does not exceed 2 to 4gr, then that is acceptable. With the same scrutiny, any neck-wall thickness that has a variation of 0.0015in or more should start the alarm bells ringing, as should any case that

had a 0.0015in variation to its outside circumference. Special ball micrometers or wall-thickness gauges are available.

Let us turn now to the primer area, primarily the primer pocket and flash hole. In European brass, such as Lapua and Norma, you will find that the cases are more consistent from lot to lot because the case heads are machined and the flash holes are drilled rather than punched. Any variation in the primer pocket depth, concentricity dimensions and flash-hole size and length and the state of the burrs present can all influence the smooth ignition of your powder column.

There will be a certain amount of burr formation on the inside edges of the primer hole as it is drilled or punched through. These will interfere with the ignition process, and one sign of this on target is a vertical dispersion of the group size due to variance in velocity. It is an easy task to remove such burrs with the correct tool, and whether you can actually see any burrs or not, it is best to deburr and uniform all the brass the same.

Next is the primer pocket itself. Keeping the

Putting it all together can at times be frustrating, but when your group sizes shrink it may all seem worthwhile.

edges uniform to ensure a correctly fitting primer is important, as is depth to ensure that the firing pin strikes are repeated for each shot. Sinclair state that most firing pins protrude within a range of 0.045 to 0.060in, and that with a primer seating variance of only 0.010in, the firing pin strike can vary as much as 20 per cent. I use a Sinclair primer pocket uniformer in small or large configuration depending on the size primer pockets I need to uniform.

Most cases when new will have a slightly sharp or burred edge to the mouth after the manufacturing process. The solution is easy with a deburring tool available from Wilsons, Redding and Lee; these tools have the bonus of having a dechamfering tool at the reverse end of them as well as a deburring end. Just insert the cone of the tool into the case neck and rotate three turns in a clockwise motion with a little applied pressure; that action will have chamfered the inside of the case neck, so reverse the tool and allow the cutters, three spurs on the Wilson model, to gently deburr the outside edge of the case, again about three turns with light pressure.

If you have an std rifle and have followed the segregation of cases by weight and neck thickness, and have therefore culled those that have fallen below specification, then you may not need to neck turn. This is because cases are neck turned to reduce the wall thickness and in turn reduce the outside diameter of the loaded round's neck dimensions. In an std chamber there is enough leeway or gap from case neck to chamber wall, but in a non-std, say a Bench gun with a tight neck, you need to turn to achieve a 0.001in gap minimum between the case neck of the loaded round and the rifle's chamber wall, on each side.

If you elect to go the neck-turning route then you must consider the tools involved, with some form of case neck uniform expander mandrel that ensures a proper fit between case neck and mandrel or pilot on the neck-turning tool. If an expander mandrel is used – I use an Expandiron – it should be 0.0005 to 0.0015in larger than the mandrel on the neck tool. By screwing the Expandiron into a press you can uniformly expand your cases inside, which therefore transfers any irregularities to the outside edge of the case's neck so that the neck-turning cutter can cleanly skim them off and therefore produce a neck with equal dimensions and thickness.

I use a K & M and Sinclair neck-turning tool, and do all the operations by hand with no powered assistance. It is slower, but you can feel your way better.

ADVANCED KIT TO AID IN BETTER RELOADS

If there is one piece of kit that every serious shooter or hand loader should own, then it is the Stoney Point overall length (OAL) gauge and bullet comparator. These two precision items can mean the difference between realizing your rifle's true accuracy potential and not, as well as ensuring that your reloading dies are set up correctly and, more importantly, safely.

It is a proven fact that most rifles shoot more accurately when the bullet is seated in the case just off the rifling lands. This means that the 'ogive' part of the bullet – the curved section of the bullet ahead of the bearing surface area or shank – is seated just shy of the start of the rifling. This ensures that the bullet has less 'jump' from case to rifling, which might upset its initial progressive flight, and that it enters the lands of the rifling concentrically, ensuring a uniform start. Also, by being seated off the lands, the chamber pressures can be drastically reduced, especially if running your loads at full throttle. A few thousandths of an inch difference in this measurement can result in fair accuracy or spectacular accuracy as the 'sweet' spot is reached – and each rifle has one.

An OAL gauge looks like a chamber bore guide with a removable sliding inner section to which a cartridge case is attached. To start using the gauge you will need to purchase what is called a 'modified case' that fits your rifle's chamber, and fits to the gauge via a threaded section at the tip. There are over sixty modified cases available, which cover the most popular calibres available to the shooter.

Select the bullet you intend to use in your reloads, and slip it into the neck end of the modified case. The inner lightweight bullet push rod made from tough glass-filled nylon is held in

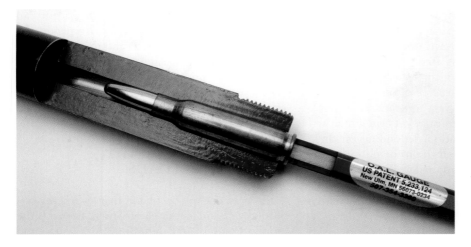

The 'overall length' (OAL) gauge allows you to seat a bullet as close as you want to the rifling in the barrel to achieve best accuracy.

place by a thumb screw at the rear of the gauge, and loosening this allows the inner push rod to be located to support the bullet and stop it falling back into the case body. Next insert the gauge by sliding it into the chamber of the rifle until it is a snug fit. Do not ram it in; you just need a surface-to-surface fit for accurate results. You can then slide the gauge's internal push rod forwards, after loosening the thumb screw, until the bullet makes contact with the lands of the rifling.

At this point you have reached the maximum OAL with that shape and ogive of bullet in the calibre of that rifle. Of course, if a different bullet were to be selected – for example a round nose instead of a soft point, or especially a VLD (very low drag) bullet – the contact length would alter considerably and the OAL would change due to the differing bullet length and ogive-to-lands contact. It is precisely these differences that ensure that the OAL of any bullet combination is the most accurate within the confines of your own gun.

Armed with this information you can now confidently transfer this measurement to your log book as a permanent record for that case and bullet type combination; more importantly, you can use this invaluable measurement in setting up your seating dies when you actually reload.

If you use a bullet comparator after the OAL gauge setting, the reading will give you a more precise and accurate result because it measures the ogive length to the base of the cartridge. You can also check bullet uniformity without a case with this tool to ascertain the base-to-ogive uniformity of individual bullets, and can then sort them accordingly. The bullet comparator can be easily attached to the blade of your callipers with the thumbscrew provided, and the interchangeable inserts' bushings allow any calibre to be measured for the bullet ogive.

NECK TURNING

I have mentioned neck turning briefly, and if you are serious about your reloads you will probably want to go down this route. In simple terms, neck turning your brass reduces the wall thickness of the cases and thus uniforms it as well as achieving a perfect fit to your own gun's chamber dimensions. In essence, you are tailor-making your brass for your own individual gun, which, after all, is what precision reloading is all about.

Reloaders who have guns with tight-necked chambers have to neck turn to ensure a correct fit, but people with standard chambered rifles also neck turn to ensure uniformity of wall thickness; however, be careful not to remove too much brass.

Neck-turning tools are usually manual and therefore laborious to use; however, very accurate case dimensions are achieved by this operation, and so it is certainly worth putting in the time to do it. To skimp on this procedure is fool-

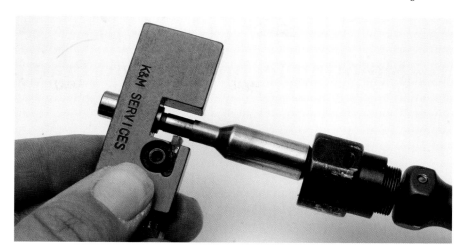

Neck turning can make neck rim thickness uniform, and may be necessary when reforming brass in a wildcat round; this K and M neck turner is very accurate.

hardy, as it can undo a great deal of the hard case prep work achieved earlier. Usually a case is supported on a pilot that is sized to be approximately 0.0005 to 0.001in smaller than the inside diameter of the cartridge. The case is then supported in the cutters and manually fed slowly into the cutter tool so that a small portion of the neck brass is removed by each even stroke until the neck and shoulder junction is met. You can use power tools for this procedure, but I prefer the hands-on manual tools because you begin to feel the actual cases you are sizing, and form a synergy between them and you.

Measuring tools are so much a part of the precision-shooting scene that a quality pair of calipers is essential if quality ammunition is to be produced. All manner of operations can be assessed by a simple caliper reading, from cases to mandrel thickness, seating depth to outside dimensions, the list is endless. Whether you opt for a dial caliper set from Starrett or others, or an electronic readout from Mitutoyo, as I do, these should form the heart of any reloading operation to check tolerances.

Regardless of the kit you buy, always remember that reloading is a potentially hazardous procedure, and one that should only be undertaken by experienced people.

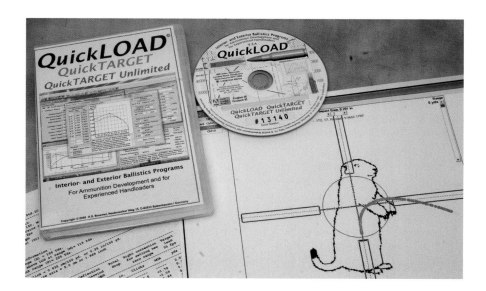

Refer to proper reloading manuals or use the excellent Quick Load Ballistics program to ascertain internal and exterior ballistics.

Chapter 10
Shooting Techniques and Practical Tips

With so many rifles on offer to the shooter, the choice can be offputting and bewildering if you do not have a clear preference. However, more important than the actual purchase is how that rifle performs, and how its individual quirks are translated out in the fields and woods where it will be put to use. Too often we sight in a rifle at 100yd (90m) from the comfort of a bench and probably a sandbag or rest, and then expect it to shoot exactly the same when we venture to the woods. The truth is more complicated, in that whether you shoot from sticks, rest on a convenient tree, or fit one of the many bipods to your rifle, you absolutely must practise in that style or position.

Why is this important? The recoiling difference and pressure variation between holds can and will affect the bullet's impact point. If a hold is made too near the end of the fore-end, then the extra upward pressure can cause any floating barrel advantage to disappear, and will not allow the barrel to vibrate freely and thus will alter your aim. The same is true with a bipod fitment, in that often the added up force is enough to close the gap between wood and barrel metal with the same consequence, so that more often than not the shots will shoot high when a bipod is fitted.

Also, too many people grip their rifle with the fingers of their supporting hand reaching round the woodwork and gripping the barrel itself – or worst still, when using sticks to steady the hold – which is good – rest the barrel on the sticks and do not use the supporting hand as a buffer. Practise stalking situations in real life: you are only fooling yourself if you can shoot good groups off a bench, and then not translate this to the game fields.

In the field, proper shooting technique can be abandoned because you have to rely on what Mother Nature gives you in the form of a rest.

Opportunistic rests often present themselves.

You should also practice with realistic targets of deer, with natural colouring and size if possible, set at any range that you typically encounter deer, and at the time of day you shoot; low light will sharpen your rifle technique, making you a more confident stalker and a safer one.

The ability to judge wind correctly is essential to achieve a successful stalk if the range is increased, so practise judging wind speeds and the effects on the bullet's path. Windmeters are cheap these days, and I familiarize myself with changing wind speed by relating what the windmeter speed is telling me in relation to the movement of the trees or leaves and bracken. Time spent honing these simple techniques will again instil confidence, and shows respect to your quarry with improved shooting and stalking technique.

Practise your Shooting Positions

In the field you have to take shots at all sorts of angles and positions and the reality is, in order to become a competent shot, you really do need to practise shooting from all manner of stances before venturing afield – sitting, prone, kneeling, standing or bending over tick-infested hummocks ankle deep in water!

Under real-life shooting conditions there is neither the time nor a suitable level from which to conduct the perfect shot. Personally in order to improve my ability at differing ranges under differing lighting conditions and from really awkward but true-to-life shots, I actually practise under these conditions. It sounds obvious, but so many shooters just zero on the range and leave it at that, and then wonder why their shot missed from that vantage point high in the craggy recesses of a wind-swept hillock.

Regardless of position, go out with a rifle zeroed under perfect conditions, and then wait for a windy day or that cold snap or incessant rain, and learn the rifle's true potential, and yours, from a variety of true-to-life shooting positions. I often put up realistic game silhouettes made from steel at unknown ranges and in all manner of angles and cover, give myself a limited supply of ammunition and a range finder, and then proceed to shoot each target. A miss is not acceptable, because in real life a trophy roe buck will not give you a second shot. The key is not, repeat not, to fool yourself. Practise like this and your game bag will always be full.

Opportunistic shots at game abound and it is you that is usually taken by surprise, so you should be ready to adapt to your environment

Use silhouette targets to hone your skill at range because they give a more realistic aiming point than a paper target, and a hit is also audible.

and use any feature or article that will help steady your aim. In the prone position any mound or bump in the terrain can help, and so can grabbing a handful of grass with the supporting hand. If time allows, your hat, roe sack or binoculars can be used to elevate your aim from any vegetation – though make sure not to rest your rifle on a hard surface or your zero will change.

EQUIPMENT

Slings

To hold a rifle whilst constantly on the move is ill advised; it should be slung over the shoulder, leaving the hands free for using your binoculars, steadying yourself or for holding a shooting stick. Slings may be of leather or synthetic material, wide or thin, but above all they must not make a sound in use so as to avoid alerting your game, and rot proof to avoid any nasty accidents.

From any position the bracing effect of using a sling slung around the outer portion of the supporting arm greatly helps in steadying the aim.

Bipods

Almost a mandatory item on rifles these days, bipods are detachable supports that can be used prone from a bench or hillock, and even from a sitting position. Some have swivel attachments to allow the rifle to tilt from the axis of the legs, which helps proper shooting on uneven ground. Always remember to check your zero before and after using a bipod, as the upward pressure they exert on the fore-end can shift your point of zero.

Their real benefit is that they are attached to the rifle and so you do not forget to leave home without them, as you can with sticks, and they fold unobtrusively under the forearm of the rifle until needed.

Sticks

I always take a good pair of sticks whether foxing or deer stalking. They provide a solid support when standing or when crossing hilly terrain, and are useful for gauging the depth of water. A telescopic pair is more versatile, and a two-legged version is better than a single because it is more stable, and quicker to deploy than some three-legged versions.

OPTIMIZING YOUR RIFLE'S PERFORMANCE

Always, and without question in a sporting situation, it is the first shot that counts. No matter how well your rifle groups on the range, if it does not reliably place that first shot from a cold barrel exactly where you aim, it has no use in my eyes as a sporting arm. This dilemma has plagued shooters for centuries, and is the most common cause for a miss in a hunting situation.

This might seem a straightforward problem to remedy, but owing to the variations in rifle manufacture, every rifle has its very own signature as to where the first shot will shoot. This is further complicated by the condition in which the rifle was left prior to the shot being taken. In this I mean, was the gun cleaned the night before? Is there still residual oil in the barrel? Is the barrel still fouled? Are the climatic conditions the same as when you shot the rifle last?

Paradoxically in order to keep a rifle shooting accurately it needs to have a spotless bore, but to store a rifle this bore actually needs a film of rust-preventing oil. Fine, but when that rifle is taken out the next morning and you forget to clean out the protective oil layer, you have instantly changed the internal conditions in which the bullet travels up that barrel, and almost always the first shot will shoot wild and away from your aiming point. The same can be true if you clean a rifle the night before and,

RIGHT: *Folding telescopic sticks from Knob loch are a great asset when no other rest presents itself.*

BELOW: *A bipod attached to the rifle offers a stable platform, but remember to zero the rifle with this on, as it may change the point of impact when fitted on a rifle with a flimsy fore-end.*

knowing you are out stalking tomorrow at first light, omit to oil the barrel. One night's lack of lube will not harm if the rifle is kept dry, but often you will find that overnight, even if that bore was spotless and patched out *dry*, a small residual trace of cleaning solvent may remain.

Similarly, if the rifle is not cleaned at all, any fouling or moisture it attracts may cause an erratic first shot.

Strangely, however, the diversion from the aim point of a lightly fouled bore is often much less than that of a clean, oiled bore, as the barrel is already 'conditioned' with shot residue and is already 'shot'-ready. But in a hunting situation you do not have the luxury of shooting off a couple of shots before you head to the woods, so to minimize this problem you need to see if your rifle exhibits these traits and how *it* actually behaves.

First test the rifle with a perfectly cleaned bore, as you usually do, and then leave a protective layer of oil in the bore as you would if the rifle were to be stored. Then shoot the rifle cold to produce a group of shots at 100yd (90m), and

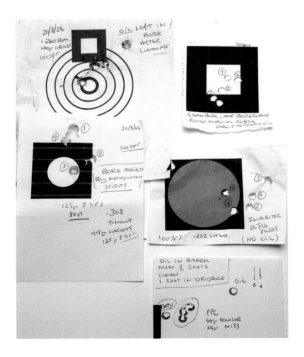

In a hunting situation it is the first shot on target that counts, not how well the other shots all group.

note each shot and where it printed in the group. Also check each shot over the chronograph to check shot-to-shot consistency.

You will notice that the first shot from each barrel exhibits a deviation from the following shots, and in some cases very markedly so – the initial shot can shoot a good 1–2in (3–5cm) away from the main body of the group. This is obviously most undesirable, and would result in a miss on small game or a poorly placed shot on large game.

Next you test under the same conditions the same rifle and load with a clean barrel with no oil in the bore. Shoot immediately after cleaning from a squeaky clean bore, and also when left overnight, to check for solvent ingress. You will find that from a dry bore after cleaning, the first shot in most cases will be much closer to the main body of the group, and repeating this but leaving the 'cleaned' rifle overnight can produce the same results.

A few remedies: if you forget to clean the oil layer from the bore prior to shooting you could use a bore snake of the right calibre with your rifle on a hunt. A bore snake is simply a pull-through cleaning system containing an integral bore brush and cleaning swap/patch, and can be very useful in these situations; it takes up no room in a pocket in its packet, and by simply pulling it through the bore a few times you achieve a dry and oil-free bore. Under these conditions the first shot behaves as though you had a rifle that was cleaned the night before and left unoiled.

Another alternative is to use Inhibitor rifle plugs. These can be inserted in the rifle as a cartridge substitute, and their vapour penetrates the bore and protects against rust. This method leaves less oil in the bore and goes some way to keeping that first shot where you aim. Alternatively you can shoot a few primed rifle cartridges prior to the stalk if you have forgotten to remove the oil from the bore, and this can give you a situation where the bore is partially 'conditioned', as stated before; as a result the first shot is much more likely to go where you aim. Similarly, a few subsonic rounds can be shot with the same beneficial results without frightening any game, and they precondition the rifle so that all-important initial shot hits home, accurately.

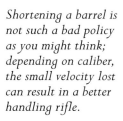

Shortening a barrel is not such a bad policy as you might think; depending on caliber, the small velocity lost can result in a better handling rifle.

Finally, a method used by many professionals, including law enforcement agencies, is to completely dry the bore with methylated spirit before shooting. If you shoot using this method every time, then you have a benchmark of your bore's condition, and the first shot should consistently shoot to point of aim. However, you have to remember always to shoot with a cleaned methylated barrel.

My advice therefore is, spend a little time learning the preferences of each rifle you own, and you will feel far more confident in your abilities on your next hunting trip.

OPTIMAL BARREL LENGTH

One of the most commonly asked questions, other than what is the perfect calibre, is how much velocity will be lost if the length of the stalking/fox rifle is reduced as an aid to a lighter rifle, and will its overall length still be manageable after fitting a sound moderator.

There are factory-set guidelines regarding the velocity loss per inch reduction of barrel length at differing velocities, but these seldom reflect the diverse range of calibres that most shooters encounter. Furthermore every barrel has its own unique internal dimensions that will affect the bullet's flight, not only in terms of accuracy but also regarding the bullet's acceleration and retardation. Bullet weight, shape and material as well as the burn rate of the propellant used also have an enormous effect on a bullet's velocity. The only really accurate way to check velocity drop is to cut a few barrels and measure the velocity drop for yourself.

I used as a reference one in .223 calibre and

the other in .308 calibre on an RPA rifle. This would give me a small calibre fox cartridge that also doubles as a roe deer round in Scotland, and muntjac and CWD in England, and the .308 is an industry standard deer calibre. In the test only velocity loss would be measured, because to quantify accuracy change at the differing barrel lengths would involve having to recrown the muzzle after each length reduction, and that would take too long, although I did deburr the cut.

Initial Results

I therefore initially started the test with the 24in (60cm) barrel lengths by shooting a string of five shots repeated twice for reloaded ammunition, and the results were then analysed.

I ended up in .223 calibre with a 52gr Speer bullet travelling at 3402fps from the 24in RPA barrel length using 24.5gr of Vit N133 powder; velocity range was only 31fps and therefore very consistent. The same rationale was used for the larger .308-calibre test barrel, with a reload of a Sierra 150gr Game King travelling at 2905fps with an overall fps range of only 27fps, thus reducing the window for inch loss analysis for the barrel reduction.

At each inch of barrel reduction for each calibre a five-shot string was recorded over a chronograph to measure muzzle velocity, and thus ascertain velocity reduction.

The .223 calibre shot a velocity of 3402fps from a 24in (60cm) barrel, which is a good starting point generating 1337ft/lb energy. Reducing the barrel inch by inch to 20in (50cm) only loses 149fps, which in practical terms is very little, yet the benefits in weight reduction

Actual velocity loss per inch reduction in the RPA rifle				
	.223 calibre (52gr bullet)		.308 calibre (150gr bullet)	
Barrel length in (cm)	*Muzzle velocity (fps)*	*Reduction in velocity (fps)*	*Muzzle velocity (fps)*	*Reduction in velocity (fps)*
24 (60)	3402		2905	
23 (57.6)	3344	-58	2879	-26
22 (55)	3299	-45	2851	-28
21 (52.5)	3275	-24	2826	-25
20 (50)	3253	-22	2792	-34
19 (48)	3235	-18	2780	-12
18 (45)	3185	-50	2748	-32
		total 217 fps		total 157 fps

and overall length are real. Taking an extra 2in (5cm) off gives a highly 'trim' rifle, but you do start to notice increased muzzle blast.

At 18in (45cm) the 3185fps velocity and 1171ft/lb energy is only 217fps short of the initial velocity. This means that when zeroed at 100yd (90m) with the starting velocity you are -2.1in (-5.3cm) low at 200yd (183m) and -9.5in (-24.1cm) low at 300yd (274m). With the shorter 18in barrel with 217fps reduction equates with a zero at 100yd and then a drop of -2.5in (-6.35cm) at 200yd and -11.3in (-28.7cm) at 300yd. So at 200yd there is only a -0.4in (-1cm) difference, and at 300yd a -1.8in (-4.6cm) difference, so in real terms the gain in weight loss and reduction in overall length far outweigh the minuscule velocity loss.

Similarly the .308 calibre 150gr Sierra Game King starting out at 2905fps generates 2812ft/lb energy and only suffers a 157fps loss for a barrel reduction of 6in (15cm). To me that is very efficient, and certainly justifies reducing a .308 barrel to 18in (45cm), as there is little real loss in velocity. Muzzle blast increases, but a moderator takes care of that.

As regards trajectory, a zero at 100yd for the 24in (60cm) velocity yields a drop at 200yd of -2.9 (-7.4cm) and -11.9 (-30.2cm) at 300yd (27m). Reduction of the barrel to 18in (45cm) with a 100yd zero has a drop at 200yd of -3.7 (-9.4cm) and at 300yd of only 14.4in (36.6cm).

In truth this doesn't really make a difference, especially when most deer are shot at 100yd or less.

Out of interest I now have that same RPA .308 barrel running at 14.5in (36.8cm) length, and it shoots a Berger 110gr bullet at 2850fps with a charge of 40gr H4198 powder and is capable of half MOA groups at 300yd with a PES Extreme sound moderator fitted.

Small Game and Fox Calibre Barrel Reductions

The rimfire is a completely different proposition: whereas a .308 may burn 46gr of powder, a .22lr commonly burns approximately 2.5gr of powder in high velocity loading and 1gr with a subsonic load, so does not require such a long barrel to achieve good ballistics – but how long is optimal? Ballistics is not only about achieving the highest velocity, and I would much rather have accurate and consistent velocities coupled to a handy rifle and moderator if this were practical.

A Sako Quad rifle was tested with both .22lr and .17 HMR barrels, and because rimfires are not reloadable I kept to Eley and RWS subsonic ammunition for the .22 rimfire and Hornady 17gr for the .17 HMR. At each barrel-length reduction five shots were fired over the chronograph to ascertain velocity.

As we know, rimfires use a small charge of powder to propel a bullet from the barrel, but how to define the optimum point where propulsion stops and barrel friction takes over?

It has long been known that for most .22 rimfires the maximum velocity is often reached at about 16in (40cm) of barrel length. This is because rimfires use a small amount of fast-burning powder that initiates burning very rapidly, and thus peak pressure rises very quickly, transferring the energy generated to the bullet to overcome the crimp from the case, to actually initiate the bullet's movement, and then engage the bullet in the lands of the barrel. The pressure does not remain constant and rises very quickly to its peak within the first 5in (13cm) of barrel, and then drops as the bullet accelerates up the barrel. As the internal volume of space increases, the gases produced from the burning powder have more space to fill, and thus cool. However, the bullet does not stop, but continues along the bore as the stored kinetic energy within the bullet from the powder burn allows it to continue its travel down the bore.

The bullet's velocity rises very quickly, then plateaus out; it does not drop off immediately, which is important here, as the kinetic energy carries it forwards. But at some point the momentum will wane and the frictional forces from the bore, and lack of bullet lube, will further retard the acceleration of the bullet. It is at what point this happens that is of interest to us.

What does this mean in real terms? This test shows what most shooters know already, that reducing a .22lr barrel to 16in (40cm) very rarely affects velocity loss. You are removing redundant barrel that only adds friction to the bullet and thus retards its velocity – the chronograph never lies. The .17 HMR round's 114fps drop is more than made up for in the barrel weight reduction and being able to keep the overall length the same when a moderator is fitted.

Based on these results, sportspersons should have no doubts about reducing their rimfire barrels or purchasing new rifles with short 16in barrels, because in real use this makes little change on the velocity of the cartridge.

Shortening a rimfire barrel is certainly beneficial, especially when you fit a moderator. Many manufacturers now offer rimfires with 14 or 16in (35 or 40cm) barrels already threaded for a moderator.

Velocity loss per inch of barrel reduction in the .22 rimfire Sako Quad rifle

.22lr Eley subsonic velocity (fps)		.22lr RWS subsonic velocity (fps)	
Barrel length in (cm)	Mean velocity	Barrel length inches	Mean velocity
22 (55)	1042	22	986
21 (52.5)	1057	21	982
20 (50)	1051	20	969
19 (48)	1061	19	995
18 (45)	1063	18	1017
17 (43)	1074	17	1043
16 (40)	1063	16	1050
Final loss/gain	+21	Final loss/gain	+64

PENETRATION TESTS

Rimfires

Most shooters will own or at least have shot a .22 rimfire in their lifetime, and often they will choose the cheapest ammunition manufacturer; however, every rifle has its own preferences as regards ammunition type, and will perform to its best when provided with the most compatible ammo. Accuracy is the key to achieving any humane shot, but you must also consider the performance of the bullet when it reaches its target. Poor penetration or expansion can mean less than perfect results.

The penetration test medium was in the form of soap bars measuring 2 × 2in (5 × 5cm) square and cut to approximately 6in (15cm) lengths. The range test was 30yd (27m), and the rifle used was a Ruger M77/22 rimfire with 20in (50cm) barrel, with the intention to measure the depth of penetration and the bullet expansion for each of the six bullets tested. I am sure the soap does not mimic actual body tissue, but it is used by certain bullet makers to test bullets, so it should give a control medium from which to *compare* each bullet's performance.

What do you want from a subsonic round with regard to actual penetration? Almost certainly their primary use is to dispatch game — that is, rabbits — as humanely as possible, yet give good exterior ballistics such as flat trajectory,

Velocity loss per inch of barrel reduction in the .17 HMR Sako Quad barrel

.17 HMR Hornady 17 grain bullet velocity (fps)

Barrel length inches (cm)	Mean velocity (fps)
22 (55)	2665
21 (52.5)	2590
20 (50)	2577
19 (48)	2634
18 (45)	2576
17 (43)	2498
16 (40)	2551
Final loss/gain	-114

accuracy and 'on game stopping power' and hopefully not too much over-penetration and carryover, where the bullet's lethality is lost.

As regards penetration depth, the RWS penetrated the least and the Lapua the most, and I repeated the test twice with the same results. This can be explained by the fact that the Lapua was the second fastest bullet tested and one of the lightest, which ordinarily would cause a rapid expansion, but it was the hardest of all the bullets and therefore failed to expand well in these tests.

The RWS had the shortest bullet path at 2.8in (7cm), which bodes well in the transferring of all its energy within the quarry. Also the actual expansion was 0.4in (1cm), the second largest from the test with a broad 0.35in (9mm) wound channel. Undoubtedly the soft, heavy lead projectile travelling at the slowest velocity performed admirably well in the tests.

The Winchesters, too, with their 40.3gr bullet, expanded well to 0.35in (9mm) and penetrated 2.95in (7.5cm) in the test medium, allowing the full 101.5ft/lb energy to be transferred to the target in the quickest possible time.

Next was the CCI round, again a 39.8 grainer with a higher velocity of 1077fps and a better hollow-point design than before. The CCI penetrated 3.40in (8.6cm), just behind the Remington round, but the bullet expansion was larger at 0.35in (9mm), probably due to the now softer lead used and larger hollow point cavity.

Eley Subsonics produced a healthy 1032fps, and when combined to a soft lead 40.2gr bullet with ample hollow point, turned in some impressive results. It did not over-penetrate like some of the bullets, and expanded to 0.45in (1.1cm) at 3.25in (8.25cm) depth with an impressive 0.5 (1.27cm) wound channel. This was the best performance of the ammunition tested.

Bars of soap show the wound channel and expansion of rimfire bullets rather well.

Finally the Remington, despite being lightest at 38.7gr, gave the second lowest velocity and energy figures, but actually penetrated to 3.55in (9cm), more than the Eley, RWS, CCI and Winchesters. This was probably due to the fact that although the bullet exhibited the classic mushroom shape at 0.25in (0.63cm), the same

Performance of common .22 rimfire subsonic ammunition available to the British shooter

Ammo make	Weight grains actual weighed	Velocity fps (mean five shots)	Energy ft/lb	Penetration inches (cm) (30yd)	Bullet expansion inches (cm)
Eley Subsonic Xtra Plus	40.2	1032	95.1	3.25 (8.25)	0.45 (1.14)
Winchester Subsonic	40.3	1065	101.5	2.95 (7.5)	0.35 (0.88)
Remington Subsonic	38.7	1029	91.0	3.55 (9.0)	0.25 (0.63)
CCI Subsonic	39.8	1077	102.5	3.40 (8.63)	0.35 (0.88)
RWS Subsonic	40.3	991	87.9	2.8 (7.1)	0.4 (1.0)
Lapua Subsonic	39.8	1071	101.4	3.75 (9.5)	0.25 (0.63)

diameter as the Lapua, it too was made of harder lead with a smaller hollow-point cavity.

You may choose a particular type of bullet based on performance, but if it is not accurate in your particular gun, then all your hard work will go to waste.

First choice should always be accuracy: there is no point going for the fastest, best expanding bullet if it does not connect with the target. Therefore looking at the results objectively, if you want a fast-expanding bullet that dumps its energy on target quickly and causes the largest wound channel and does not over-penetrate too much yet has good exterior ballistic characteristics, the Eley Subs Xtra Plus or the RWS would be my choice based on these results.

.17 Mach 2 and .17 HMR

The .17 rimfires are a different proposition altogether, transcending the rimfire world into higher velocities, utilizing fast-expanding, light copper-jacketed bullets most akin to centrefire ammunition.

There are two ways to look at this: on the one hand you have a highly frangible varmint bullet in the 17gr V-Max loads that make for a safe but close-range vermin bullet, but as velocity drops, fails to expand reliably at extended ranges and lacks the kinetic energy levels for foxes. The 20gr projectile with a hollow point goes some way to alleviate this problem and provides a greater energy figure and more controlled expansion for better penetration.

The only way to test this in real time is to shoot some more bullet expansion medium.

The .17 Mach 2 has a muzzle velocity of about 2100fps depending on barrel and the rifle's chamber, and utilizes the same 17gr V-Max bullet as the .17 HMR cartridge. Even at 2100fps, the speeding, highly volatile bullet expands very rapidly at ranges from 0–75yd (0–68m), where a deep, almost instant hydraulic expansion occurs, causing the V-Max to rupture with only the rear-led core section and base continuing to penetrate. As the range passes beyond 75yd (68m) or so, the velocity drop causes the V-Max to expand less violently and actually penetrate deeper, and beyond 100–125yd (90–114m) the bullet can often act as a full metal jacket with complete pass-through on small game and thus

little hydrostatic shock, but still deadly as a head or neck shot. The .17 HMR starts out faster at 2500–2650, depending on the rifle, but you have a choice of several 17gr bullet types with V-Max, TNT and also a 20gr XTP bullet weight.

At these velocities the 17gr V-Max literally disintegrates at ranges up to 100yd (90m) on small game, causing instant and humane first round kills with very little chance of ricochets. On foxes it penetrates sufficiently first to enter the rib cage before expansion, but a poorly placed shot on a shoulder, quartering away, would result in a surface wound.

The Speer 17gr TNT bullet has a hollow-point light-jacketed design, but shows a much milder and more controlled expansion, with good penetration but lacking real explosive effective, like the 17gr V-Max bullet. The 20gr XTP load gives the small game shooter a much better fox load, as penetration is deep with really good controlled expansion like a deer bullet, mushrooming controllably and still imparting a better kinetic energy punch than the lighter 17gr bullets at longer range.

Centrefire Varmint Loads

This category covers a wide range of velocities, making the correct choice of bullet design and construction of paramount importance. If you want to be able to eat a rabbit shot at 50yd (45m) it will require a totally different bullet from one that is needed to expand rapidly to dispatch a fox. With the same token, the larger the animal, the more controlled expansion is necessary to allow penetration into the vitals before the bullet fragments. This can cause a lot of problems when choosing a bullet for centrefire work, because unlike the 17 rimfires, the velocities are usually a lot higher and the bullets, however fragile, need to withstand the pressures in the barrel and the rotational twist of the rifling.

Some bullets of this exact nature – the Sierra Blitz Kings, Hornady V-Maxes, Speer TNT or Nosler Ballistic Tips – are designed to withstand the high rotational speeds yet still stay intact and perform predictably on target. Bullets designated for cartridges such as the .22 Hornet have a velocity ceiling – for example the Hornady SX bullets – because they are more fragile than

The bullet test tube gives very accurate information with regard to bullet performance, and can be a real aid to determining the best bullet for use against a certain species.

other .224 bullets and are designed to expand at Hornet velocities, not .22-250 speeds.

Also check that any hollow-point bullets are designated for 'varmint' use, as many match-grade bullets have hollow-point designs but have a thicker jacket wall towards the tip and expand more slowly. You have to judge for yourself the range at which you most encounter game to best select a bullet, as more aerodynamic bullets with high BC figures – such as those with polymer tips, boat-tail or VLD designs – will give you better performance down range, whereas a close called-in fox or crow needs a faster expanding, lighter bullet type.

Deer Calibres

For deer by law you must have a bullet that is designed to expand with a soft or hollow point. Any match-grade bullet, even with a hollow point, is illegal to use on deer in this country, however good their accuracy or indeed down-range performance.

Deer vary enormously in size, and again choice of bullet has to reflect the game you will encounter. However, bigger is not always better, because with all deer there is the consideration of valuable venison to harvest, and although fast-expanding varmint-type bullets may appeal for

their lethality, in reality they will either ruin a carcass or cause nasty surface wounds without proper penetration.

There is no reason you cannot use a varmint bullet for the smaller deer species, but I would reload the cartridge to shoot them at a lower velocity to gain *good* expansion and not *explosive* expansion. In my .308 Tikka I regularly use 125gr Nosler Ballistic Tips loaded to just above the Scottish velocity minimum of 2450fps, and have found this normally fragile bullet to work very well on muntjac and roe as well as reds at close range. Conversely to save meat damage I tend to use a heavier bullet per calibre class at a lower but deer-legal level for the same reasoning: to deliver a predictable penetrating but expanding bullet with high sectional density to cause lethality but minimal venison damage. However, there will be times when that extra velocity and bullet expansion is necessary for stags or fallow bucks that know how to stay out of your normal shooting range, and you need all the speed possible to connect.

Bullets such as the Nosler Partition are very good controlled expansion bullets, as are the Sierra Game Kings and the Hornady Interbonds. I really like the Hornady SST bullets that always have shot accuracy and perform perfectly on game, and the newer Nosler Accubond

.308 bullets showing the differing expansion rates well in the test tube media.

is probably the best all-round deer bullet for British deer I have used. It combines good BC figures with a strong, rear-bonded core section to drive home the thinner jacket front section of the bullet to allow perfect mushrooming of the lead core in the bullet's tip.

The only way to truly assess a bullet's performance is to shoot it! Accuracy is paramount, but to test the down range performance I use a ballistic medium called the 'Bullet Test Tube'. This is a tube 12in (30cm) long containing a waxy medium that mimics tissue sufficiently to allow a bullet to expand and be captured, and when sectioned reveals the bullet wound channel that is the giveaway to proper bullet performance. Only in this way, by comparing the individual bullet's performance against another, can you really achieve the goal of which bullet suits you and your circumstances.

UPHILL AND DOWNHILL SHOOTING

If you reload or shoot factory ammunition you should choose a load you like that shoots accurately and with enough energy, and then shoot it over a chronograph to gain the true velocity reading and thus energy reading from that load under your individual conditions. Barrel length, rifling twist, groove diameter, rifling land size and a number of other factors all have a bearing (literally) on the true ballistics of a load, and that is why even the same calibre from a differing rifle can shoot so differently. With this information you can then plot your rifle's trajectory over the distance that you

Shots taken at a large angle either up or down will result in your shots going high.

expect to shoot, and thus compensate for any drop to ensure a hit.

This is all very fine, but those trajectory values are only valid when you shoot on a horizontal plane (also with unaltering climatic conditions), but as soon as the muzzle is inclined or declined at an angle, the trajectory alters with increasing severity as the angle becomes greater. To understand the problem is just a simple method of physics and how gravity affects a bullet's flight in any situation. In fact in both scenarios the bullet will always shoot high on a sloped shot when compared to a horizontal one. This is because the trajectory is flatter as the angle reduces the horizontal distance the bullet travels, and thus the effect that gravity imparts on the bullet.

In this way it is the horizontal distance travelled that will count, and not the linear distance. This is because gravity always works perpendicular to a horizontal line; it neither increases nor decreases the velocity of a projectile as some people think.

If you look at the diagram you can see that a shot taken at 345yd (315m) from point a to b at an inclined angle of 40 degrees actually only has a gravitational effect on the distance the bullet travels parallel to the ground where the gravitational force is at its strongest. This means that the distance c to b has the true gravitational force acting, and not from a to b. In real terms this means that although your range to a target is 345yd, the true gravity force acting is only 266yd (243m), and being a shorter distance the bullet will drop less and thus shoot high. This is the same whether shooting up- or downhill, but the angle you shoot at will affect, more or less, the trajectory depending on its acuteness.

Consider a .308 calibre rifle shooting a 165gr bullet at 2640fps that has been zeroed at 100yd. At 345yd the bullet has dropped -24.6in (62.5cm) when shooting from a horizontal position. Fine, but that afternoon you take the rifle up on the hill and a stag presents itself at 345yd, but this time you are shooting from a high vantage point with an angle of 40 degrees between your rifle and the stag: so where does the bullet impact now? We know from earlier that at 40 degrees the bullet's path is actually like

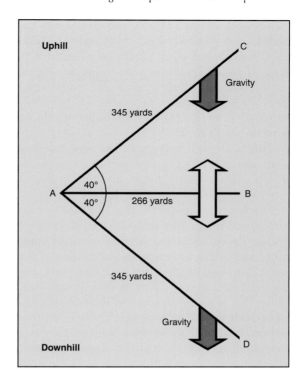

Diagram to show gravitational force on a bullet when it is fired up- or downhill.

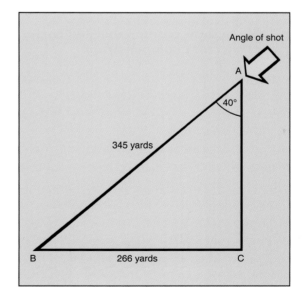

A 345yd (315m) shot at a 40-degree angle will result in trajectory compensation as though you were shooting at 266yd (243m).

shooting at 266yd (243m), and this places the bullet *not* -24.6in low, but only -12.5in (31.74cm) low, a clear 12.1in (30.7cm) difference. If you did not compensate for the angled shot you would think your bullet would drop 24in (60cm), where in reality it has only dropped 12in (30cm) and the bullet would go over the stag's back!

This is all well and good, but how can you with any reliability gauge the exact angle at which you are taking a shot, and thus compensate for your trajectory accordingly?

Firstly you will need the true distance to your target, and this is best achieved by a laser range finder. These items are becoming more common, and prices have tumbled accordingly. The weak link is estimating the angle correctly, and for this I use a device called an angle cosine indicator. This is a scope-mounted slant-angle indicator with a readout in cosine. There is another option, and that is to buy one of the new rangefinders with a built-in angle indicator, which in some cases will actually work out your trajectory drop based on your bullet type and velocity. This is achieved by a table of slant angles and multiples based on cosine arithmetic.

This sounds difficult, but is really easy. For example, if you spot a fox at 345yd (laser range found) and determine that your shooting angle is 40 degrees downhill (uphill will be the same value), the equation is this:

345yd × 40 degree cosine value,
which is 0.77 from the chart,
so 345 × 0.77 = 266,
which is the new range setting for your scope
(as stated earlier)

If this is all a bit much, then a quick-fix three-number cheat is all you really need, and you can tape a card with this information to your scope or rifle:

30 degrees   90 per cent of distance

45 degrees   70 per cent of distance

60 degrees   50 per cent of distance

Remember this may seem irrelevant, but if it means the difference between a hit and a miss, and more importantly, avoiding a shot that will

---

Table to show cosine value and corresponding slant angle for trajectory compensation

Degrees	Cosine value
0	1.00
10	0.98
20	0.94
25	0.91
30	0.87
40	0.77
50	0.64
55	0.57
60	0.50
65	0.42
70	0.34
75	0.26
80	0.17
85	0.09
90	0.0

The wind is the biggest unknown to affect your bullet connecting with your game; it is best to practise in all weather conditions, and with a wind meter.

wound and not kill, it has to be worth it. You can see that at shorter and less severely angled shots the range difference is not that significant, and shots below a 30-degree angle become less of a problem, especially if you own a flat-shooting rifle.

JUDGING THE WIND

More than any other influence to you taking the shot, correct wind estimation is crucial. You can have all the latest kit, laser rangefinders to precisely know the distance and hand-held computers to compensate for trajectory drop, but if your knowledge of wind speeds is lacking and how to estimate them, even with a windmeter, all your efforts will be in vain and a poor shot will result.

Any good ballistics program such as Quick Load and Quick Target can predict the wind effect on your bullet down range at varying wind speeds and directions. This is great, but the wind rarely blows constantly as you take the shot, nor does it remain a constant force on the bullet for its entire trajectory. Wind tends to blow in rhythmic waves with lulls and peaks, and it is these you need to learn, and how the varying topographical features that the bullet's path will take can influence its progress.

The bullet travels down a very small window through the atmosphere along its trajectory, so I judge the wind speed not from the swaying trees but from the indicators closest to the bullet's actual path. Wind has many layers, and a shot close to the ground will fly differently to that shot over a clear glen.

Think of yourself cycling down a track with a variety of trees and bushes on either side: in a strong gale you will lean into the wind a little to stay in line, and the amount of divergence corresponds to the severity and strength of the wind, and whether a tall tree or bush is blocking the path. Along your journey it is highly unlikely

Use any available vegetation as an aid in judging the wind: here are two readings, one at a slight 2mph (3.2km/h) flutter and one of 10mph (16km/h); knowing the wind drift will make you a better shot.

that the wind conditions will remain constant, even at the speed a bullet travels. The best advice is to shoot when the wind conditions are constant and *not* at their calmest, as it is easier to read *some* wind rather than what you think is nothing.

You will never substitute actual practice in windy conditions. I practise in differing locations with differing ranges with varying degrees of obstructions and clear ways, and set up steel silhouette targets of rabbits and foxes at unknown distances. This helps you practise trajectory compensation, and an audible clang indicates a hit if you have judged the wind correctly. I find silhouettes more reactive, and better than paper targets in this respect.

Wind drift is not linear, and gets worse as the range increases, with the worst effects at the closest part of the bullet's path without any other influence; but if the wind is slight at the muzzle and then strong down range, this will have the greatest effect. It is also important to judge wind not only for its strength but also for its direction, as this will greatly affect the degree of influence it has on a travelling bullet.

Most shooters think of a clock with themselves in the middle. Wind from 12 and 6 o'clock affects the bullet little. From 9 to 3 o'clock the wind effect is 100 per cent, from 2, 4, 8 or 10 o'clock it is only 90 per cent, and from 1, 5, 7 or 11 o'clock only 50 per cent. Wind directions between the values of, say, 6.30 are 25 per cent strength of the wind. So if you know that a wind speed of 10mph (16km/h) blows your bullet 2in (5cm) off at 100yd from a straight cross-wind of 9 to 3 o'clock or vice versa, then a wind blowing from 7 o'clock to 1 o'clock needs 50 per cent less compensation.

Problems occur with fishtailing winds from behind that change left to right. There is no 'quick fix' I am afraid, you just have to learn the effects on your bullet. Similarly a headwind can cause vertical shift, as can a wind behind you, and a wind from 3 o'clock will cause the bullet to go up slightly, and from the left, down slightly – and this is all exaggerated at longer range.

If you have a wind meter with you this helps a lot, but it is no good for judging speed or direction down range. In this case Mirage can help you by the way the lines caused by light refractions from humid air bend when observed through a scope. Turn the scope's magnification to full: on a calm day the lines are straight up, but as the wind speed increases they bend with more severity.

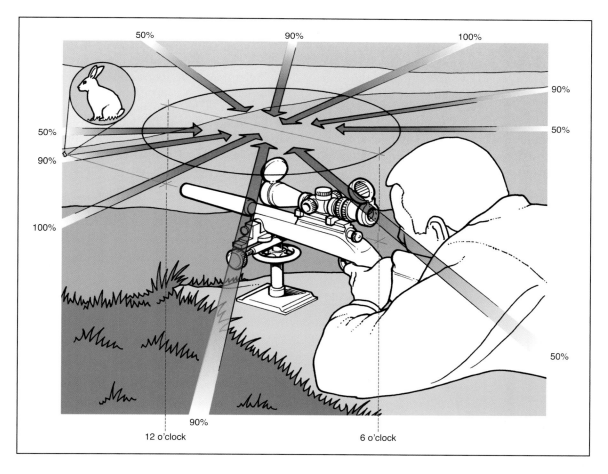

Imagine yourself at the centre of a clock face: how the wind relates to it will have a greater or lesser influence on your bullet's trajectory.

Chapter 11
Care and Maintenance

As modern technology increases seemingly day by day, there continues to be an ever-bewildering array of cleaning products for our rifles. Whether you believe the hype or not, one thing that is still paramount for anyone shooting a rifle, you will not achieve optimal accuracy if you do not clean your rifle correctly. There is no miracle product designed for perfect cleaning, however, and you still have to put in the effort, use the correct solvents and equipment and establish a good cleaning routine. This is actually the key point, as no two rifles require the same cleaning routine mainly due to the different materials used in their construction. Much as you would hand load ammunition to achieve peak accuracy from your cherished rifle, so should you draw up an exact cleaning regime for that individual firearm.

Whether it is a hard-used stalking rifle, a fox gun or a long range varmint rig, the detrimental effects of copper fouling in a rifle's bore are well established. The internal surface of any rifle's bore undergoes intense and aggressive erosive forces. Pressures of nearing 50,000psi are generated when the bullet travels up the barrel as it undergoes a controlled swaging effect as it engages the lands of the rifling. It is therefore hardly surprising that copper residue from the bullet's jacket is deposited inside the barrel as the bullet concludes its travel along the barrel's entire length. That is just the first bullet: on top of this now lies the unburnt powder residue, and as the second shot is fired this leaves another layer of copper fouling over the existing powder residue and further compacts the bottom layer of copper. Remember this all happens under

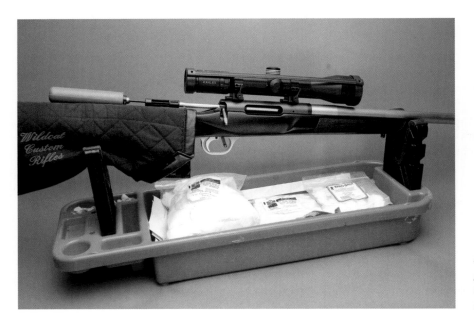

An MTM cradle is a great aid in supporting a rifle during cleaning.

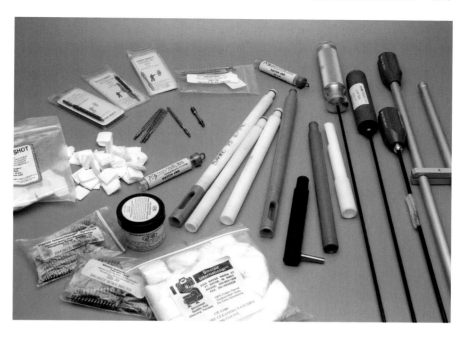

To keep your rifle shooting well you need to buy some good cleaning kit.

very high pressures and temperatures, and without routine cleaning this fouling will certainly be detrimental to the rifle's accuracy.

There are three main types of cleaning regime: chemical action, manual or mechanical cleaning or by use of an electrochemical device. The former two are straightforward, but the electrochemical route is more expensive and requires specialist equipment such as the Foul Out product.

The same is true for rimfire shooters, although many may beg to differ and suffer the consequences of poor accuracy and reliability from leaded up bores and powder build-up. Rimfires have their own set of criteria, but the principles and kit are basically the same as for full bores. I will detail the differing cleaning regime at the end of the chapter with that of the full bore rifles.

Just because most stalkers only take one shot at a time, unlike a target or crow shooter, this does not mean the same precautions into rifle cleanliness should not be heeded. The harsh environments experienced by most stalkers, crawling through bogs and burns and in all weathers, will only exacerbate any deterioration to the inside of the bore. Over time, or even overnight, the deadly rust may take hold, with

subsequent pitting of the bore, which is irreversible.

Careful routine cleaning takes time and is probably the last thing on your mind after an arduous stalk, but if you clean your rifle regularly then it will reward you in the long term with continuing accuracy and reliability.

CLEANING EQUIPMENT

It is of paramount importance to choose the correct cleaning equipment, because it is just as easy to wreck a barrel with poor kit as it is to maintain it with the right kit. Some of the essentials you will need include cleaning rods, bore guides, jags, brushes, solvents, mops and lubricants.

• The **cleaning rod** is the most important tool; it must always be one piece in construction and coated in a synthetic material, because a coated rod has far less wear effect on the barrel during cleaning. Every rod flexes as you clean the barrel, and it is this bending and possible contact with the all-important rifling that you must try to minimize. Certainly a coated rod can suffer from ingress of dirt, and therefore throughout cleaning keep a rag handy to wipe the rod periodically. An uncoated rod will last longer than a coated one, but if you buy an uncoated rod and it then wears a groove in the rifling, you will curse the day you bought it. The rods that I use are made by Dewey or ProTech and are available in all calibres from .17 up to .35 and above.

- Just as important and often forgotten is the use of a quality **bore guide**. This protects the throat of the rifling from damage by centring the brush/jag with patch and rod within the bore, and stops the protective coating from a coated rod being damaged by the rifle's action. Most bore guides are no more than a synthetic tube that replaces the bolt and seals in the rifle's chamber by 'o' rings, with the solvent port extending out the back of the action; this stops any loose debris and solvent from seeping into the action and stock area. I use either a Sinclair custom fit or the more universal and very adaptable Stoney Point model, which has a changeable bush that can be matched to your rifle's action size. I also always fit a stock sock, a simple slip-on protective cover to stop spillage of the solvents from stripping that beautiful walnut finish.
- **Patches** are usually flannel and serve to push out debris and carry the cleaning solvent within the bore. Buy the right patch to fit your cleaning jag; most manufacturers have a guide chart to achieve a good safe fit.
- A **jag** to hold your patches: it is commonly a pierce type, where the patch is speared to the jag. There are many types, but I use the Dewey or Sinclair pierce style, with either male or female threads depending on the calibre of rod used.
- Whereas a jag and patch are used to carry the solvent, the **brushes** are used for actual cleaning. Be sure to buy brushes with a brass core and bronze bristles, and not stainless steel brushes, which may cause internal damage. Brushes will wear, and as soon as their bristles become loose, discard them. Nylon brushes can also be used where a particular solvent may attack the bronze bristles, but they are not as effective as bronze bristle brushes.

Patches tell a story as to the cleaning progression in your bore. I keep mine for reference purposes.

- A **wool mop** is used to soak a barrel in solvent where stubborn copper persists, or to coat the barrel in lubricating oil against rust after the barrel cleaning procedure.
- Some sort of **cleaning gun cradle** allows a hands-free cleaning operation because the rifle is supported, usually in an angled position. I really like the MTM Maintenance Centre: it is tough and reasonably priced.
- **Cleaning solvent**: there is a huge choice, as you would expect; some are copper solvents, some are copper and powder residue solvents, whilst others just target lead fouling. I use Butch's Bore Shine, as this can be left in the bore to soak for bad fouling, and I also like KG products, KG1, 2, 3 are a simple all inclusive series of cleaning products or KG12 can be used for really stubborn copper fouling.

- A **protective lubricant** must be used to protect the bore between shooting outings; this is largely a personal choice, as most work equally well. I use Butches Gun Oil to compliment the solvent product, or Inhibitor V80, which really soaks into all the crevices.

With the hardware sorted you need to establish a set procedure to clean your rifle. There is no hard or fast rule here, but the following routine is the one I have used over the years, and it works for me.

CLEANING REGIME FOR FULL BORE RIFLES

Set up the rifle in the rifle cradle with a downward muzzle angle, attach a stock sock and insert a bore guide. Then proceed as follows:

1. Soak a correctly sized patch in copper solvent and run it through the bore. This will be quite tight and it comes out black as it takes out a lot of powder residue first.
2. Repeat the above, and leave to soak for 10–15 minutes.

3. Soak a bronze or nylon brush with copper solvent and pass through the barrel ten times. Make even, pressured strokes and if possible remove the brush at the end of the stroke and reattach to the rod for the next pass. If you do not, as the brush exits the bore at the muzzle fully, on re-entry it can scuff on the barrel's crown, and after a time will wear a groove. I know it is finicky, but it is well worth the attention in the long run.
4. Remember to wipe the rod between applications to stop contamination.
5. Soak another patch with copper solvent and push through to remove debris from the bore. It should come out blue if copper is present with certain solvents. Wipe the rod.
6. Repeat step three.
7. Soak two patches with copper solvent and pass them through the bore after each other. Wipe the rod.
8. Run clean, dry patches through the bore until they come out clean. They start off blue and turn to black, and then tail off as the fouling is removed.
9. Soak one patch or wool mop in rust-inhibiting oil and pass it through.

A bore guide will save you damaging the throat in the barrel due to a bent or damaged cleaning rod.

10. Sit down and have a coffee! Clean all the rods and brushes by soaking in boiling water if using an ammonia-based solvent, otherwise it will eat the bronze in the brushes; hence the use of nylon.

CLEANING REGIME FOR RIMFIRE RIFLES

It is a perverse truth that rimfires, unlike full bores, actually shoot better with a certain amount of fouling in the barrel, though how much depends on each rifle make. This is mainly because, unlike the severe copper fouling from jacketed bullets in full bore rifles at high velocity, rimfires shoot lead-lubricated bullets at lower velocities, although the .17 HMR and .17 Mach 2 rounds need a different approach. Powder residues are dirty and leave a lot of unburnt flakes within the barrel and blackened chambers and bolts.

The rationale behind rimfire barrel cleaning is twofold: one, clean the barrel's metal surface completely; and two, apply an interim carbon and fouling removal only. The differences are as follows:

.22 Lead Bullet Cleaning

After removing the bolt and magazine if the rifle has one, it is a good idea to dislodge any loose debris such as unburnt powder and grimed-in waxy deposits. Then proceed as follows:

1. Swab the ejector slots with degreaser such as Gun Scrubber or KG3, and allow to soak so as to loosen any stubborn fouling. Take care not to allow any dislodged grime to fall into the trigger area.
2. Insert a correctly fitting bore guide (this is especially important on a rimfire due to the small diameter of the cleaning rods that can bend very easily).
3. Run two to three (more if necessary) wet patches soaked with either Butches Bore Shine or·Kroil, which removes the loose grime in the bore. Remember a loose patch is beneficial here – you do not want to embed the grime back into the bore.
4. At this stage waxy deposits should be minimal. Attention is now drawn to the carbon fouling and lead. Replace the patches with a brush. Phosphor bronze is good, but a nylon brush can be 'worked' a lot more easily. Soak

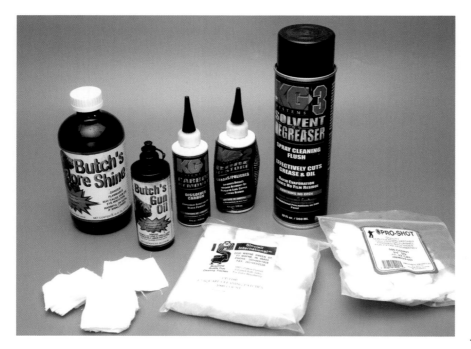

There are many good cleaning solvents and oils on the market; I tend to keep with those that work best for me.

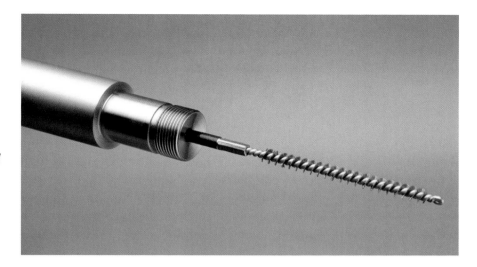

The barrel's muzzle is relatively delicate, and you want to avoid damage to the rifling lands; aggressive and improper brush action can cause problems in this area.

the brush in Butches Bore Shine, and then make long, slow strokes back and forth about twenty times.

5. Remove the brush and swab the barrel with a patch soaked in Butches Bore Shine to remove loosened dirt.
6. Follow up with dry patches until they come out clean.
7. Oil the bore to stop rust.
8. If your rimfire is used at high volume, as in a repeater, then after the cleaning in steps three to seven above, you may wish to scrub the bore with JB Bore Shine on a patch or nylon brush to remove really stubborn fouling.
9. Then run Kroil-soaked patches, and then dry patches until they come out clean.

.17 HMR, .17 Mach 2 and .22 WMR Rimfire Cleaning

Due to the copper-jacketed bullets used in these calibres the cleaning differs from that of the lead-bulleted .22 rimfire ammunition. Couple to this the higher velocities – past 2550 fps for the .17 HMR, as compared to 1050fps for a subsonic .22lr – and the lack of wax lubrication, and it is clear there is a difference. Whereas .22 rimfires prefer a 'shot-in' barrel, .17 calibres will shoot better with a clean barrel after a couple of fouling shots.

A good copper solvent such as Butches Bore

Shine or KG12 should be used after the wet/dry patches for removing loose fouling, as in the .22 rimfire clean.

Allow the barrel to soak for twenty minutes, then follow up with wet patches of Butches Bore Shine, then dry patches to remove the loosened copper fouling, if any. There will be typical blue-streaked copper deposits if copper was present in the bore.

Running back in a rimfire barrel after cleaning is important, as rimfires tend to perform best from a slightly fouled barrel. The best way to do this is to set up a chronograph and shoot your rifle off a bench, and shoot five shot groups at a target until the velocity variation is consistent with the accuracy level that suits you. Every rifle is different, and in this manner your own individual rifle's preferences can be recorded. Usually twenty to thirty rounds are sufficient to get your rimfire shooting at its peak.

ACTION AND MECHANISM CLEANING

It is just as important to keep a rifle's bolt and action running smoothly and safely, and this is especially true with some of the high tech, very close tolerance custom actions we are increasingly seeing in the game fields. Particular areas to look at are the bolt race ways, bolt body, shroud, locking lugs and bolt face, and the action

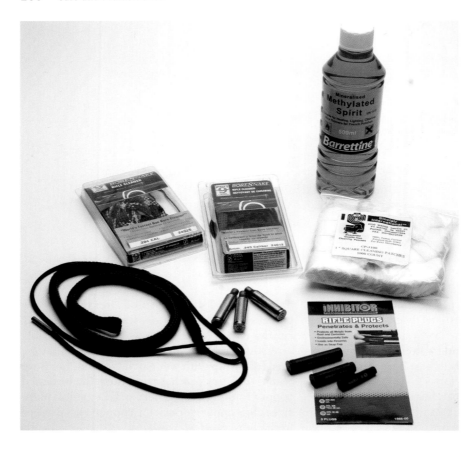

If nothing else, a pull-through bore snake should be used after each shooting session to get out the worst of the fouling.

well and stock area should be checked for the ingress of oil.

In fact too much lubrication in the wrong place can be just as detrimental as too little. Oil and grease will attract powder residue and debris, and too much can freeze an action or even slow down the lock time of the firing pin in extreme cases.

Little and often is the best policy here. You should start with the removal of the bolt from the action and give it a thorough degrease with Gun Scrubber or KG3; because these products are in aerosols, this will dislodge a lot of muck from crevices. Be sure to use them in a well ventilated room, and work on a cleaning mat to avoid unwanted stains to surfaces.

It is a good idea to remove any hardened fouling with a phosphor bronze brush, particularly around the bolt face and in the ejector or extractor areas to maintain positive action.

Where the bolts lock up into the action of a full bore rifle can become incredibly dirty, and this part will need regular cleaning with special tools. I use a Sinclair bolt lug recess rod, which utilizes felt pads the same shape as the bolt; when soaked in solvent and rotated (as you would the bolt) these pads clean these hard-to-get-at recesses. Repeat the process until the felt pads come out clean; you will be amazed at how often they come out dirty.

At this stage you can also clean the barrel's chamber, which becomes blackened and dirty; a simple solvent and chamber brush is all that is necessary here.

Be advised to leave the trigger well alone; all I will do is blow out debris with an air line from the filler tank/divers bottle of a pneumatic air rifle. If there is a problem, take the rifle to a competent gunsmith, because fooling with a trigger if you have no experience can have disastrous consequences.

One area that is often overlooked is where the

wood meets the metal action. Any ingress of cleaning solvent or oil here can make a wood stock degrade to a point where the bedding integrity becomes soft, and so a solid cohesion between action and stock is lost. This will certainly affect the accuracy and consistency of your rifle, and some bore solvents are very aggressive and will take off that lovely lacquered or oiled finish.

When reassembling the bolt back into the action, use a light oil or grease such as Montana X-treme to lube the backs of the bolt lugs where they engage the action, on the body itself and action race ways; a dry moly-type lube is also very good.

CLEANING MAXIMS

Cleaning can be a chore, but it will keep your rifle in tip top condition and ensure that its accuracy is maintained for its natural life, and not one dictated by neglect. At the very least after a day's stalking or rabbiting clean it with a pull-through such as the bore snake to get most of the dirt and grime out, and then clean it properly as above when you have the time later.

It is also important to realize that every rifle

needs its own specific cleaning regime to keep it working in the best condition. The varying barrel dimensions and the different grades and types of metal used in firearms require a different approach to cleaning, and in order to keep your rifle accurate and safe you should learn its preferred oils and solvents, and how frequently you need to clean it.

SCOPE CARE

As a general rule ensuring your rifle is in good shape comes as a matter of course, but how many of us spend as much time on our scopes and optical equipment? Although most good scopes state they are waterproof and shock-proof, it would be wrong to assume that they do not need maintaining. There are many good products that can be used to prevent problems, largely by keeping the British climate out, whilst others rectify a problem after it has occurred.

Preventing Problems

Most scopes come with some form of lens cover. These can range from two separate plastic

It is important to keep your scope functioning properly, and there are some good products on the market to this end.

cups with some form of see-through plastic insert held together by elasticated cord, screw-in lens covers, or rubberized stretchable one-piece units.

The plastic cups and cord covers in my view are not satisfactory. If it is raining and you leave them on to stop rain contacting the lens surface you can bet this is when a deer or fox will appear, and will be spooked as you fumble to remove the plastic inserts, or worse still try to peer through them. You certainly won't have time to remove screw-in caps, although rubberized one-piece covers go some way to solve the problem. With these, the edge of each rubber cap, front and rear, is a flap/tab: when you pull on these, the stretch rubber around the eyepiece or objective lens is released and 'pings' off quickly.

This is certainly a lot quicker than the normal covers, and being a stretchy rubber it seals the ends of the scope very tightly against moisture, dust and debris. However, be careful that in the heat of the moment when you remove it, you don't let it drop and it becomes fouled. I usually place a rubber band around the mid-section of the scope by the scope rings, which prevents the cover from falling off the rifle but still allows the lens to be uncovered.

The Scope Coat

In a similar vein there is a product called the Scope Coat, a cover that shields the scope but is made from a stretchable neoprene material which covers the scope much more comprehensively. There are three sizes available that cope with most scope lengths, and an extra benefit is that all the lens ends and scope body and turrets are covered, which not only protect from rain but also against knocks and scratches. Again, just tug on the eyepiece end and the scope coat can be peeled off and the shot taken. It is a bit fiddly, but better than no protection at all.

Pop-up Lens Covers

The best bet for the sportsperson is to obtain a system that stays permanently attached to the scope ends, but can be speedily opened without spooking the quarry. The option here is to use a pop-up lens cover, and there are very good covers available now, in particular Polar Caps from Weaver and Flip Open from Butler Creek. Both these systems are very similar, and offer a huge range of sizes to accommodate any scope made today.

The Butler Creek system uses a tough, black plastic lens end cover sized to match your scope with a flip-up hinged front section. On the objective lens part there are two protruding tabs: when pushed with the rifle's supporting thumb, the sprung hinged cover pops open instantly. At the same time your thumb from your hand on the pistol grip pushes down on a red button and thus opens the eyepiece cover. This allows instant access to viewing from the scope, with minimal movement of the hands. This also means the lens covers are closed for maximum protection throughout the stalk, only needing to be opened at the instant of the shot.

The Weaver Polar Caps differ in that the main body of the lens cover is stretchable rubber to fit a differing diameter of lens, and the pop-up cover is made from polarized see-through plastic lens. In an emergency you can see through the scope without popping open the covers, though for best clarity they should be open.

All-in-One Cleaners

The Swarovski Cleaning Kit

Swarovski, famous for scopes from Austria, make a great all-in-one lens cleaning kit. It comes in the form of a green cordura-type pouch with pockets, which hold a lens cleaning fluid bottle, a lens brush pen, moistened lens wipes and a packet of lens tissues. It contains all you need, and has a convenient belt strap. For a quick clean you remove the dust with the brush, akin to a lipstick applicator, and then use one of the moist wipes to clean the lens, working with a circular action, starting from the centre of the lens and working outwards.

For a more thorough clean, again brush away the dust/dirt, then place a few drops of the lens cleaning fluid on the lens tissue and clean the lens surface in the same circular manner as before.

This is a very useful kit that takes all the hassle out of keeping your scopes clean, and can be easily stored away in a pocket or on its belt strap.

Swarovski produces a useful scope-cleaning kit in wallet form, with everything you need.

The Leupold Lens Pen

In similar vein, Leupold produce a lens pen system, a double end application in the shape of a pen with a brush at one end and a non-fluid lens cleaner at the other. It represents good value for money and is easy to use, and can be kept in a coat pocket until needed. Simply slide the green barrel on the pen's body to reveal the brush, and remove the cap on the other end to expose the cone-shaped lens cleaning tip; this has a chamois insert that uses a non fluid-based cleaning agent. Use in the same circular motion as described above, and you can remove smudges and fingerprints in a trice.

The Bushwear Spudz

Another really convenient piece of kit is the Bushwear Spudz, a cleaning cloth that is stitched into a protective elasticated waterproof pouch measuring no more than 2 × 1.5in (5 × 4cm) with the Bushwear logo on it. Pull out the cloth, a triangular lint-free fabric, clean your lens and pop it back in. Because there is an ABS clip attached it makes for easy location on any rifle sling or clothing, so it is always to hand. This is a very useful item to have with you. How often when stalking are you fumbling to clear your lens, especially in the Highlands?

Photography Cleaning Kits

Last but not least you can use photography cleaning equipment to clean your scopes,

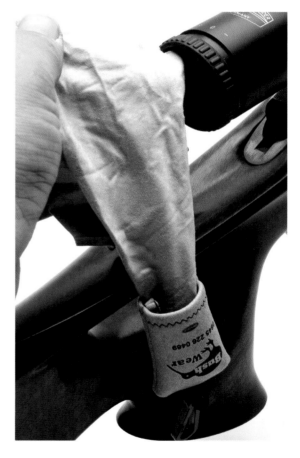

The Spudz is a cleaning cloth that attaches to your rifle so it is always at hand should you need it in the field.

purchased as single items such as brushes and cloths, or bought as kits. I use a company called Speedgraphic for all my photographic supplies, as they carry a vast array of items.

Hama also make a kit of brush, paper and cleaning fluid, giving you all you need to keep your rifle scope in order. The end of the brush is like a bellows, which when squeezed provides a useful jet of air when brushing. I also carry a small 85ml canister of Kenair, an aerosol-type dust remover with CFC-free gas that blasts away dust and debris from the lens surface. I also use it for removing grit, grease and dirt from bolt race ways, mounting dovetails and gummed-up rifle magazines.

Finally for a really good clean or service of the scope, when I return home or when the rifle is being serviced, I use Kodak lens cleaner and Kodak lens cleaning paper. The 37ml fluid and fifty sheets of soft, lint-free tissues last for ages and give the lens surface a really good clean.

In Summary

Regardless of what product you choose, scopes are expensive items with expensive lenses and coatings, and they deserve better treatment than a quick clean-out in the field with a scrunched-up old tissue, or worst still, shirt tail end! Treated well, your lenses – not only on your scope, but also on your binoculars and range finders – will perform to their intended optimum. As with your rifle, cleaning takes only a few minutes, but it is time well spent.

Chapter 12
Safety, Law and Close Seasons

Safety is everyone's concern when dealing with firearms, and the unexpected can, and will, happen if fundamental precautions are not taken. Thankfully deaths and serious injuries are not common, but the unpredictable terrain and natural hazards one encounters whilst out in the hills or woods can catch out even a seasoned shooter. However, by observing the following few simple guidelines the chance of mishaps will be significantly reduced:

- With regard to firearms, always assume that a rifle is loaded and never point it at anyone.
- Unload the rifle when crossing ditches, climbing high seats and fences, and when storing it in a car. It is also advisable to remove the bolt from the rifle whilst in transit.
- Before you load your rifle when you arrive at your shoot, check it over for faults and make sure the bore is unobscured.
- When the rifle is loaded, apply the safety catch and only release it prior to taking the shot.
- Always be sure of your backstop, especially when out lamping at night; if in doubt, do not shoot.
- The backstop must be thick enough to stop the calibre of rifle you are shooting. Branches, scrub and thickets will not suffice, and who knows what lurks within them?
- Similarly, make sure the bullet will not hit any intervening branches or foliage on its way to the target, as this will alter the trajectory unpredictably.
- Where possible shoot at game on the ground and not in trees, as even .22 rimfires can carry for great distances. Better still, shoot from an elevated position such as a high seat so the shot angle is less likely to ricochet.

- Remember to identify your quarry correctly, and make sure that you have the legal rifle calibre and are shooting in the open season.
- A shot taken must be followed up, even if you feel it was a miss; learning the animal's reaction to the shot only comes with experience. Go to where the animal was and look for signs of blood or hair, and then search for it if you think your shot has downed it.
- Shots at running game should not be taken unless the animal is wounded.
- If in doubt, never shoot.

FIREARMS LAW

Firearms law and law of ownership in Great Britain are both very strict, and for good reason: we live on a small island with an ever-increasing population. The firearms law is there to keep you and the public safe, and to ensure that suitable rifles and ammunition are used for specific game. England and Wales, Northern Ireland and Scotland all have their own interpretations of the law, but if you are in doubt, seek advice from your firearms liaison officer from your local police force: they are there to help, so use them.

Firearms Ownership

In Great Britain, firearms and ammunition come under the restrictions laid out in the Firearms Act of 1968 and subsequent amendments to date. Essentially a firearms certificate only allows the holder to own the specific rifles, ammunition or sound moderators detailed on the certificate, and the holder has to prove good reason for ownership. This involves a degree of knowledge of what firearms and calibres are suitable for each specific species, and you need proof of permission from landowners to shoot on their land. It can be a little daunting at first as the forms are quite complex, but again you can ask your firearms liaison officer for help.

A firearms certificate (FAC) lasts for five years, and as you have to state what rifles you wish to own prior to purchase, it is important to enter the correct details of the firearms you are likely to want over this five-year period. The grant of an FAC costs £50, whilst renewal is £40, and changing any details will cost you £26.

First-time certificate holders will probably be subject to certain restrictions until they have established a track record, which is wise; however, usually over time one's certificate becomes less restrictive, usually with regard to the land you can shoot over. This is called an 'open' certificate, where the onus is on you to determine whether a piece of land is suitable for shooting over with a certain calibre – as long as you still retain the owner's permission to shoot.

To start with, for pest control you would probably apply for a .22 rimfire of some sort, and it is reasonable that a sound moderator will also be required. In this case it is best to specify on your certificate whether you want a .22lr or .22 magnum entry, because when you come to purchase a rifle, a gunsmith will not sell you a .22 magnum if your licence states .22lr. You can avoid this problem by entering a .22 rimfire rifle to cover you for both, but check that your firearms department will allow this.

This becomes more pertinent with the larger calibres, as you may want a 6mm calibre rifle for deer work but are undecided on the specific cartridge. In other words, if your certificate specifies one 6mm/.243 rifle, it will cover you for any 6mm/.243 calibre chambered rifle – a .243 Winchester, 6mm Remington or 6mm BR.

Similarly you need to specify the ammunition calibre you want to buy and the quantity you intend to hold as well as purchase. For .17 and .22 rimfire ammunition, due to the probable frequency of use, plus the fact that this type of ammunition is sold in containers of 500 rounds, you should be able to hold 1,000 rounds and purchase 500 rounds at a time. This allows you to buy all from the same lot number to keep consistency between each round.

For fox or deer ammunition it is reasonable to hold less ammunition on your certificate, say 200 rounds, but if you reload you will want a provision to add expanding bullets also, and as these can come in boxes of only 50 or 100 units, I would double your centrefire ammunition allowance.

This brings up an important point, that for sporting use you will require a provision on your certificate to allow you to purchase expanding ammunition, which is a prohibited item. However, for sporting use, as long as you have a clause to include the right to purchase and use such ammunition under the conditions of the certificate for sporting purposes, the police will grant this. For deer, expanding ammunition is mandatory, however for foxes and vermin there is no such requirement, although with regard to effectiveness and safety – namely fewer ricochets – expanding ammunition is preferable.

Your certificate will also state for what purpose each rifle is to be used with regard to species type and also zeroing a weapon. Both these points are very important. Just because you use your .22 centrefire for foxes, this does not entitle you to shoot rabbits too, unless it expressly says so in the wording on your licence; for instance: 'The .17 PPC rifle and sound moderator and ammunition shall be used for shooting foxes, shooting vermin, ground game and zeroing on ranges and land (name of approved land).'

It is important to have zeroing on the land or ranges you have permission to shoot, because you will want to test your rifle with the ammunition you intend using in the rifle.

It is all right to change your mind, and if you find you do not need a rifle of a certain calibre and that some other calibre would be suitable, then the licence can be swiftly changed. But remember, if you sell a rifle or sound moderator, it does not entitle you to buy another item of the same, and you must have your certificate changed to allow you to purchase another specified rifle or sound moderator again.

Every time you purchase ammunition or expanding bullets you are lawfully required to enter it on to your certificate. This also acts as a record as to how frequently you use your rifle, and if there have been few ammunition entries (unless they were large bulk purchases), when renewal time comes you are likely to be asked whether you actually need such a rifle. Use it or lose it!

Prohibited Weapons

I have touched on the relevant rifle actions the law allows at the beginning of each chapter describing the various rifle types, but there are some important facts you also need to know before you make a purchase. Most gunsmiths can give very good advice to a prospective, new or even seasoned shooter regarding the relevant law requirements or changes that seem to happen all too frequently. Ignorance of the law is no excuse for committing an offence. There are bans on weapons such as rocket launchers and weapons disguised as other objects, but with regard to sporting weapons the most pertinent are as follows:

- Any weapon that is modified or designed to shoot two or more shots without repeated pressure on the trigger.
- Any self-loading or pump-action rifled gun except those chambered for .22 rimfire rounds. This means all .22 rimfire ammunition including .22 magnum but *does not include* .17 Mach 2 or .17 HMR, which at the present time are illegal as semi-automatic weapons in Great Britain.
- Any firearm with a barrel less than 12in (30cm) in length or which is less than 24in (60cm) in overall length.

Sound Moderators

Sound moderators, whether they are for rimfire or centrefire use, have to be entered on your firearms certificate as a matter of law. You need to have permission to acquire the moderator on your certificate in the first place, and usually it is necessary to specify the calibre of firearm to which the moderator relates. If a name or serial number is visible or discernible, then this must also be entered on to the certificate in order to identify the unit.

If you want to sell or exchange a moderator, then you can do so, but only to a gunsmith or private certificate holder who has the relevant 'right to acquire' for that calibre or type of moderator; moreover you need to inform your police of the transaction, and have your certificate changed to allow you to acquire another moderator *before* you make a new purchase. You cannot simply buy or swap items, one for one as it were. This is also true of firearms on your licence.

Security

All Section One firearms and ammunition must be stored as securely as is reasonably practicable to stop use or taking by unauthorized persons. It is an offence not to comply with these requirements, and contravention evokes a maximum of six months imprisonment and/or a fine.

Whether in use, for transfer or for sale, the safe custody of the rifle and ammunition still applies.

Regarding a grant of, or a renewal of a firearms certificate, your local firearms liaison officer can advise you as to the level of security required. This usually involves a steel security cabinet that meets the British standard BS 7558 for gun cabinets. Although not compulsory, the cabinet should be a minimum of 2mm steel sheet metal with all seams welded continuously. Hinges should be on the inside unless a blocking bar or bolts on the reverse side of the locks are used. The locking mechanism should be on the inside, with five lever locks to BS 3621 standard regarded as a minimum, although hardened padlocks can be acceptable in some cases. Your own circumstances and location and home layout can be a factor in the level of security required, which the police will advise on. The security has to be in place and to the police's satisfaction before your FAC is granted.

Ammunition can be stored within the cabinet if it is contained within its own lockable container. I always feel it is better to have a separate cabinet, and for added security I would remove the bolts and magazines from the rifles where possible and store these separately also.

It is also important to secure the cabinet/cabinets to the fabric of the building that is built from brick or concrete, and in a room that does not have access from the outside, where possible. If you can disguise the location of the cabinet, so much the better. 21st Century Antiques and GunSecure companies make some superb, authentic-looking period furniture that look like Wellington chests or display corner cabinets, and contain a high security gun cabinet within.

Security is a very real issue, and the above should be viewed as only a minimum; prudent shooters will want the extra security of upgraded cabinets with thicker steel construction, or the gun vault-type cabinets that use a nine lever mapping key and multiple locking lugs around the circumference of the door. There are some very good, well priced, high security vault cabinets from Sentry that have 1in (2.5cm) thick doors, fireproof linings and electronic or combination locking systems.

As regards transporting rifles, the certificate holder must take reasonable precautions to make sure that the firearms and ammunition on the certificate are kept safe. In real terms this means that if a car is left unattended, then a vital piece of the rifle should be taken off, namely the bolt, and taken with you. The rifle should be out of sight and kept in a suitable case. There are some really good gun cabinets for use in cars, and Napier of London sell a gun case that comes with a padlock and securing cable, to lock the rifle to the superstructure of the car.

Law Restricting Young Persons

Those aged seventeen years and over can apply for a firearms certificate, and if this is granted, can purchase firearms and ammunition to which the certificate relates.

Those aged between fourteen and seventeen years can apply for a firearms certificate to own a rifle, but cannot buy a rifle or ammunition, but can be given or lent either to which the certificate relates.

Those aged less than fourteen years cannot possess firearms or ammunition but can carry either under instruction by the certificate holder when using them for sporting purposes.

Estate Rifles

A person without a certificate may borrow a rifle from an occupier of private land as long as certain conditions are met:

- They must be seventeen or older.
- The rifle can only be used on land occupied by the person lending the rifle.
- The lender has to be the occupier of the private land or be a servant of the occupier.
- The rifle has to be on the lender's firearms certificate.
- The rifle has to remain in earshot and sight of the lender.
- Only species specified to shoot on the lender's certificate may be taken by the borrower.

Night Shooting

The night shooting of deer is illegal unless under special licence, but fox, rabbit or hare may be shot at night. Night is defined as one hour after sunset and one hour before sunrise.

Knives

The carrying of knives is restricted by the Criminal Justice Act of 1988 and the Violent Crime Reduction Act of 2006. You have to be eighteen years or over to purchase a knife, and it is now illegal to have on your person a sharply pointed or bladed device in a public place without good reason or lawful authority. This would involve a shooter, whether recreational or professional, who carries a knife when they are expecting to use it whilst pursuing a lawful activity such as deer stalking. However, you must not leave a knife in a car or pocket until next time you use it for a sporting use, and this is no defence if you are stopped and are in possession of a knife whilst out shopping at your local supermarket.

An exception is with regard to folding pocket knives, which must not have a blade more than 3in (7.5cm) in length and the blade must not lock; however it can be viewed as an offensive weapon if you were to carry it in a restaurant, club, school or suchlike.

Rights of Way

Shooting on or near rights of way across land you have lawful permission to shoot over will inevitably come up. In England and Wales it is deemed an offence without reasonable excuse or lawful authority to shoot a rifle within 50ft (15m) of the centre of a highway, if from these actions a user of that carriageway is injured, stopped from continuing, or endangered. It is an offence to disrupt the users of a public right of way when shooting near that right of way.

Common sense dictates to note all rights of way and carriageways on the shoot, and to observe great care and vigilance whilst shooting near them, and if the public are encountered, to stop shooting and be courteous at all times.

The police have the powers to seize any firearm if you do not show a valid FAC for the rifle and ammunition you are stopped with. This is why you should always carry your FAC, maps and copies of permissions or shooting rights just in case this situation occurs, because it can defuse a potentially negative situation.

QUARRY SPECIES

The lawful control of quarry species is governed by the Wildlife and Countryside Act of 1981, which allows certain species to be shot all year without control. General licences are issued by statutory bodies in England, Scotland, Wales and Northern Ireland with regard to certain bird species. You do not need to apply for a general licence, but you must abide by the terms and conditions stipulated within the licences. Copies are available from www.basc.org.uk

Species that can be shot at all times are rabbits, feral pigeon, woodpigeon, collared dove, magpie, rook, crow, jay, jackdaw, rat, great black backed and herring gull, house sparrow and starling. Depending on your location some species are not applicable, so it would be prudent to contact Natural England who has taken over responsibility for the general licences.

You as an individual must have the authority to actually use the general licence over the land you intend to shoot, and this involves written permission from the landowner who holds the sporting rights. You have to comply with at least one of the criteria on the licence, such as prevention of serious damage to livestocks, foodstuff, crops, fruit, vegetables, timber, giving

justification to shoot pigeon, rat or squirrel, or the prevention of the spread of disease, or conserving wild birds with relevance to controlling the corvid family of crows, jackdaws, jay, magpies and rooks. There have to be reasonable grounds that the authorized person has found that non-lethal methods such as scaring are not an effective control before you can start shooting.

There are also restrictions on shooting on Christmas Day or Sundays where Sunday shooting is prohibited in certain areas, so check first.

Just because you can shoot the above species it does not mean you have to or want to: it is better to concentrate on the primary field species included in this book.

Some of these listed species are lawful to shoot, although in some areas it may not represent such a problem as in other more highly populated areas. Here it would be prudent to determine whether you want to shoot such species possibly on the grounds that they present a hygiene problem or are causing crop damage.

Hares have no close season but must not be shot on Sundays or Christmas Day. On moorland and unenclosed non-arable land, hares can be shot by the occupier and authorized persons designated by him from 1 December (1 July in Scotland) to 31 March.

There is no law governing fox shooting as long as you have permission to shoot such a species on land owned by the occupier and to which your firearms certificate relates. Most police licensing authorities will now allow you to use your deer rifle on approved land for foxes also, which is sensible and precludes the need to buy a rifle for deer use and another for fox use.

You can use the same ammunition as for deer use if the ground is safe, but in preference you may want to reload or use some lightweight bullets that will be more frangible and less likely to ricochet.

Due to the complexities of the law this is just an outline of the requirements. Your own specific requirements, situation, location and circumstances as to suitability with regards to experience, lawful land to shoot over and its size and whether the calibres of the rifles are suitable for each quarry species, will ultimately be determined by your own county's police authority. To make sure you are up to date with regard to the latest law, the British Association for Shooting and Conservation (BASC), British Deer Society (BDS) and Home Office have downloadable fact sheets detailing all the relevant sporting laws.

Deer Law

To shoot deer there are restrictions not only on calibre size but also the muzzle velocity or energy that a bullet produces, and the expanding nature of a bullet, depending on what part of the country you live in.

Rifle restrictions for deer in England and Wales

Rifle	**Muntjac and Chinese Water Deer** Minimum calibre of .220in Muzzle energy not less than 1000ft/lb Soft- or hollow-nosed bullet not less than 50gr
	All other deer species Minimum calibre of .240in Muzzle energy not less than 1700ft/lb
Rifle ammunition	Soft-nosed or hollow-point bullet

Rifle restrictions for deer in Northern Ireland

Rifle	Minimum calibre of 0.236in
Rifle ammunition	Minimum muzzle energy of 1700ft/lb Bullet weight minimum of 100gr Bullet designed to expand in a predictable manner

Rifle restrictions for deer in Scotland

Rifle	No specified minimum calibre
Rifle ammunition	**Roe deer** Minimum of 50gr bullet weight and minimum muzzle velocity of 2450fps and minimum muzzle energy of 1000ft/lb
	All other deer species Minimum of 100gr bullet weight and minimum muzzle velocity of 2450fps and minimum muzzle energy of 1750ft/lb
	Bullet designed to expand in a predictable manner

Close seasons for deer in England and Wales

Species	Sex	Dates close season
Red and red/Sika hybrids	Male	1 May–31 July
	Female	1 April–31 October
Sika	Male	1 May–31 July
	Female	1 April–31 October
Fallow	Male	1 May–31 July
	Female	1 April–31 October
Roe	Male	1 November–31 March
	Female	1 April–31 October
Chinese Water Deer	Male and Female	1 April–31 October

Close seasons for deer in Scotland

Species	Sex	Dates close season
Red and red/Sika hybrids	Male	21 October–30 June
	Female	16 February–20 October
Sika	Male	21 October–30 June
	Female	16 February–20 October
Fallow	Male	21 October–30 June
	Female	16 February–20 October
Roe	Male	21 October–31 March
	Female	1 April–20 October

Glossary

Accuracy A rifle's capability to place a bullet where it is aimed.

Action Sometimes called a receiver, the portion of the rifle where the barrel is secured and the round is loaded and fired and the bolt operates.

Anneal To soften the brass case after sizing or reforming in wildcat cartridges.

Anvil Point in the primer where the primer compound is crushed and ignited by the firing pin.

Arbor press Small reloading press for use with hand dies.

Ballistics Projectiles in motion, either within the bore or externally.

Ballistic coefficient A bullet's ability to pass aerodynamically through the air.

Barrel Part of the rifle where the bullet is accelerated from the chamber through the bore.

Barrel vise Clamp used to exchange a rifle's barrel in a switch-barrel rifle.

Bearing surface Portion of the bullet that contacts the barrel's rifling.

Bedding Method of precisely fitting the action to the stock with synthetic epoxies and pillars for a precise fit.

Belted case Cartridge that has a raised ridge in front of the extractor groove and headspaces off this.

Boat tail Efficient streamlined design to bullet with rear portion resembling a boat's aft end.

Body Main portion of the case.

Boil Vertical heat haze or mirage.

Bolt Contains the firing pin, locking lugs, extractor and operating handle.

Bore The diameter of the barrel's interior that is measured before the rifling is cut.

Bore guide Device to ensure the cleaning rod remains centralized whilst cleaning.

Bullet Projectile, the only part of the cartridge that makes contact with the target.

Burn rate The relative speed at which smokeless powder burns.

Calibre The diameter of the groove or bore of the barrel; described in metric as 6mm, for example 6mm PPC, or in decimals of an inch as 0.243.

Cant Movement from the vertical position of sight to bore axis.

Cartridge Complete loaded round of ammunition with all components.

Case Usually brass, to hold the powder charge, primer and bullet. It can be reloaded after use.

Case trimmer Device to trim the case neck back to specifications after firing and before reloading.

Centrefire Primer located in the centre of the case head.

Chamber The void in the barrel that supports and contains the cartridge on firing.

Charge The amount of powder loaded in the case.

Chronograph Device to measure the velocity of a bullet.

Cleaning rod Long rod usually coated in plastic or carbon fibre and smaller than the bore diameter used to clean the barrel and remove fouling after firing.

Concentricity Term to describe the precision between two components so that their centres are parallel, namely bullet-to-bore axis: the better the concentricity, the more accurate the load.

Copper fouling As the bullet passes up the bore it leaves deposits of copper behind, which is bad for accuracy.

Creep Trigger movement but without the trigger breaking cleanly.

Crimp The case mouth is pressed inwards slightly in order to grip the bullet.

Deburr Removal of burrs around the case mouth, both inside and out.

Die Reloading tool used to re-form a case after firing and to seat new bullets.

Double-based powder Powder made from nitro-glycerine and nitrocellulose.

Drop Bullet drop from the barrel and a distant target caused by gravity.

Ejector Item that ejects the case from the rifle either in bolt or action.

Elevation Vertical adjustment to sights.

Energy Ability to transfer force from the bullet to the target expressed in ft/lb.

Erosion Hot gases on firing cause metal erosion to rifling in the throat and baffles to moderator if fitted.

Extractor Item that removes the case from the barrel's chamber.

Eye relief The distance from the eye to the eyepiece of the scope to obtain a correct full sight picture.

FPS Feet per second, the measure of a bullet's velocity.

Fire forming Achieves maximum expansion of the case in the chamber, common when blowing out wildcat calibres.

Firing pin Also called 'striker', the part of the bolt that contacts the primer to cause initial ignition.

Flash hole Aperture in the web of the case to allow primer gases through to ignite the powder charge.

Foot/pound (ft/lb) Unit to describe the striking power/energy of a bullet.

Free bore Portion of the bore in front of the chamber that is unrifled to accommodate differing lengths of bullet.

Grain Unit weight of powder used: 437.5gr is 1oz.

Groove Major diameter of internal barrel: .30 calibre is .308 or .224 for .22 calibre.

Handloading Manual assembly of a cartridge using case, powder, bullet and primer.

Headspace Correct cartridge fit within the chamber as measured from the bolt face to section of the chamber that stops forward motion of the case.

Hollow point Area at the tip of the bullet that has no core.

Ignition Primary burning of powder by the primer flame.

Improved cartridge Modification of a standard case usually to increase case capacity; requires fire forming in the chamber to fully form the new dimensions.

Jacket Outer portion of the bullet used to contain the core and allow expansion of the bullet at terminal velocity.

Lands Measurement of the bore diameter from the raised section of the barrel from the grooves.

Leade As throat.

Line of sight A straight line from the axis of the scope that will coincide with the bullet's impact point.

Locking lugs Part of the bolt that locks the bolt into the receiver or barrel section to support the cartridge on firing.

Lock time Time elapsed from the firing pin release to the point of the pin striking the primer; the faster the lock time, the better.

Magnum Larger capacity of a case for a certain calibre to achieve greater velocity.

Meplat Diameter of the blunt end of a bullet.

Minute of angle MOA, $\frac{1}{60}$ of a degree, which relates to 1.047in at 100yd. Therefore the minute angle group at 100yd is 1.047in, and at 200yd 2.094in, and so on.

Muzzle The barrel's end where the bullet emerges on firing.

Muzzle blast Gas release from the muzzle as the bullet exits the barrel causing a loud noise, heat and flash.

Neck Section of the case that grips the bullet.

Neck down To reduce the size of the neck dimensions in the formation of a wildcat cartridge using smaller die bushings.

Neck sizing Resizing the neck portion to its original dimensions.

Neck tension The amount of grip a neck has on a bullet.

Neck turning Reducing the thickness of the neck for uniformity and fit into non-standard rifle chambers.

OAL Overall cartridge length, the base of the case to the tip of the bullet.

Objective Light-gathering forward section of a scope.

Ogive Curved section of the bullet forward of the shank.

Parallax Image in a scope moves when the eye is moved from the centre of the scope.

Powder Propellant part of the cartridge that transfers energy to the bullet to gain velocity in the barrel.

Pressure The force produced by the burning powder.

Primer Metal cup containing priming mixture to start powder ignition when struck.

Primer pocket Recess in the case head to hold primer.

Projectile A bullet in flight.

Rebated case Case whose rim is smaller than the diameter of the body.

Receiver *See* Action.

Resizing die Reloading die that reforms the case after firing to its original dimensions.

Reticule Lines in a scope used to aim with, such as cross hairs, dots.

Rifling Spiral grooves in the barrel to spin a bullet and impart stability.

Rim Section of the case behind the extractor groove to allow a case top to be extracted from the chamber.

Rimfire Primer content is placed in the rim not in a central primer, and ignition is caused by the firing pin striking the rim.

Round Complete assembled components of a cartridge.

Sabot Discarding portion of a projectile to allow higher velocity for a given calibre; 'sabot' means 'shoe'.

Seating depth Measurement of the depth of the bullet within the case.

Seating die Adjustable reloading device to seat a bullet tin case at varying lengths.

Sectional density Ratio between the bullet's weight and the square of its diameter; gives a degree of the bullet's penetrating potential.

Semi-rimmed case Case with the rim just larger than the body diameter.

Shank Straight portion of the bullet.

Shell holder Holds a case's head when used in reloading press.

Shoulder The sloping portion of the case from the body to the neck section, often described in degrees.

Single base powder Powder made only from nitrocellulose.

Swaging To form a material under pressure, *ie* reform a case in a wildcat round.

Throat Beginning of the rifling, a tapered section cut at an angle to allow correct bullet forward movement.

Time of flight Usually expressed in seconds, the time it takes for the bullet to travel over any given distance.

Trigger Device to release the firing pin sear, which starts the firing cycle.

Turret Scope knob to adjust elevation and windage, and even parallax if side mounted.

Twist rate 360-degree rotation of the bullet in the rifle's barrel *ie* 1-in-10 is one complete turn in 10in (25cm) length.

Varmint American term for pest or vermin.

Velocity The projectile's speed measured in fps (feet per second) or m/s (metres per second).

Web Solid portion of the case at the head.

Wildcat Cartridge design of non-commercial origin, but often using another parent case.

Windage Lateral adjustment to the sights to compensate for left/right correction for aim.

Wind deflection Degree the bullet is shifted off course by the strength of the wind.

Zero The point of impact and the point of aim coincide.

Useful Contacts

SUPPLIERS

Alan Rhone Ltd
6 Coed Aben Road
Wrexham Ind Est
Wrexham
LL13 9UH
Tel: 01978 660001
alan@alanrhone.com

A K Sports Optic
31 Hillgrove Business park
Nazeing Road
Nazeing
Essex
EN9 2HB
Tel: 01992 893001
enquiries@light-stream.co.uk

Attleborough Accessories
Morley St Peter
Norfolk
NR18 9TX
Tel: 01953 454932
sales@attacc.com

Brock and Norris
The Buttery Farm
Kynnersley
Telford
TF6 6EG
Tel: 01952 670198

BushWear
7 Glen Tye Road
Stirling
FK7 7LH
Tel: 0845 226 0469
info@bushwear.co.uk

BWM Arms Ltd
Unit 2
Moorbrook Park
Didcot
Oxon
OX11 7HP
Tel: 01235 514550
sales@bwmarmsltd.com

Callum Ferguson
PRS Ltd
Strathavon Lodge
Tomintoul
Ballindalloch
Banffshire
Scotland
AB37 9AR
Tel: 01807 580422
www.precisionrifles.com

C H Westons
12 East Street
Brighton
Sussex
BN1 1HP
Tel: 01273 326338
sales@chweston.co.uk

Edgar Brothers
Heather Close
Lyme Green Business Park
Macclesfield
SK11 0LR
Tel: 01625 503669
www.edgar-brothers.co.uk

F A Andersons
49 High Street
East Grinstead
Sussex
RH19 3AF
Tel: 01342 325604
faanderson@btconnect.com

Frank Dyke and Co
1–7 Ernest Avenue
West Norwood
London
SE27 0DG
Tel: 020 8670 2224

Garlands
Raddle Lane
Edingale
Tamworth
Staffs
B79 9JR
Tel: 01827 383300
info@garlands.uk.com

GMK Ltd
Bear House
Concorde Way
Fareham
Hampshire
PO15 5RL
Tel: 01489 579999
sales@gmk.co.uk

Highland Outdoors
PO Box 8640
Market Harborough
Leics
LE10 0DB
Tel: 01858 410683
sales@highlandoutdoors.co.uk

Jackson Rifles
Parton
Castle Douglas
Scotland
DG7 3NL
Tel: 01644 470223
www.jacksonrifles.com

Jagersport
Westmark Cottage
Petersfield
Hants
GU31 5AT
Tel: 01730 263477
sales@jager-sport.co.uk

John Rothery
Bedford Road
Petersfield
GU32 3AX
Tel: 01730 268011
www.bisley-uk.com

JLS and Co (1959) Ltd
Scoltock House
Perry Street
Wednesbury
WS10 0AZ
Tel: 0121 556 1322
sales@jls-wednesday.freeserve.co.uk

JMS Arms
Merrivale
Handcross
Sussex
RH17 6BA
Tel: 01444 400126, 07771 962121
julian@jsavory.freeonline.co.uk

Kammo
Freepost Kammo (that is all you need to write!)
Tel: 0800 783 7382
sales@kammo.co.uk

LEI
PO Box 328
St Albans
Herts
AL4 0WA
Tel: 01727 826607
lei@lei.co.uk

Leica Camera Ltd
Davy Avenue
Knowhill
Milton Keynes
MK5 8LB
Tel: 01908 256400
www.leica-camera.co.uk

Napier of London
3 Moorbrook
Southmead Park
Didcot
Oxfordshire
OX11 7HR
Tel: 01235 812993
sales@napieruk.com

Norman Clarks
19 Somers Road Ind Est
Rugby
Warwickshire
CV22 7DG
Tel: 01788 579651
info@normanclarksgunsmith.com

Open Seasons Ltd
Unit 58 Monument Park
Warpsgrove Lane
Chalgrove
Oxfordshire
OX44 7RW
Tel: 01865 891773
rupert@openseasonltd.com

Otmoors
Hudson Street
Deddington
Oxon
OX15 0SW
Tel: 0845 631 0119
otmoors@hotmail.co.uk

Pantiles Vintage Guns
8 Union Square
The Pantiles
Tunbridge Wells
Kent
TN4 8HE
Tel: 01892 544063
www.pantilesguns.co.uk

Reloading Solutions Ltd
6 Cherwell Business Centre
Rowles Way
Kidlington
OX5 1LA
Tel: 01865 378200
www.reloadingsolutions.co.uk

R Macleod and Son
14 Lamington Street
Tain
IV19 1AA
Tel: 01862 892171
sales@rmacleod.co.uk

RPA International Ltd
PO Box 441
Tonbridge
Kent
TN9 9DZ
Tel: 0845 880 3222
info@rpainternational.co.uk

RUAG
Upton Cross
Liskeard
Cornwall
PL14 5BQ
Tel: 01579 362231
enquiries@ruag.co.uk

Sentry Trading
PO Box 1250
High Wycombe
HP11 9DB
Tel: 01494 463466
sales@st.uk.com

Speed Graphic
Unit 2
Old Aylesfield Buildings
Froyle
Road
Alton
GU34 4BY
Tel: 08453 305530
sales@speedgraphic.co.uk

Sportsman Gun Centre
19 Apple Lane
Trade City
Exeter
EX2 5GL
Tel: 01803 558142
www.sportsmanguncentre.com

Steve Bowers
Specialist Rifle Services
Gables Farm
Badgeworth Lane
Shurdington
Cheltenham
Glos
GL51 4UJ
Tel: 01242 863005

Swarovski UK Ltd
Perrywood Business Park
Salfords
Surrey
RH1 5JQ
Tel: 01737 856812

Swift Precision
11 Holly Grove
Bromsgrove
Worcestershire
B61 8LH
Tel: 01527 871620

Tim Hannam
Peckfield Lodge
Great North Rd
Leeds
LS25 5LJ
Tel: 01977 681639
sales@timhannam.com

Thomas Jacks Ltd
Unit B2
Bridge Business Centre
Timothys Bridge Road
Stratford upon Avon
CV37 9HW
Tel: 01789 264100
info@thomasjacks.co.uk

UK Custom Shop
PO Box 11809
Bromsgrove
Worcs
B61 9YS
Tel: 01527 832549
enquiries@wildcatrifles.co.uk

V-Mach
PO Box 4582
Stour Bridge
DY8 3WT
Tel: 07850 296360
v-mach@blueyonder.co.uk

Viking Arms
Summerbridge
Harrogate
North Yorkshire
HG3 4BW
Tel: 01423 780810
info@vikingarms.co.uk

Carl Zeiss Ltd
15–20 Woodfield Rd
Welwyn Garden City
Herts
AL7 1JQ
Tel: 01707 871200
www.zeiss.co.uk

SUPPLIERS AND MANUFACTURERS AND THEIR PRODUCTS

Rifles

Alan Rhone Ltd	Blaser rifles
BWM Arms Ltd	Browning and Winchester rifles
Edgar Brothers	Remington, CZ rifles
F A Andersons	Full range of rifles new and second hand
Frank Dyke and Co.	Anschutz rifles
Garlands	Savage, Sauer, Weatherby rifles
GMK Ltd	Sako, Tikka rifles
Highland Outdoors	Howa, Mossberg rifles
JLS and Co. (1959) Ltd	Krico, Rossi rifles
Pantiles Vintage Guns	Classic sporting rifles
R. Macleod and Son	Extensive range of rifles both new and second hand
RPA International Ltd	RPA rifles
RUAG	RWS rifles
Sportsman Gun Centre	Steyr rifles
Viking Arms	Ruger, Merkel, Thompson Center, Henry, H-S Precision rifles

Scopes and Binoculars

A K Sports Optics	Light Stream scopes
Carl Zeiss Ltd	Zeiss scopes and binoculars
F A Andersons	Schmidt and Bender scopes, laser rangefinders and binoculars
Garlands	Tasco scopes
GMK Ltd	Leupold, Burris scopes and binoculars
Highland Outdoors	Nikko Stirling Scopes
Leica	Leica binoculars and rangefinders
Open Seasons Ltd	Kahles scopes and binoculars
Sentry Trading	EAW/Apel scope mounts
Speed Graphic	Quality lens cleaning kit
Swarovski UK Ltd	Swarovski scopes, binoculars and rangefinders
Thomas Jacks Ltd	Night Vision Specialist
RUAG	Nightforce scopes

Reloading Kit

Edgar Brothers	Nosler and Hornady bullets and cases, Hodgdon and Alliant powder
GMK Ltd	Barnes and Speer bullets, RCBS reloading kit and CCI primers
JMS Arms	Quick Load, Quick Target and Quick Design ballistics software
Norman Clarks	Large range of reloading equipment plus bullets, cases, powder and primers. Specialist bullets stocked
Reloading Solutions Ltd	Comprehensive range of reloading equipment plus bullets, cases, powder and primers
Tim Hannam	Comprehensive range of reloading equipment

Custom Gunsmithing

Brock and Norris	Custom rifles, rebarrelling and bedding, load development
Callum Ferguson	Full custom rifles, bedding, rebarrelling and wildcat work
Norman Clarks	Full custom rifles, traditional gunsmithing, rebarrelling, bedding
Steve Bowers	Full custom rifles, bedding, custom stock designs, rebarrelling, threading and wildcat speciality
Swift Precision	Custom rifles, rebarrelling and one-off custom items

Sound Moderators

Jackson Rifles	BR Toute, ASE Utra and SAK full bore and rimfire
JMS Arms	PES/MAE full bore, small bore and fully suppressed
John Rothery	Parker Hale rimfire
LEI	LEI full bore, rimfire and fully suppressed
Swift Precision	Carbon fibre and custom units
UK Custom Shop	Wildcat full bore and rimfire
V-Mach	Custom rimfire units

Accessories

Attleborough Accessories	Absolutely everything you could possibly need!
Bush Wear	Extensive range of stalking, sporting and outdoor accessories
C H Westons	Knives, clothing, scope covers, cleaning kit and targets
F A Andersons	Alan Wood custom knives, slings, cases, bipods, shooting sticks, calls and decoys
Jackson Rifles	McMillan and Robertson synthetic stocks, C G Universal, Jewell and Timney triggers
Jagersport	Everything the stalker or sportsperson needs in the field
John Rothery	Gun bags, cases, cleaning kit
Napier of London	Oils, cases, gun bags, cleaning kit cartridge bags, ear defenders
Otmoors	Cleaning kit, cases, knives, clothing

Clothing

Bush Wear	Stalking jackets and trousers, boots and outdoor clothing
C H Westons	All major outdoor clothing stocked
F A Andersons	Extensive range of outdoor clothing, boots, hats gloves
Jagersport	Quality specialist outdoor clothing and boots
Kammo	British-made weatherproof clothing

Index